The Theology of Post-Reformation Lutheranism

Volume II

The Theology
of Post-
LUTHER

God and His Creation

Robert D. Preus

Reformation
ANISM

Volume II

CONCORDIA PUBLISHING HOUSE / Saint Louis London

Concordia Publishing House, St. Louis, Missouri
Concordia Publishing House, Ltd., E. C. 1
Copyright © 1972 Concordia Publishing House
Library of Congress Catalog Card No. 70-121877
ISBN 0-570-03226-1

MANUFACTURED IN THE UNITED STATES OF AMERICA

CONTENTS

PREFACE

The present study is the continuation of what I began in a previous volume entitled *The Theology of Post-Reformation Lutheranism.* That volume dealt with the origin and development of theological prolegomena and with the doctrine of Scripture as taught by the great Lutheran theologians of the Post-Reformation era. It also provided a certain amount of necessary historical introduction into the era. There is no need to repeat what was said there about the spirit and characteristics of the era and about the personalities who played formative roles in the formulation and presentation of Lutheran doctrine. But a few introductory remarks might be made about the period which I intend to cover.

The period spans more than a century, continuing from the time of the writing of the Formula of Concord in 1578 to the first quarter of the 18th century. This period has been called the era of Lutheran scholasticism, or the age of Lutheran orthodoxy. It was an age typified by strict adherence to the Lutheran Confessions, a deep interest in theology and concern for the truth, a piety and seriousness in worship and Christian life, a remarkable unity in doctrine, and an intolerance of any heterodoxy. The spirit and posture of the theology of this era does not differ greatly from that of the Reformation era. In fact, the Lutheran theologians who were active after the Formula of Concord made every effort to preserve the theology and spirit of the Reformers and the Lutheran Confessions and to remain faithful to their heritage. But much of the flush of discovery which marked the Reformation was not so apparent in this period of conservatism.

My specific purpose in this present study is to present as completely as possible the teaching of post-Reformation Lutheran dogmatics on two articles of faith, the doctrine of God and the doctrine of creation. In addition to presenting objectively the historic Lutheran teaching on two important articles of faith, I hope to offer some insight into the dogmatic methodology of the era, and into the manner in which the old Lutheran teachers thought and organized their material. It is my hope also to provide some understanding of their dogmatic and exegetical procedure.

There are good reasons for choosing those two particular articles which in dogmatics are usually the first to be given special attention. There have previously been no studies made in the classical Lutheran doctrine of God or of creation. Perhaps it was thought that the Lutheran theology of the orthodox period had little that was new or significant to offer on these subjects. But this is only partly true, and it is my hope that this study will help to fill a lacuna in the history of Protestant doctrine. Furthermore, the study of classic post-Reformation Lutheran theology as it treats these articles will portray a fair picture of Lutheran theology as a whole during this era. Much of the theology of the day was developed in a definite polemical setting or from an almost servile dependence upon Luther and the Lutheran Symbols (for example, the articles of justification, Christology, and the Lord's Supper). This is much less true of the two articles which we have chosen for study. Here we may observe the Lutheran theologians of the post-Reformation era as they are compelled to work independently and for the most part dispassionately — without polemical motives. This does not mean that we will observe them at their best. Polemics does not always bring out the worst in a theologian, but sometimes the best. But we will, I believe, see the constructive side of Lutheran dogmatics, its strengths, and its weaknesses.

There are about one hundred Lutheran theologians whose works could have been consulted in a study such as this. I have tried to draw from as broad a representation of theologians as possible, but I have also thought it necessary to concentrate attention on those who were the dominant figures of their particular time and place: men such as Chemnitz, Selnecker, Gerhard and Mentzer, Calov and Quenstedt, and Dorsch and Sebastian Schmidt, and of course Hollaz, who is the last of the great orthodox dogmaticians. I have refrained from considering contributions of Lutherans like Calixt who were not confessional Lutherans in the strict sense. I have also not consulted the works of the Pietists of the late 17th century and early 18th century. But I have restricted my research rather to those theologians, almost all professors, from such centers as Jena, Tübingen, Leipzig, Wittenberg, Strasbourg, and Copenhagen, whose confessional loyalty was unquestioned. My findings will reveal a remarkable doctrinal unity among the Lutherans from 1580 to 1715. But there are also differences to be noted, differences in emphasis and approach if not in doctrine, differences due as much to place (Strasbourg as opposed to Wittenberg) as to time. When one considers the tremendous literary output of such men as Chemnitz, Gerhard, Calov, and Schmidt, one will immediately realize that I have been forced to be highly selective in drawing from the sources; and I can only hope that I have succeeded in presenting a fair picture of the theology of the era.

One more word by way of introduction. One can only regret that in a study of this kind one cannot give more attention to the exegesis of the Lutheran teachers, for it is here that the strength and weakness of the old Lutheran theology often becomes most clearly apparent. But it is simply beyond the scope of this study to go deeply into the massive exegetical works of the old Lutherans. The best I could do was to draw from exegetical works when it seemed necessary for completing a true picture of the Lutheran doctrine on a given point. I have tried to compensate for this deficiency by citing hundreds of the Scripture passages as they are quoted by the dogmaticians themselves. In *every case* the passages I cite are those cited by the Lutheran theologians themselves. Such a procedure may seem a bit pedantic, for the reader can hardly be expected to check out all these passages. But if checked out, I believe the Lutheran teachers' choice of Biblical proof and their way of employing Biblical proof will be most revealing. In some cases the Biblical evidence presented for a certain position reveals a deep grasp of the whole of Scripture; in other cases one can only wonder whether there is any rationale at all in the way the old Lutherans cite Scripture, for they often shy away from what we would consider to be the real *sedes doctrinae* for an article of faith.

What I am saying at this point applies to all of the post-Reformation Lutheran dogmaticians to some extent. This inconsistency in their use of Biblical evidence in their dogmatics works is all the more curious in light of the fact that most of the Lutheran dogmaticians also did extensive work in exegesis and were well acquainted with the Scriptures, to say nothing of the usual *sedes doctrinae*. A partial explanation to this problem may be found in the fact that their work in dogmatics was sometimes hastily or even carelessly done; but such an explanation cannot be pressed, for a hasty worker would have simply followed the citations of his predecessors, and there is a noticeable lack of this kind of thing among the Lutheran dogmaticians.

In conclusion I would like to express my deep thanks to the staff of the Bibliothèque Nationale et Universitaire de Strasbourg for the helpfulness shown me during my research into the sources which this library so richly possesses. And I state my deep appreciation to Prof. François Wendel of the Faculté de Théologie Protestante of Strasbourg University for his encouragement and many helpful suggestions on the improvement of my study.

PART ONE

The Doctrine of God

INTRODUCTION

Following the ancient creeds and the Augsburg Confession, Lutheran orthodoxy begins dogmatics with the doctrine concerning God. With most theologians the treatment of this article represents an elaboration of the brief statement of the Augsburg Confession concerning God. Although Scripture as the source of theology has already been discussed in a prolegomenon or as a separate *locus,* the doctrine of God belongs properly as the first article of theology.[1] For God is the source of the existence of all things, including theology and Scripture, which contains His Word of revelation. Moreover, God is the center of the entire Scripture, the nucleus of all theology, and the goal of all our knowledge and desires. We have been created by God that we might know Him and serve and worship Him (Acts 17:27). And after man had fallen into sin and spiritual blindness, God, out of His immense goodness, came forth from the hidden abode of His majesty to reveal Himself. This He did for no other purpose than that man might know Him and have fellowship with Him (Ex. 29:43). God makes Himself known by gathering a church and by teaching sinful man about divine redemption from sin, about true worship, judgment, death, and eternal life.

---

[1] John Gerhard, *Loci Theologici* (Tübingen, 1762—81), III, 1. Cf. also Abraham Calov, *Systema Locorum Theologicorum* (Wittenberg, 1655—77), II, 2; also John George Dorsch, *Synopsis Theologiae Zacharianae* (Strasbourg, 1655), II, 139 ff. John Conrad Dannhauer, *Hodosophia Christiana* (Strasbourg, 1649), is an exception, who treats the article on God after presenting the doctrine of the church, an excessive concession to the analytic method.

This procedure of beginning dogmatics with the doctrine of God is by no means a mere submission to tradition. God is the starting point and the terminus of every article of faith and of all Christian confession. And all Christian theology has to do with God and leads to Him.[2] Likewise, the doctrine of the Trinity is the basis of all Christian doctrine; as Lutheran theology throughout the whole of dogmatics portrays the mighty *opera ad extra* of God, these are clearly seen to be the works of the triune God *(opera Trinitatis)* as are the *opera ad intra*. God's external acts can be summed up under the themes of creation, redemption (Christology), and soteriology.

Chemnitz, for instance, in one of his schemata for dogmatics [3] lists the works of God as follows: creation, the preservation of the fallen creation, the restoration of fallen man, conversion of man, justification, sanctification, and glorification. These works which summarize the activity of the triune God constitute the themes under which the whole of Christian doctrine can be subsumed. As God seeks to establish fellowship with man and to save him, Chemnitz in another schema relates the following activities of God: He accuses and terrifies man by the Law, He comforts and lifts up the sinner by the Gospel, He saves the sinner through Christ, renews him through the Spirit, sanctifies him through Word and sacrament, tests and exercises his faith through crosses, and glorifies him by the resurrection of his flesh to eternal life.

Christian doctrine cannot be rightly understood or taught, neither can Law and Gospel be rightly divided, apart from the doctrine of the Trinity. If it is important for Lutheran theology to make the foundation of faith Christ, who has brought man forgiveness of sins and offers this in the Gospel, it is equally necessary to list as the first fundamental article of faith the doctrine of the triune God who is "the effective cause of our faith, of our righteousness, and our salvation."[4] To know God as triune God is to know Him as the creating, sustaining, saving God; and to know God as Creator and Savior is to know God as Father, Son, and Holy Spirit.

Although there is complete agreement on the doctrine of God among

---

[2] In one of his schemata of *loci theologici,* Chemnitz represents all theology as dealing either with God or the deeds of God. Martin Chemnitz, *Loci Theologici* (Wittenberg, 1653), I, 13.

[3] Chemnitz, *Loci Theologici,* I, 13.

[4] David Hollaz, *Examen Theologicum Acroamaticum* (Rostock and Leipzig, 1741). Prol. II, q. 20 (I, 50—51). See Chapter II, p. 1.

the evangelical Lutherans from Selnecker and Heerbrand to Hollaz, there is little uniformity in the order or mode of presentation. At the turn of the 17th century a new approach to the doctrine develops, and a rather marked difference in emphasis is discernible. We might say that Lutheranism as a whole covers four main points in dealing with the doctrine of God: (1) our knowledge of God and the ways He has made Himself known, (2) the description and nature of God, (3) the attributes of God, and (4) the Trinity. The earlier theologians: Heerbrand, Chemnitz, Aegidius Hunnius, and even Hutter, give only perfunctory attention to the natural and revealed knowledge of God, offer no discussions of the attributes of God, and devote their attention for the most part to the doctrine of the Trinity.

Gerhard, whose discussions more or less standardized the treatment of the doctrine of God among the later Lutherans, goes more deeply into the subject of how God is proved and makes Himself known; and following the medieval scholastics, he introduces detailed discussions on the attributes of God. Such an innovation was bound to make its appearance sooner or later, for the attributes of God were given insufficient attention by the earlier Lutherans. But the innovation as it was handled by Gerhard was not always helpful, for it introduced much objectionable scholastic terminology and some really knotty problems relative to the classification of the attributes. In the case of the later dogmaticians all four points were treated at length — but in the light of the rapidly changing philosophical and theological milieu of the 17th century, for example, the advent of Cartesianism, Socinianism, Quakerism, Deism, etc. All in all we must say that the doctrine of God as presented by evangelical orthodoxy is one of the least satisfactory. Among the earlier theologians the doctrine is not wholly presented, and the discussion in some cases is not sufficiently thought through. Among the later Lutherans there is greater balance, but their preoccupation with the attributes of God and classifications of these attributes tends at times to abstract God from His works.

If the Lutheran treatment of the doctrine of God seems inadequate, this is at least in part due to the inherent difficulty connected with the presentation of the *locus de Deo:* for everything that can be said in theology pertains to the doctrine of God, and the doctrine of God embraces every theological *locus.* Now for purely didactic reasons the article on God, of His nature and attributes, must be separated from His works which embraces the rest of Christian doctrine. Such a procedure which commences with a distinction between *Deus per se* and *Deus ad hominem* is at the very outset fraught with serious dangers. For strictly speaking there is no revelation of God *per se*. God's revelation, as was clearly taught by Lutheran orthodoxy, was in Law and Gospel.[5] And Law and Gospel speak of God only in relation to His creatures. Furthermore, the distinction between *Deus per se* and *Deus ad hominem* is a distinction without a difference. God does not want us to think of Him in any other way than as He has revealed Himself *(omnino vult Deus ita cognosci & invocari, sicut se patefecit);* indeed, as He has revealed Himself, so is He.[6] For instance, the Trinity is not a mere trinity of revelation (Schleiermacher), but is *Deus per se,* as Lutheran theology clearly perceives.[7] What we are trying to say is that one cannot speak about God without at the same time speaking about His works. Thus, when the Lutheran theologians in their *locus de Deo* seek to speak of God apart from His works, they are attempting the impossible; and they are well aware of this and of the grotesque caricature which would result if they were to be successful in their attempt. It is just that they feel that to speak first of God (and His works) and then of His works (and of God) is the only way open to them. The alternative which would try to give adequate attention to the works of God under the *locus* on God would extend the *locus* to the whole of dogmatics or reduce all dogmatics to one *locus.* And there is really no way out of this dilemma. When Hollaz[8] says that the knowledge we have of God through revelation includes His existence, His essence and attributes, His trinity and His deeds, he is eminently correct, but he is compelled in the nature of the case to treat the works of God in subsequent *loci.*

[5] F. Balduin, *Commentarius in Omnes Epistolas Pauli* (Frankfurt, 1664), pp. 26—27.

[6] Chemnitz, *Loci Theologici,* I, 24.

[7] Chemnitz, *Loci Theologici,* I, 13.

[8] *Examen,* P. I, C.1, Q.12 (233 ff.).

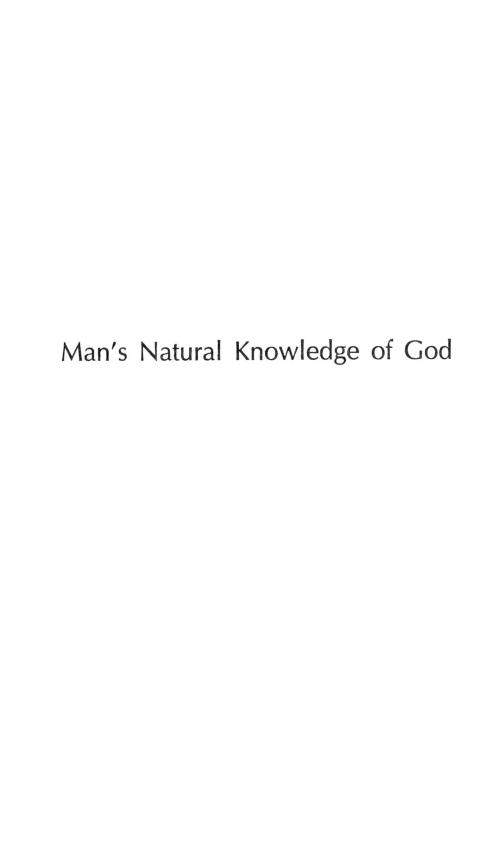

Man's Natural Knowledge of God

CHAPTER ONE

Lutheran dogmatics has a way of becoming expanded as time goes on. Old issues die slowly and new issues and problems arise with regularity. And quite naturally Lutheran theologians develop and build upon what their confessional forbears have taught. This is particularly so in respect to what has been taught concerning man's knowledge of God. The theologians of the 16th century give only cursory attention to this question in discussing the article concerning God. This does not imply, however, that the earlier dogmaticians felt the subject of man's knowledge of God to be of minor importance.

Chemnitz maintains that the summation of all theology is simply man's knowledge of God; and the knowledge of God is of such importance to man that eternal life is contingent upon it (John 17:3).[1] Man has been created and redeemed in order to know God and worship Him as His temple and image. Since God wishes to be known and worshiped (Ps. 118:17; 149:1), man's first concern is to teach the true doctrine concerning God. The knowledge of God is never a matter of academic concern to Lutheran theology but a matter of ultimate and eternal moment. God must be known.

"Without a knowledge of God," writes Giles Hunnius,[2] "no one can be saved. Indeed the knowledge of God is the hinge on which our

[1] *Loci Theologici,* I, 19.
[2] Giles Hunnius, *Opera Latina* (Wittenberg, 1607), I, 81.

salvation hangs, as Christ Himself testifies when He says, This is life eternal, that they might know Thee the only true God, and Jesus Christ whom Thou hast sent. Now, as I have said, this knowledge is imperfect and partial in this life. But it will be made perfect in the life to come, where we will behold Him face to face and know Him even as we are known."

But how is God known? Heerbrand, followed by Hafenreffer,[3] poses this question in the following apologetic form: "How does one prove that God exists?" The answer is: by the book of nature and the book of Scripture. The entire universe, and man as a microcosm, give witness to a wise, powerful, and beneficent Architect who has created and who preserves and governs all things. "The work vouches for the artificer." There can be no effect without a cause. The world comes from another source (*aliunde*) than itself; it is not the result of "a fortuitous collision of atoms." And this is all Heerbrand says about our knowledge of God from nature; everything else that can be known about God, everything which pertains to our salvation, is drawn from the book of Scripture. Hafenreffer says little more, except to list Rom. 1:20 and 2:15 as proof of the fact that God is known from the book of nature.

Chemnitz wisely chooses not to speak about proving God, but refers rather to the natural and revealed knowledge of God. To him it is only because of the great corruption of human nature that man asks such questions as whether there is a God or whether there is Divine Providence. These are illegitimate questions which only indicate the darkness into which the human mind has fallen, a darkness which only God can penetrate with a special divine revelation (1 Cor. 1:21), with a wisdom which the world ridicules as fables, with a wisdom of the Gospel, made known in the Old Testament (Ps. 110) and revealed finally in His Son. Only one who has seen the Son sees the Father (John 14:9). And no Turk or Jew, but only one who honors the Son honors the Father. (John 5:23)

Chemnitz objects to the attempts to prove God's existence because of the sinful concession to skepticism from which all such "proofs" proceed. But he also objects on the ground that our natural knowledge of God is only defective *notitia legalis* which leads to doubt and despair rather than

---

[3] Jacob Heerbrand, *Compendium Theologiae* (Tübingen, 1573), p. 3 ff. Matthias Hafenreffer, *Loci Theologici* (Wittenberg, 1601), pp. 2—3.

to faith. Indeed the natural knowledge of God is *nothing*, he says, for the whole of philosophy knows nothing of the Son of God and His promise of forgiveness in the Gospel. Even as a true *notitia legalis* such knowledge is *imperfect*, relative only to the Second Table of the Law and often commingled with many absurdities. Finally the natural knowledge of God is impotent and *sluggish (languida)*: although men know that God exists, their assent is not only feeble but often shaken with severe doubts.

It might strike us as strange that Lutheran theology would construct its whole doctrine of the natural knowledge of God on the basis of statements from Scripture, the source of the revealed knowledge of God. What is the reason for this surprising procedure? Why should one even bother to prove the natural knowledge of God from Scripture, if it is evident from nature? If the existence of something (for example, the sun) is known from nature, would anyone feel constrained to prove from some authority that one can know of the sun's existence from nature?

There is a reason for this procedure which is not apparent on the surface and unfortunately is never explained by the dogmaticians. Although from God's creation the evidence for His existence is as clear as daylight and is definite and true, the dogmaticians see no need as theologians for bothering with arguments from empirical data when the Biblical proof is so easy and available. Scripture not only tells us what is knowable about God *(quod de Deo cognosci debet)* from the things He has made (Rom. 1:20), but it offers God's interpretation of what nature tells us about Him. And whereas the natural man, as he contemplates God's handiwork, indulges in guesswork and arrives at all sorts of misconceptions, the witness of Scripture is clear and unassailable. "What is more definite," asks Calov,[4] "more certain, less open to question, than what the clear testimony of Scripture presents concerning the natural knowledge of God (Rom. 1:19, 20; Acts 14:25; 17:12; Job 12:7-10)? Of course the revealed knowledge of God is more complete than the natural knowledge, but it is no more firmly and certainly grounded in the testimonies of Scripture." Thus it is perfectly in order (according to the *sola Scriptura* principle) that the Lutherans appeal to Biblical evidence for the natural knowledge of God. Just as their doctrine of man as he exists *coram Deo* is not taken from empirical investigations but from Scripture alone,

---

[4] Abraham Calov, *Consideratio Arminianismi* (Wittenberg, 1655), p. 37.

the same procedure is correct in establishing man's natural knowledge of God.

Following Melanchthon and Chemnitz, Gerhard and all the orthodox Lutherans subdivide the *natural* knowledge of God into innate knowledge *(notitia insita)* and acquired knowledge *(notitia acquisita)*.[5] For the most part their discussions repeat what they have already said in their treatment of natural and revealed theology. Innate knowledge is defined by Gerhard in the following manner: "Innate knowledge has its origin in the common notions (κοιναὶ ἔγνοιαι) which are more or less obscure vestiges of the lost divine image and traces of that lost light which shone in man's mind before the Fall. By means of these notions which are like little sparks the common and accepted notion that there is a God is naturally rooted in the minds of all men." The acquired knowledge is gained discursively by a contemplation of God's handiwork. Just as many letters contribute to make up a book, God's many creatures are letters, so to speak, written by God's hand; and by reading them we can know something of God. If in every walk of life a great work gives knowledge of its master, only a fool would deny this in the case of the most illustrious works of creation.[6] Innate knowledge was called subjective by the Lutheran teachers; acquired knowledge was called objective. The former was found in all men, even infants; the latter was not. The former was inherited; the latter was the result of teaching and investigation.

The Biblical proof for the acquired knowledge of God was easily found by the Lutheran teachers in such passages as Rom. 1:17-20; Acts 14:17, and Acts 17:17-28. Corroboration was sometimes brought from Is. 40; Ps. 19:1; Job 12:7-25. In each case the intimation was that something was knowable about God from His works. Little exegesis was offered on the above passages, the dogmaticians apparently feeling quite confident of their position. It was another matter when they assembled Biblical evidence for the innate knowledge of God. In the case of the

---

[5] See Robert Preus, *The Theology of Post-Reformation Lutheranism* (St. Louis: Concordia Publishing House, 1969), pp. 173—5. Cf. Chemnitz, *Loci Theologici*, I, 20. Cf. also Gerhard, *Loci Theologici*, III, 42—43; John Andr. Quenstedt, *Theologia Didactico — Polemica sive Systema Theologicum* (Wittenberg, 1685), P.I, C.4, S.1, Th.11 (I, 253); Jerome Kromayer, *Theologia Positivo-Polemica* (Leipzig, 1711), I, 89.

[6] Balthasar Meisner, *Philosophia Sobria* (Rintelen, 1626), I, 596.

notitia insita the orthodox Lutherans were hard pressed to defend their position, and therefore they indulged in some rather extensive exegesis of the passages which they considered pertinent. For the most part two *sedes doctrinae* were brought forth: Rom. 1:18-19 and 2:14-15 (also Acts 17:27: Chemnitz).

In the case of the first passage it was generally maintained by the Lutheran theologians [7] that the κατεχόντων, "*holding* the truth in unrighteousness," indicates that in the heathen there is "an innate practical knowledge" of God's righteous judgment against them. The things knowable (τὸ γνωστόν) about God are manifest in them (ἐν αὐτοῖς), that is, in their hearts, "and known without any discursive operation." The implication is that the τὸ γνωστόν includes the righteous rule of divine justice which is evidenced in the Law (Rom. 1:18, 25). This knowledge is sufficient to render the heathen without excuse. It will be seen that this entire interpretation hinges on the understanding of ἐν αὐτοῖς as "in them" rather than "to them." The possibility of the latter rendering is not entertained. Calov simply says, "In those upon whom the wrath of God will be manifest a knowledge of God is manifest."

More convincing is the exegesis of the second passage, Rom. 2:14, although here an inference is drawn from a knowledge of the Law to a knowledge of the Lawgiver. In this passage the apostle speaks of a Law which is not proclaimed or known by external manifestation or information, but by an inner perception. The Gentiles who do not have the external Law are nevertheless a law unto themselves. They show the work of the Law written in their own hearts. And he who knows by nature God's law knows by nature that there is a God. The testimony of the conscience, then, gives evidence of an innate knowledge of God. Wherever man is, he is preoccupied with the Law, but there can be no law without a lawgiver. This is the burden of the Lutheran argument for an innate knowledge of God. It was also sometimes averred that man's innate religiosity indicates an awareness in man that God exists.

According to Lutheran orthodoxy there was a definite but limited content to the knowledge of God provided in God's creation, viz. His Godhead, power, wisdom, and goodness. And this knowledge is true, so

---

[7] Gerhard, *Loci Theologici*, III, 54. Cf. also Calov, *Apodixis Articulorum Fidei* (Lüneberg, 1684), p. 52; John Andrew Quenstedt, *Theologia Didactico-Polemica sive Systema Theologicum* (Wittenberg, 1685), I, 253.

far as it goes (Rom. 1:25). It is because men have stifled this "truth" that God's wrath is revealed against their unrighteousness (Rom. 1:18). This position was maintained by the orthodox Lutherans against Flacius and Daniel Hofmann, who, because of their peculiar anthropology and their extremely negative attitude toward philosophy, concluded that all "natural knowledge" of God is false. For the most part Lutheran theology countered pretty much as follows, in the words of Hollaz,[8] "Although the true God, Father, Son, and Holy Spirit is not known by the natural knowledge of God, still something about the true God is grasped in that way, viz. His existence, His goodness, His wisdom, justice, etc." This fact is seen in the case of the Jews and Mohammedans, who correctly but confusedly teach that God is powerful and wise, but utterly distort and restrict the Godhead by insisting that He is only one Person, thus worshiping an idol and figment of their own imagination. Put differently, the natural knowledge of God is true in itself (per se), but because of man's imperfection and proclivity toward error such truth is *per accidens* annulled. (Rom. 1:18)

In the case of the so-called *notitia insita* the Lutheran theologians are much more cautious, and they never say that there is any specific content to this knowledge. What, then, is this "knowledge"? Again the dogmaticians are quite cautious in their answer. It may be likened to an instinct, a tendency, a faculty, a disposition *(habitus).*

Calov [9] grants that there is no notion in man by nature concerning God before the exercise of reason, no particular thought about God which man has actually known since birth, but there is a definite capacity, or disposition, for such thought. And this "habitual knowledge" may by the use of reason flower into an actual knowledge about God.[10]

Hollaz,[11] who is extremely careful to dissociate himself from Platonism and Descartes' ontological proofs, exercises even greater caution in discussing the nature of the *notitia insita.* He says, "Although man does not have a knowledge of God before he exercises and makes use of the powers of reason, at least to the extent of having an express image or definite idea formed in the mind; still we feel that it cannot be denied

[8] *Examen,* P.I, C.1, Q.5, p. 208.

[9] *Theologia Naturalis & Revelata,* pp. 149—50.

[10] Calov, *Socinismus Profligatus,* p. 108.

[11] *Examen,* P.I, C.1, Q.5, p. 204 [193].

that there is some disposition in man, something analogous to a *habitus*, namely some τελείωσις of intellectual capacity remaining in man after the Fall. With the benefit of this capacity man without a teacher can to a certain extent know God."

With the reservations which the above statement implies, Hollaz is willing to go along with the "trite" axiom of Locke and the empiricists that there was nothing in the intellect that was not in the senses. The opinion that an innate idea or image of the essence of God was necessary before man could in any sense know God from nature is simply rejected as a "sweet dream of the Cartesians." But Hollaz feels compelled to break with the other extreme position of the empiricists and the Socinians,[12] which on empirical grounds denied a *notitia insita* altogether. Adam was possessed of a concreated knowledge which was not limited to what he observed through the senses. And after the Fall there are remnants of this divine image and they do not depend upon the senses. "Wherefore that axiom must be taken as referring to simple intelligible ideas which since the Fall are not naturally implanted in the intellect, but hold true by virtue of abstractions. It does not pertain to concreated and innate tendencies *(habitus)* which inhere in the intellect prior to the process of forming ideas." If there is little definite in what Hollaz asserts here — and he is following Calov — [13] he must at least be given credit for trying to steer a middle course between the apriorism of Descartes and the strict empiricism which would restrict all knowledge to what is the result of sense perception. Both of these extremes are exceedingly dangerous, and not merely because they conflict with the Biblical evidence concerning the natural knowledge of God; in the case of these two extremes a special divine historical revelation which conveys a saving knowledge is either unnecessary or impossible.

[12] The Socinians accepted a virtual Lockean epistemology. See Conrad Vorst, *Tractatus Theologicus de Deo* (Steinfurt, 1606), p. 128: "We do not think that there is any innate knowledge of God in us. Strictly speaking, there does not seem to be any knowledge of anything inborn in man. But all knowledge is acquired in its own time through the senses or by the operation of the intellect." The atheist of Ps. 14:1 (cf. Ps. 10:4) is a fool, according to Vorst, not because he does not know, but because he fails to think. The nonexistence of a *notitia insita* in man is proved in discussions with the Brazilian Indians, Vorst observes, who have not the slightest notion of God. Vorst argued that too great an emphasis upon natural knowledge depreciated the importance of faith. (Ibid., p. 144)

[13] *Systema*, II, 80. Cf. Kromayer, op. cit., I, 90—91.

It was pointed out[14] that the Lutheran doctrine concerning the natural knowledge of God virtually denied the possibility of a theoretical atheist, i. e., one who honestly could not believe in God. To be sure, Scripture speaks of the fool who says there is no God (Ps. 14:1), but the psalmist here is not speaking of one who does not know God, but of the fool who maliciously wishes there were no God. In like manner, when Paul says (1 Cor. 1:21) that the world does not know God, he is not speaking of an absolute ignorance of God (Gal. 4:8) but is saying that the world did not know God as Savior. In this sense the heathen are called atheists. (Eph. 2:12)

Of course there are practical atheists who deny God by their lives. Specifically the question of theoretical atheism and its relation to *notitia insita* is answered as follows: No man is a speculative atheist by nature; it is rather that unrepentant men have been justly abandoned by God and blinded by the devil, and then they deny God's existence. The *habitus*, the innate religiosity, has not been eradicated but stifled.

Concerning the atheist, Hollaz says, "Because such a person will not submit to the law of nature, a fixed and firm belief clings to him that there is no God. But although the mind of the godless man slumbers away in its morbid drowsiness and does not consider God, still there can be no one whose conscience does not assert itself and accuse him, especially when he faces death, of ignoring God."

The old Lutheran doctrine of the natural knowledge of God has sometimes been censured for being too intellectual and rationalistic, as though the dogmaticians made too much of man's ability to prove God, as though there were in their view only a short step from the natural knowledge of God to the revealed knowledge of God, or as though there was little left for revelation to supply after the natural knowledge of God had been established.[15] Such criticism seems strange in the light of what has been shown above.

The Lutheran teachers were really only trying to be faithful to the Biblical data in presenting their doctrine of the natural knowledge of God. They were convinced that Scripture taught a natural knowledge of God. And they exercised extreme caution against making extravagant claims

[14] See Robert Preus, op. cit., p. 193.

[15] See, for instance, Jaroslav Pelikan, *From Luther to Kierkegaard* (St. Louis: Concordia Publishing House, 1963), p. 64 ff.

concerning the extent or benefit of the natural knowledge of God. For all of them the most important concern was to confute the ideas of Zwingli and particularly Lord Herbert of Cherbury that certain noble heathen might be saved — those who made the most of the natural knowledge of God. There was little of the apologetic which Gerhard briefly indulged in, and no attempt whatsoever to present the mysteries of faith as knowable apart from special revelation or to make these mysteries rational in the manner of the 18th-century Wolffian theologians. The entire Lutheran position was really extremely conservative. With its doctrine of anthropology and monergistic soteriology evangelical orthodoxy has no reason to exalt the benefits of natural knowledge.

Calov, for instance,[16] grants that by considering God's creation one can come to some knowledge *about* God and His providence, one can know facts concerning God, for example, that He fills all things, that He has made the world, that He is Lord of heaven and earth (Acts 17:22-28; 14:15-17). But without the revelation of the Gospel, Calov says, one cannot know God *(ignorare Deus)* in the personal relationship of faith. No consideration of nature can help one to know God as Savior. Without divine revelation man is without God (Eph. 2:11-12), not knowing Him (Gal. 4:8; 1 Thess. 2:5 [sic]), and living in blindness and impenitence. (Acts 17:30)

A bit more moderate, and yet more surprising and unfair, coming as it does from such a knowledgeable scholar, is the criticism of Elert.[17] He alleges that Lutheran dogmatics divorced penitence from the natural knowledge of God, forgetting that this knowledge only leads to doubt and unbelief. In this way the appearance was given, although unintentionally, that the evangelical knowledge of God was innate in man, and the church in preaching the Gospel needed only to clarify what was more or less self-evident to every man by nature. Such sweeping criticism is without foundation. Lutheran theology never divorced the natural knowl-

16 *Socinismus Profligatus,* p. 103.

17 Werner Elert, *The Structure of Lutheranism,* trans. Walter Hansen (St. Louis: Concordia Publishing House, 1962), pp. 50—52. A different conclusion is that of Jörg Baur. See *Die Vernunft zwischen Ontologie und Evangelium,* Eine Untersuchung zur Theologie Johann Andreas Quenstedts (Gütersloh: Verlagshaus Gerd Mohn, 1962), pp. 76, 82, 181. Admitting that Quenstedt's study of natural theology is one of his weaker discussions, Baur shows that the theocentric character of Quenstedt's theology and his emphasis on the blindness of human reason really safeguarded his theology from the charges Elert makes.

edge of God from repentance. Rather the very purpose of God's revelation in nature was to establish to all men their inexcusability before
God, to convince them that they were sinners under God's wrath.[18] As
he perverts the natural knowledge of God, the natural man is aware that
something is radically wrong with him and he is under judgment. Moreover, the Law written in man's heart functions to accuse the natural man
and show him his lost condition;[19] it is always the purpose and result of
the natural law to render every man inexcusable before God, to produce
horror in man's soul before he does wrong, and shame after he has committed wrong.[20]

As for the allegation that the Lutheran doctrine of *notitia insita* could
easily lead to the idea that an evangelical knowledge of God was somehow innate in man, this was the very antithesis of what the Lutheran
teachers were driving at. They were vehemently outspoken in their con-
demnation of the heresy that heathen could be saved by cultivating the
natural knowledge of God.

And the later dogmaticians were equally adamant against Robert
Barclay and the Quakers with their doctrine of an inner light which was
supernatural and saving. There is no spiritual light in an unregenerate
man at all, but only error and darkness (Eph. 2:1; 5:8). The doctrine
of an inner light undermines both the material and the formal principles
of theology; faith in Christ becomes no longer crucial and the power of
the Word and sacraments is nullified.[21]

According to Lutheran dogmatics the faith of Christians and the
knowledge of the heathen concerning God do not differ merely quantita-
tively; rather there is a radical qualitative and formal difference between
Christian faith and a *notitia Dei naturalis*.[22] Those who have charged

---

[18] Gerhard, *Loci Theologici,* III, 66; John Adam Osiander, *Collegium Theologicum Systematicum* (Stuttgart and Frankfurt, 1684), I, 247 ff; Calov, *Systema,*
II, 27.

[19] F. Balduin, *Commentarius in Omnes Epistolas Pauli* (Frankfurt, 1664),
p. 36.

[20] Hollaz, *Examen,* P. III, S.2, C.1, Q.11.12.

[21] Cf. Hollaz, *Examen,* P.I, C.1, Q.7, who polemicizes at length against
Barclay, especially the statement that "God has given to each a measure of saving,
sufficient and supernatural light." See Robert Barclay, *An Apology for the True
Christian Divinity* (London, 1825), Prop. V,VI, par. 14, p. 133. Hollaz used the
Latin edition, *Theologiae vere Christianae Apologia* (Amsterdam, 1676), cf. p. 97.

[22] The view of certain Arminians that Christian faith and the heathen knowl-

that Lutheran orthodoxy made too much of the natural knowledge of God have somehow missed the most important point of the Lutheran doctrine, viz., that by nature and through nature man knows nothing of the Gospel, of Christ, of grace or forgiveness. Evangelical orthodoxy fervently held that Christianity was an exclusive religion. Only judgment and hell awaited those who possessed merely a natural knowledge of God. The classic Lutheran doctrine of the natural knowledge of God must be viewed in the light of the Lutheran doctrine of man, sin, and God's wrath. Man is altogether a sinner and under the wrath of God. By nature he is spiritually blind and ignorant; and original sin involves not merely ignorance and a lack of righteousness, but the deepest corruption of all man's powers, error, and hatred of God.[23] On no point does Lutheran orthodoxy go beyond the Lutheran symbols in its teaching concerning the natural knowledge of God.[24]

Why then do the later orthodox Lutherans emphasize the natural knowledge of God far beyond the scant attention given in the Lutheran Confessions? Primarily for polemical reasons: to counter the extravagant views of Calixtus, the Quakers, the Cartesians, and many Roman Catholic theologians, and to refute the denials of the natural knowledge of God which were voiced by Flacius, the Socinians, and the empiricists (Locke).

But it was not merely to defend a traditional position that the doctrine was enunciated so carefully. There was definite practical use to which the doctrine could be applied. In respect to those who are outside the church the natural knowledge of God incites them to search after the living God (Acts 17:27), to restrain themselves from violence, and to live at peace with their neighbors according to their innate knowledge of right and wrong; and it teaches them that they are without excuse in not recognizing the true God and glorifying Him (it is a Law preachment)

edge concerning God differed only *gradu perfectionis* is explicitly condemned (cf. John Adam Osiander, *Theologicum Systema seu Theologia Positiva Acroamatica,* I, 249). Faith is different in its very nature from a natural knowledge of God: faith is born of the Gospel and is a gift of God. Faith is not in what is seen, but in the impossible and what is against all evidence. What faith believes is regarded as utter foolishness by the natural man. Jesper Erasmus Brochmand, *Commentarius in Epistolam ad Hebraeos* (Copenhagen, 1706), p. 489.

[23] Quenstedt, *Systema*, P. II, C.2, S.1, Th. 24 (II, 60): *totius naturae omnium virium profundissima corruptio, error in mente, in voluntate rebellio, odium Dei.*

[24] Edmund Schlink, *Theology of the Lutheran Confessions.* Trans. Paul F. Koehneke and Herbert J. A. Bouman (Philadelphia: Muhlenberg Press, 1961), pp. 50—51.

(Rom. 1:20). Such a knowledge could serve as a point of initial contact for the church in preaching Law and Gospel to unbelievers. (Acts 14: 15 ff.; 17:22 ff.)

However, the greatest value of the natural knowledge of God has nothing to do with apologetics but pertains to the Christians themselves. As Christians we ought to cultivate the natural knowledge of God, even with all its imperfections, and subordinate it to our revealed knowledge. It is a pleasing act of worship, Calov says,[25] for a believer to recognize God's glory and goodness from His ποιήματα [works] and to praise Him for His marvelous handiwork. Again and again the psalms and prophets allude to God's creation as a mark of His glory and munificence; and that this is a fact for all to see and apply is manifested from the frequent appeal made to animals and inanimate objects to praise God (Psalm 19; 103:22; 104; Job 38). The book of nature, says Gerhard,[26] is replete with miracles of divine power, indications of divine goodness, and proofs of divine wisdom. In six days God created the world and on the seventh day He rested from His labor. "Therefore we on six of every seven days ought to reflect with our mind's eye upon the wonders of His six-day creation, and then on the seventh day of quiet our souls ought to take their rest in God the Creator."

The notitia insita also should not be neglected by Christians. "For our innate knowledge of God comprises the book of conscience, and our acquired knowledge is taken from the book of nature; and therefore we ought to devote ourselves diligently to both books." Conscience is our own "domestic witness" of our words and actions, our own intimate and inseparable companion. And we ought not grieve or insult this witness and friend. So we see that the natural knowledge of God is considered to be of a certain limited practical value in the theology of Lutheran orthodoxy. It is rightly associated with the doctrine of creation and providence. It is by faith that we acknowledge God as Creator; but a grateful consideration of His work of creation is a part of our praise and worship of the Creator God. Only when the natural knowledge of God is linked with the church's doxology is it rightly understood and estimated.

[25] Socinismus Profligatus (Wittenberg, 1652), p. 103.
[26] Loci Theologici, III, 67.

God's Existence and Essence

CHAPTER TWO

It might seem strange that a discussion of the revealed knowledge of God is not included by the Lutheran theologians in their *locus* on God, especially since they have said at least something about man's natural knowledge of God.[1] There are two reasons for this omission. First, in the case of some theologians (for instance, Calov [2] and Hollaz) the idea of revelation and revealed theology was discussed at great length in their prolegomena, and any lengthy consideration of man's revealed knowledge of God within the very next *locus* on God would be redundant. Second, and more important, man's revealed knowledge of God is actually treated in everything which follows the discussion of the natural knowledge of God: the whole of Christian doctrine is the summation of the knowledge of God which man has by revelation.

This is clearly the thinking of Gerhard in his *Loci Theologici.* In his first two volumes he affirms the fact of divine revelation and defends the principle that Scripture, which is God's revelation in writing, is the source of our knowledge of God *(principium cognoscendi).* He then begins his *locus* on God with a discussion of man's natural knowledge of God, but

---

[1] David Hollaz, *Examen Theologicum Acroamaticum* (Rostock and Leipzig, 1741), P.I, C.1, q.10 ff., p. 220 ff. Hollaz does offer a short discussion of the subject "de notitia Dei revelata," but actually it is all a polemic against the many forms of mysticism (ideas favoring a direct, noncognitive, nondiscursive revelation) which he saw in his day.

[2] See Robert Preus, *The Theology of Post-Reformation Lutheranism* (Saint Louis: Concordia Publishing House, 1970), p. 180.

he is careful to make it clear that only through the Gospel does man learn to know who God is and to know Him as Savior.[3] The implication is that everything which follows in his dogmatics concerning God, Trinity, creation, sin, redemption, etc., is known only by revelation. And in fact Gerhard never returns to the subject of the natural knowledge of God but attempts to support everything he says from Scripture alone.

Before proceeding, however, to a consideration of the attributes of God and the doctrine of the Trinity as revealed in Scripture, the Lutheran dogmaticians feel obliged to face a few preliminary questions which pertain to the existence and essence of God.

1. The Apologetic Problem

Are there formal proofs, totally apart from any historic revelation, for the existence of God? This question, as we have seen (p. 20), was already posed within the discussion of man's natural knowledge of God. And the answer was that God's existence was shown by His creation and His activity in history.

Heerbrand,[4] for instance, offers a very brief discussion, dropped by the later Lutherans, of the question, "How the sacred Scriptures testify that there is a God." In six ways, says Heerbrand: (1) From His works, from the marvels of His creation. (2) From His marvelous deliverance of His people at the Red Sea. (3) From the many special miracles which accompany His deliverances, e. g. manna, resurrections, the sun standing still. (4) From frequent apparitions (theophanies). (5) From His prophecies and promises which He always keeps. (6) From the promise to send Christ who came and revealed God. What Heerbrand speaks of here, however, is a far cry from what we might call formal proofs.

Nicolaus Selnecker,[5] writing at the same time as Heerbrand, is even more conservative as he speaks on the same subject. He offers no less than nine arguments drawn from the Psalms and Romans 1, arguments of an a posteriori nature, which point to God's existence and power and justice. But these arguments, he says, only indicate the weakness of the human

---

[3] Loci Theologici, III, 44 passim.

[4] Jakob Heerbrand, Compendium Theologiae (Tübingen, 1573), p. 4.

[5] Nicolaus Selnecker, Institutiones Christianae Religionis (Frankfurt, 1573), p. 51 ff.

mind. The universal knowledge of God, that which is knowable about Him, to which these arguments testify, only renders all men without excuse before God. And the contemplation of such arguments does not lead one to the true God, but only to shadows, and it shows the need of a special revelation. Only the Gospel can teach that all religions are not equal and that only through Christ is salvation to be found. In short, only the Gospel can tell us who and what God is and save us from the "infinite opinions" of heathen speculation. Having said this, Selnecker launches into a polemic against the overweening opinions of heathen philosophies.[6]

It is with John Gerhard[7] that formal a posteriori proofs for God's existence begin to take shape in Lutheran dogmatics. In a rather perfunctory manner, and leaning quite obviously on the arguments of Thomas Aquinas,[8] Gerhard lists five observations from experience to show that there is sufficient empirical proof for belief in God's existence. (1) The orderly succession of moving objects leads to one first mover. (2) The chain of efficient causes which we observe in the ordered world leads to a first efficient cause "which we all call God." Like Thomas Aquinas, Gerhard assumes at this point that an infinite regress cannot be accepted logically (cf. Aristotle, *Metaphysics*, II, 6). (3) One may argue from sufficient reason: there must be a sufficient reason for all possible things being what they are, and the only sufficient reason which would not be merely another possibility is God, who is per se necessary. This proof, which again discounts the possibility of an infinite regress, is a slight variation of Thomas' argument from contingency and bears a similarity to Leibniz' argument from sufficient reason.[9] (4) We observe reason, care, wisdom, and teleology in the process of all things. This could hardly be

[6] The arguments from nature and history (interpreted in the light of Scripture) which Selnecker has used to show that God exists, Melanchthon (*CR* 7, 1078) and David Chytraeus (*Opera* [Leipzig, 1594], I, 1 ff.) had used to show that Christianity was superior to other religions. But Selnecker is rather more cautious in his approach. To him other arguments for God's existence serve in the only valid way as a Law preachment.

[7] *Loci Theologici*, III, 41 ff.

[8] *Summa Theologica*, P.I, Q.2, a.3.

[9] See ibid., p. 43. Gerhard also leans on Richard of St. Victor (*De Trinitate*, L.I, P.1 [*MPL* 196, 894]). Richard spoke of a mode of being which is not from eternity and not of itself, a mode of being which is of eternity and of itself, and a mode of being which is from eternity but not of itself.

due to accident, but is rather according to the intention and direction of an intellect. (5) There is a natural inclination in man, when he is in extreme difficulties and without help, to call upon God in prayer.

These five arguments make up Gerhard's entire effort to go the empirical route in proving God's existence. And it might be added that the existence (τὸ ὅτι) of God is all he attempts to prove — not any particular attribute.

But why does he bother to do this? Why does he attempt to prove empirically what the Christian already believes? It is significant that the later Lutheran teachers do not usually trouble themselves with such proofs, although they sometimes go to rather great lengths to show that people of all nations and cultures have some conception, vague as it is, of God.[10] They return rather to the less ambitious program of Chemnitz and restrict themselves to a discussion of the natural knowlege of God.

Gerhard feels that there is some justification for proceeding as he does. Although the existence of God remains an article of faith, and not a mere preamble to the articles of faith, as Thomas has said (*Summa Theologica,* P. I, Q. 2, a. 3), there appear nevertheless to be three justifiable reasons for offering such proofs for God's existence. (1) Not all believe in God, and certainly not all behave as if they do. Proofs for God's existence serve as a refutation of such theoretical and practical atheism. Gerhard does not tell us at this point whether such refutation is done for the sake of the unbeliever as a sort of law preachment, or for the sake of the church. He does mention, however, that Scripture itself does not bother with any such proof but rather establishes the fundamental article of God's existence for the comfort of God's people by pointing to God's works and in particular to His creation. (2) Since all men in times of extremity and temptation tend to become either Stoics or Epicureans, proofs for God's

---

[10] Even Chemnitz (*Loci Theologici,* I, 20) mentions the opinions of Cicero and others. Perhaps the most elaborate attempt to show that people at all times and everywhere had notions concerning God is offered by Calov, *Theologia Naturalis et Revelata* (Leipzig, 1646), p. 150 ff. He mentions, among others (without citing their works): Zoroaster, Homer, Hesiod, Thales, Pythagoras, Anaximander, Simonides, Anaximenes, Xenophon, Parmenides, Zeno, Anaxagoras, Empedocles, Protagoras, Pindar, Sophocles, Euripides, Aratus, Socrates, Plato, Demosthenes, Theophrastus, Cicero, Seneca, etc. Calov is not so much interested in what doctrine these ancient thinkers held as in the fact that their writings reflect an awareness of God. Calov's method (against the Socinians primarily) is to cite Scripture verses which teach a natural knowledge of God (e. g. Acts 17:22-29; 14:15-17; Ps. 19:1; Heb. 11:6; Ps. 10:4; 14:1 et al.) and then to offer corroborating evidence from examples of ancient heathen philosophers and thinkers.

existence may serve at times to bolster their faith. If such an assertion seems at first blush to be utterly rationalistic, we must bear in mind that it is never Gerhard's intention to establish the existence of God only or even primarily from such formal proofs as he now offers, but from Scripture which "supplies more numerous and more certain proofs *(fundamenta)* for God's existence and thus makes our knowledge which is based upon divine revelation more full and firm." (3) The knowledge of God which we possess from nature will be enhanced by these arguments. That is to say, these proofs will enable us better to see and appreciate God's workings in nature. Gerhard, like the other Lutheran dogmaticians,[11] envisages the pursuit of natural theology as the legitimate activity of the Christian as he applies the doctrine of creation.

In Gerhard's five proofs for God's existence we have the most developed presentation of such apologetics to be found in Lutheran theology. But actually his approach is rather modest when compared with the elaborate arguments of the philosophers of the day. Whereas Descartes and Spinoza and Leibniz start *de novo,* as it were, using variations of the ontological proof or, in the case of Leibniz, a posteriori proofs as well, Gerhard starts from the point of the natural knowledge of God acquired *(acquisita)* from the contemplation of His creation. Unlike the philosophers of the day, he and Lutheranism as a whole begin from a definite and frank Christian perspective, from the point of view of faith.[12]

[11] Calov, *Systema,* II, 51.

[12] This is true even of the Lutheran philosopher, Cornelius Martini, who, following Heerbrand, goes no farther than Gerhard. Martini feels that one is quite justified in working out a posteriori demonstrations for God's existence, based on Romans 1; this is within the spirit of Paul's utterances there. And Martini uses David's confession that he was wonderfully formed in his mother's womb (Ps. 139:13) to show that man is not formed by some fortuitous concurrence of atoms or in any accidental manner. See Cornelius Martini, *Compendium Theologiae et Epitome Theologiae Naturalis* (Wolfenbüttel, 1650), p. 57. One might assume from the foregoing that some form of ontological argument for God's existence could have been derived from the Lutheran teaching of a *notitia Dei naturalis insita,* but one does not find such arguments worked out. The Lutherans are content merely to affirm the fact of an innate knowledge of God without going any further and without expatiating apologetically.

The Calvinists of the 17th century, even with their sometimes strong neo-Aristotelian bent, dealt with the proofs for God's existence from the same point of view, from the perspective of faith. Matthew Martini, the Reformed theologian and Gerhard's contemporary, for instance, begins his large study of theology proper with a series of formal proofs for God's existence, something no Lutheran did. See Matthias Martini, *De Deo, Summo Illo Bono et Causa Omnis Boni, Libelli Duo* (Bremen, 1616), p. 9 ff. To him "nothing can be more certain than

By the existence of God, Lutheran theology, whether using rational arguments or proofs from Scripture, means simply that God is.[13] Gerhard's formal proofs are brought forth to show this. But such proofs can never bring forth faith in God's existence. Faith can only be wrought by the Word of God.

Against Thomas Aquinas, who denied that God's existence was an article of faith but said it was only a presupposition for all the articles of faith (*Summa Theologica,* P. I, Q. 2, a. 2), Calov contends that the very chief article of faith is that God is.[14] True, philosophers have spoken of God's existence and attributes apart from any Christian revelation. But faith in God can only be wrought by the Word of God. Calov assumes a complete distinction between the theory or opinion of a philosopher and the faith of a Christian. In spite of the fact that they speak of the same thing, faith and philosophy remain in two completely different and distinct categories. Calov is thinking of faith in the sense of personal trust. Philosophy, proofs, reason cannot produce such faith. Faith, even in things which seem clear and true to the natural man, is always based upon a special word or revelation of God. Whatever views one may entertain about God apart from revelation are mere opinions; they may be called knowledge, but they are not faith. Here in Calov we observe a strenuous rejection of natural religion as being in a class with Christianity. To Calov it is important that we learn both who God is and that He is by faith from

that God really exists." Martini adds to the stock proofs of Thomas the arguments that all pagans have a propensity for religion, that there are events of judgment and deliverance in history which cry out for divine authorship, that prayers have been answered, and many other evidences.

However, with the Socinians the approach was different. In spite of their rejection of an innate natural knowledge of God — or perhaps because of it — they presented the most detailed a posteriori proofs for God's existence. And whereas the Lutherans and Calvinists for the most part were interested in what Christians could know about God from nature and how to use this knowledge, the Socinian concern in using such rational proofs was more directly and optimistically apologetic. Among the Socinians John Völkel offers perhaps the most elaborate causal, cosmological, and teleological arguments for the existence of God — again at the very beginning of his large work on the Christian religion. See *De Vera Religione Libri Quinque* (Cracow, 1630), pp. 7—46. Völkel also argued at length for God's existence from miracles (p. 57 ff). Whereas the Lutherans were interested chiefly in the knowledge of God we as Christians have from nature, what its significance is, and how we Christians are to use it, Völkel is concerned about proving God's existence to any doubter — his purpose is much more clearly apologetic.

[13] Calov, *Systema,* II, 110.

[14] *Systema,* II, 140.

His Word — and not from philosophy. This is in keeping with Heb. 11:6: "He that cometh to God must believe that He is." [15]

Of course, simple existence in itself is never comprehensible. Therefore Scripture, in attesting God's existence, always tells us also something about Him and His works. This is done when Scripture ascribes names to God and rehearses oracles of God and manifestations such as theophanies and appearances. God's miracles tell of His majesty and power, His gifts tell of His grace and mercy, His acts of judgment tell of His infallibility and omniscience, and His creation and preservation of all things tell of His wisdom and goodness.[16] In the light of such an approach of Calov's we can see how very limited formal proofs for God's existence really are in Lutheran theology. For faith and salvation depend upon our learning to know of God's existence and works from His revelation in Scripture.[17]

2. THE SEMANTIC PROBLEM

Can we talk cognitively and with meaning about God who is utterly transcendent? Can terms be ascribed to God and created things (such as men and angels) meaningfully and without denying God's transcendence? These questions, which were considered by the medieval scholastics and are discussed today with renewed vigor and interest by theologians and linguistic analysts, were reintroduced by the Lutheran theologians of the 17th century.

The most thorough answers to the questions are offered by Quenstedt and Hollaz.[18] Their position is that terms such as Spirit, substance, essence, and the like (it makes no difference to their argument whether the terms are Biblical or not) can be predicated of both God and creatures. The terms, however, are not to be predicated univocally or equivocally, but analogically, according to the analogy of intrinsic attributes. Both theologians follow closely the conclusions of Jacob Martini,[19] who had offered

[15] *Systema*, II, 142: "Oportet ergo id e verbo Dei, non ex philosophia addiscere, quod Deus sit (et multo magis reliqua si credendum sit)."

[16] Calov, *Systema*, II, 110.

[17] See Robert Preus, loc. cit., 178—79.

[18] Quenstedt, *Systema*, P.I, C.8, S.2, q.1 (I, 293); Hollaz, *Examen*, P.I, C.1, q.18 (I, 258). Both theologians present a refined version of Thomas Aquinas' position (*Summa Theologica*, P.I, Q.13, a.5).

[19] Jacob Martini, *Partitiones & Quaestiones Metaphysicae* (Wittenberg, 1615), p. 635.

a long and detailed study of the formal logico-semantic aspects of analogical predication.

According to Martini the concept "being" *(ens)* can be employed only analogically when ascribed to God and creatures. If the term were used equivocally we could know nothing and say nothing cognitive about God; God's entire revelation of Himself would thus be undermined. If the term were used univocally the priority of God's being would be threatened; theologically this would tend to deny the infinite distinction between God and His creatures. Therefore to speak cognitively about God without denying His transcendence we must speak by analogy. But what sort of analogy do we employ? For there are many kinds of analogies.

Martini distinguished between an *analogia proportionis* and an *analogia attributionis.*[20] The former is the analogy which is represented by any relationship between things, an analogy which is always somewhat metaphorical and inexact, for example, the analogy between a laughing man and a blooming meadow. The *analogia attributionis* obtains when certain terms are predicated of many objects because of some order or relationship they have in respect to one to whom these terms can be attributed in the original or primary sense *(ex primaria constitutione).* Thus certain attributes of man are analogous to the same attributes in God, and being is predicated of man and God; but always principally of God as the *ens primum.* For the creature always depends upon God and derives his being from God, and not vice versa.[21]

The position of Quenstedt and Hollaz is that there is a formal justification for analogical predication in addition and in contrast to equivocal and univocal predication. And in the case of language which applies to both God and rational creatures they argue for more than a mere *analogia proportionis* which is too vague and indefinite, but insist that such language is according to an *analogia attributionis.* This is not merely an analogy of outward attributes, attributes really extrinsic to both God and man, but of attributes which are intrinsic to both God and man. In other words, the terms Spirit, essence, being, etc. are predicated of God and man and angels — God is a Spirit and so are angels — but of God absolutely *(absolute,* πρώτως), of men and angels in a contingent and posterior sense (δευτέρως, *per dependentiam*) in that they have their existence in Him.

---

[20] Martini, p. 770.
[21] Martini, p. 636.

What about the charge that analogical language undermines the infinite difference *(infinita distantia)* between God and man, a doctrine which Lutheranism wished ardently to uphold? — And ironically the use of analogical language was an attempt to uphold this very doctrine. Or to pose the objection somewhat differently, if God is utterly transcendent, infinitely distinct from His creatures, as distinct as being from nothingness, then there can be no analogy *(proportio)*, no likeness, no common features between God and any creature. This denial of all analogy between God and any creature Quenstedt attributes to Arminius. And today the entire school of logical positivism would voice its agreement.

Hollaz answers the objection in the following way. There is truly an infinite distinction between God and man, but this is not an infinite negative difference as between being and nothingness. "Between God and His creatures there does obtain an infinite positive distance," he says, "in that God in His absolute perfection and majesty infinitely excels His creatures. But we must not conclude from this that God and His creatures have no attributes in common and that no concept will fit them both. For since God is one who shares His goodness and perfection, He has imparted many streams of His goodness and many rays of His perfection to His creatures, with the result that they possess a certain, though limited, degree of perfection." Hollaz remarks that God's creation did not always exist, and some of it will not always exist. It is therefore unlike God; it does not exist of necessity. But it does have being. And therefore being can be ascribed to God and man even though God is absolutely infinite.

A more sophisticated twofold answer to the objection is offered by Quenstedt. First he points out that the analogies between God and creatures are never absolute but always comparative. Created beings are quite clearly not nothing. They behave in a certain way, they think, they feel, they have definite properties. Therefore they are beings. Quenstedt says, "Now although being, as it is in God, is infinite, nevertheless the idea of being can be separated from infinity itself. God differs from creatures totally, not however in respect to the *existence* of being, but in respect to the nature of His being which is infinite."

Second, Quenstedt maintains that when being is attributed to God and creatures, this is not done according to strict mathematical analogy; but certain features and relationships exist between the one and the other, such as the relation of cause and effect. It is quite apparent that Quenstedt,

particularly in his first argument, is making a concerted effort not to confuse ontology and predication (meaning) at this point. Although there
is an infinite distinction between God and man, still man can know something about God and make cognitive, literal — not merely metaphorical
or symbolic — statements about Him. God's transcendence makes neither
revelation or meaningful discourse about Him impossible.

But have our two theologians really answered the objection? It is clear
that their conception of analogy is based upon a prior assumption that
there is a God who has made Himself known to us through the medium
of language so that we can speak cognitively about Him and thus describe
Him and His actions to some extent. This means that God has condescended to come to us and speak to us at our level, so to speak. And
therefore we must know something about His creatures before His speech
to us will mean anything to us and before we can speak meaningfully
(analogically) about Him. This does not imply that we are creating a God
after our own image; for all our language about God is normed by His
verbal revelation which was made particularly concrete through the Incarnation.

Hollaz had previously made it clear that we can only grasp God conceptually according to human thoughts. This is why our speaking God
calls Himself King, Father, Redeemer, etc.: terms which are generally
within the experience of men. And it is not a false picture which God
offers of Himself through such verbal revelation — God does not make
Himself known as a mere phenomenon — it is God as He really is, *Gott
an sich*, whom we know and describe, God who *is* King, Father, and
Redeemer. Quenstedt insists that only the notion of analogy can be made
to fit with this assumption: that the living God has actually spoken to
us about Himself.

Given this assumption, the Lutheran position regarding analogy seems
both well taken and impregnable logically. But the objection, at least
as our modern positivists would pose it, has not been answered. For the
charge is that those who argue for analogical predication beg the question
when they assume that God has made Himself known verbally to man.
Since they were not confronted with this particular challenge, I do not
know just how the old Lutherans would have reacted, except by an appeal
to the historical witness of God's revelation (namely, Scripture) and to
its inner power and criteria and to the witness of the Spirit through the

Word of the Gospel.[22] It is interesting, however, and amusing that Quenstedt accuses the very ones who object to analogical predication of begging the question. Their objection, he says, is based upon a rejection out of hand of the possibility of cognitive language about God. Quenstedt saw clearly what was at stake in the issue, even as we do today, namely the possibility of theology as doctrine, language about God; and he tried his best to defend his position with the Thomistic concept of analogy. God is totally transcendent, but He is not totally indescribable; these two facts must be upheld.

There has been a good deal of discussion of Quenstedt's position on this point, and it might be well to trace this discussion in order to make his position more clear. Karl Barth has been quite critical.[23] Jörg Baur, in a very detailed study of Quenstedt's theology,[24] has been quite sympathetic. According to Barth, Quenstedt's insistence on the notion of *analogia attributionis intrinsicae* and his insistence that man possesses the same attributes as God (but only *dependenter et per participationem*) presupposes that only the grace of revelation can make this predication of a creature. And Barth agrees with this. But he faults Quenstedt for not bringing in the doctrine of revelation at this point and for not speaking in good Lutheran fashion of justification by faith and of an *analogia attributionis extrinsicae* of the righteousness of faith, Christ's imputed righteousness. For only on the basis of revelation and justification, according to Barth, do we know God and our relation to Him, certainly not from a mere understanding of the notion of analogy.

It seems that Barth has missed something of the point Quenstedt is trying to make in his entire discussion. The question to which Quenstedt addresses himself is not primarily cognitive, as Barth assumes, or ontological, but linguistic and semantic. He is speaking of our language about God, not our knowledge of God. This is the reason the question is posed where it is within the *locus* on the essence and attributes of God and the reason it is posed as it is, namely, whether certain terms can be "predicated" of God and creatures. Of course our language about God cannot be dis-

[22] See Robert Preus, loc. cit., p. 300.

[23] Karl Barth, *Church Dogmatics,* trans. G. T. Thomson, G. W. Bromily, et al. (Edinburgh: T. & T. Clark, 1936—), II, 1, 237—43.

[24] Jörg Baur, *Die Vernunft zwischen Ontologie und Evangelium: Eine Untersuchung zur Theologie Johann Andreas Quenstedts.* (Gütersloh: Verlagshaus Gerd Mohn, 1962), p. 181 ff.

sociated from our knowledge of God, inasmuch as the predications we make of God are descriptive and cognitive, but the question of our knowledge of God is not the specific point of discussion for Quenstedt.

Neither is Quenstedt speaking of an ontological question, of our creature relationship to God. Of course the question might be put: Can God and man be comprehended under one concept such as being? But again, when Barth says that for Quenstedt the answer is a simple yes, he is not, according to Baur, being completely true to Quenstedt. For Quenstedt is not asking this question. He insists, in fact, that the terms which describe both God and man (such as essence, substance, Spirit, and others) are used in the present context conceptually, not ontologically. In other words, there is no ontic reality (called essence, substance, or what have you) prior to God and under which both God and man can be subsumed.[25] It is just that man does and must conceptualize and speak of God. And the question is whether this can be done without denying God altogether (univocal language, pantheism) or whether it can be done at all. It is the position of Lutheran theology that terms can be ascribed analogically — and that means meaningfully — to God, and this on the basis of God's revelation which is conceptual and verbal — a revelation given that man might worship and confess Him.[26] This is the only concern at this point.

But what is Quenstedt's answer to the question posed above? Can God and man be comprehended under one concept such as being? Quenstedt does not answer the question, nor do the other Lutherans, possibly sensing that the whole use of analogical language in speaking of God will be undermined if the question is answered yes or no.

Actually Barth's criticism is not really so much against the theology of Lutheran orthodoxy at this point as against the very method of beginning a dogmatics with the doctrine of God unless done Christologically, as Barth himself attempts to do. This is well taken. But one's doctrine

---

[25] Quenstedt, *Systema,* "Nihil Deum antecedit, aut antecedere potest, prioritas vere illa conceptuum tantum fit per mentis nostrae operationem." In the light of this statement and of Quenstedt's whole careful discussion Barth's criticism (p. 241), as Baur points out (p. 182), is not true to Quenstedt, when Barth says: "The consequence is surely inescapable that the criterion of all truth in this relationship is not God at all, but the being in which God and man — the former absolutely, the latter relatively — participate. And everything that is to be said in this relationship and in consequence of it will necessarily lead up to an explication of this participation, not of man in God, but of God and of man in this final truth of being which is ultimately superior to God" (sic).

[26] Cf. Chemnitz, *Loci Theologici,* I, 24.

of God cannot be taken only from one's first chapter in dogmatics; all theology is theocentric and Christocentric. That classical Lutheranism believed and tried to practice this principle just as Barth did will become apparent as we proceed in our studies.

Although some of the same attributes and works can be predicated of both God and rational creatures, this cannot be done with the proper names of God.[27] The tetragrammaton, for instance, can be only ascribed to God and is incommunicable. For it infers His essence which is independent and omnipotent "and is therefore appropriate to nothing except the one God." [28] In Scripture the divine name is ascribed to God in direct opposition to false gods and creatures and idols. It denotes God Himself. There was more at stake in maintaining this Biblical principle and practice than first meets the eye. Against what they thought to be a latent pantheism among the Socinians, Lutheran theologians were attempting at this point to stress the absolute uniqueness of God, that He is wholly different from all that is not God.

Calov [29] fears also an inherent nominalism in Socinianism which tended to make "God" a proper name for the Deity but only as a *nomen dignitatis et officii.* To Calov such a view could actually lead to atheism (although using the name God), to a denial that God had His own nature — a view not dissimilar to that of modern pragmatism or of Neo-Kantianism. The names of God have the function, among other things, of pointing to His existence; and God exists on account of Himself *(Deus ob naturam divinam solum Deus est).*

3. THE CONCEPTUAL PROBLEM

Can God's essence be defined? Following Thomas Aquinas (*Summa Theologica,* P. I, Q. 3, a. 5), Lutheran theology makes no attempt to define God and His essence.[30] To attempt any definition would place God within

---

[27] Calov, *Systema,* II, 148. See also Joh. Guiliemi Baieri, *Compendium Theologiae Positivae,* ed. Carol. Ferd. Guil. Walther (St. Louis: Luth. Concordia-Verlag, 1879), II, 14-32. Hereafter listed as Baier-Walther.

[28] Calov, *Systema,* II, 161.

[29] Ibid., II, 218.

[30] The first of the Lutherans to go into a lengthy discussion of the question is Gerhard (*Loci Theologici,* III, 68), and we shall base our comments on his discussion. Prior to that time theologians like Giles Hunnius (*Opera Latina* [Wittenberg, 1619], p. 94) lists three reasons why God cannot be defined: (1) Only

some genus or other, make Him univocally similar to His creatures and deny the infinite distinction *(infinitum intervallum)* between God and His creation. It must not be granted that God has something even analogous to a genus. For whatever has its own genus is finite and composite (Aristotle, *Topica,* 6, 3). But God is infinite, He is *simplicissimus* which means absolutely without parts, without many operations, and therefore absolutely unanalyzable. He cannot be comprehended under the categories of matter and form, genus and difference, subject and accident, potency and act, being and becoming, person *(suppositum)* and nature.

Dannhauer [31] offers a typical explanation of why a definition of the divine essence must be avoided. His reasons are quite practical and doxological. Any attempt to define God would undermine His transcendence and illicitly probe the mystery of His essence. Ultimately it would destroy both the unity and the trinity of God and our worship of Him. He says, "You cannot define what is infinite and subsume it under certain categories like genus and difference, much less can you represent the infinite with any one concept. Strictly speaking, every genus along with its species and individual parts may be multiplied so that it becomes plural in number. For instance, Abraham is a man, Isaac is a man, Jacob is a man. Therefore Abraham, Isaac, and Jacob are three men. But in divine things it is wrong to talk like that; you cannot say, for instance, the Father is God, the Son is God, the Holy Spirit is God; therefore the Father, the Son, and the Holy Spirit are three Gods."

It is quite clear that Lutheran theology in its refusal to make any attempt at defining God's essence is simply trying to uphold the absolute uniqueness of God and His transcendence.[32] For instance, if God and

finite things are capable of definition. (2) Something infinite cannot be comprehended by a series of predicates. (3) God who is infinite cannot be classified according to any genus; He is unique. Calvinists had already discussed this point in some detail. See Bartholomew Keckermann, *Systema Theologicus* (Geneva, 1602), L.I, p. 6.

[31] *Hodosophia Christiana* (Leipzig, 1695), p. 92.

[32] Both Gerhard and Dannhauer owe much in their discussion to a well-known statement of John of Damascus (*De Fide Orthodoxa*, I, 4 [*MPG* 94, 799]) which deserves to be cited here. "It is impossible to say what God is according to His substance. It is better to make statements about God's being far removed from all things. For He is not of the same class as those things that are *(Nam nihil eorum, quae sunt, est)*, but He is above all beings *(entia)* and above being *(ens)* itself. For if all forms of knowledge have to do with what exists, certainly that which is above knowledge must be also above essence (ὑπὲρ οὐσίαν, *supra substantiam*) . . . God then is infinite and incomprehensible, and all that is comprehensible about Him

angels had a genus in common, even analogically, there would be some sort of comparison *(proportio)* between God and angels. But there is no comparison between the infinite and the finite (Is. 40:12 ff.). The term spirit is indeed attributed to both God and angels, but never in the sense of a genus, of an overarching classification. The term Spirit when applied to God denotes His limitless majesty, His οὐσία ὑπερούσιος which can neither be restricted nor limited nor defined.

But if God cannot be defined, how can He be known? To this question which is still very much alive today, Gerhard replies in the following manner. Although no logical definition is possible, an ample description of God may be drawn from the Scriptures. Although we do not understand and know God perfectly,[33] we do know Him with a knowledge which is sufficient for salvation. Thus a logical definition cannot be given, but an essential definition which amounts to a description is possible.

Following Chemnitz, who offers a more lengthy Biblical description of God, Gerhard describes God as follows,[34] "God is a Spiritual Being. He is absolutely without composition and infinite, of immense goodness, wisdom, and power. He is righteous and true. He is the Father who from eternity begat a Son in His own image and through the Son and the Holy Spirit has established and still preserves all things. He is the Son who was born of the Father from eternity and in the fulness of the time took

is His infinity and incomprehensibility. Now when you speak affirmatively of certain things being in God, you are not talking of His nature, but of those things which pertain to His nature (τὰ περὶ τὴν φύσιν). For if you say that God is good, righteous, wise, or speak of any other power in God, you are not talking about God's nature but of those things which pertain to His nature." The concern of Lutheran theology at this point is the same as that of John of Damascus, to preserve the absolute transcendence of God. This protects the Christian doctrine of God from all forms of pantheism and retains belief in the unity of God.

[33] Here too Gerhard is no doubt taking much from the church fathers. Basil, for instance (Ep. 234, *PMG* 32, 867—68), says that although God is not comprehended, He is still known. Although we do not know His essence, we know Him; but we know Him only in part.

[34] See Chemnitz, *Loci Theologici,* p. 18. Heerbrand and Selnecker give a description of God very similar to that of Chemnitz, a description which is slightly longer than Gerhard's and with an emphasis upon the church and God's revelation to the church. Dannhauer (*Hodosophia Christiana,* p. 178) makes much more of creation, providence, and God's lordship in his description; but then in his dogmatics he had already discussed the doctrine of the church. The later dogmaticians, Calov (*Systema,* II, 177), Baier (Baier-Walther, II, 14), and Hollaz (*Examen,* P.I, C.1, q.16) give the very shortest description such as "God is an independent Spirit" or "God is an infinite spiritual essence of three Persons, Father, Son, and Holy Spirit."

on a human nature and in that nature accomplished the work of redemption. And He is the Holy Spirit who in an indescribable manner proceeds from the Father and the Son, who was visibly poured out upon the apostles and in our day is invisibly sent into the hearts of believers, and who through the preaching of the Gospel gathers a church from our whole human race and sanctifies it to the glory of His name and to the eternal salvation of all who believe."

This description, which sounds like a brief summary of Christian doctrine, is highly significant. Gerhard is describing the acting, speaking, saving God who has made Himself known in His acts of redemption and who is even now acting and speaking in the church. Like Chemnitz, Gerhard wants no part of that "mutilated" description of the philosophers: "eternal mind," "the cause of all good in nature," etc. God's revelation, His mighty works, *Deus pro nobis* must enter into the description. For "This description rightly tells us who God is and leads us to the divine revelation." [35] Divine revelation and the church as the recipient of revelation must be woven into the description of God. And the divine revelation is that God has sent His Son who came in the flesh, was crucified, and rose again for sinners. Every description of God must include this fact; it must first of all be a Trinitarian description,[36] but it must also be an evangelical description which sets the church apart from every heathen opinion or fancy.

In a word, love, divine love, must mark the description of God. And so as a practical description one might simply say with the apostle, "God is love" (1 John 4:8). For all the works of God, says Gerhard, spring from His love. Love prompted the creation of all things. Love sent the Son to carry out the work of redemption. Love gives the Holy Spirit who kindles love in the hearts of believers. In eternal life love will bring us face to face with God. The *Deus absconditus* in the category of substance is incomprehensible, ineffable, beyond our understanding and knowledge, bewildering and frightening; but the *Deus revelatus* in the category of His relation to us is rightly described as love. For in love and from love He does all things. Moreover, our practical knowledge of God consists in love. For God has manifested His mighty works and goodness among men that they might love Him. When we consider that God in love not

---

[35] Chemnitz, ibid.
[36] Calov, *Systema,* II, 282; Hollaz, *Examen,* P.I, C.1, q.16.

only created all things for me but in His love became Himself man for men, we must respond in kind. The heart which is not softened by such a great fire of love must be harder than iron.

In the light of Gerhard's entire discussion of the Christian description of God one is surprised to read Elert's bitter denunciation of Gerhard at just this point.[37] Noting that Gerhard calls God *"summum ens,"* [38] Elert comments, "Here, therefore, God is, in the first instance, a neuter — the characteristics that make up the person are accidental. He who defines God in such a way is no longer conscious of responsibility for what he thinks about Him. Those definitions leave out of consideration the unavoidable alternative between unbelief and belief." But these terms *(summum ens, actus purus)* are not Gerhard's *starting point* in his doctrine of God. Gerhard has already offered a long and fruitful discussion on the names of God. Nor do the terms belong to a definition of God, as Elert implies; rather they occur in a section in which Gerhard is trying to show that God cannot be defined. And that Gerhard, in using a term which may be applied to God and to creatures, employs a term which happens to be neuter *(ens)* is utterly irrelevant (when Gerhard later describes God as love *{charitas}* he is hardly making God feminine). It is merely Gerhard's way, ill-chosen though it may be, of speaking of the absolute transcendence of God, of saying that God is holy and perfect in every direction and not to be confined within any human categories. A more just criticism by Elert would have been to fault Gerhard for employing the old scholastic terminology, as he spoke to this particular issue, and for not seeing the advantage and necessity of returning *ad fontes Scripturae* also at this point — and then to let it go at that.

In this respect Calov, who does rather little with the whole problem of the definition and description of God, is no doubt on safer ground. Calov only indirectly touches upon the subject of the essence and description of God in his treatment of God as Spirit (John 4:24).[39] That God is Spirit means for Calov that God is incorporeal in any materialistic sense (Luke 24:39); but for Calov it means more. It means that He is infinite and almighty. It means also that He is invisible (John 1:18; Col. 1:15; 1 Tim. 1:17). But the term bears also positive connotations, according

[37] *The Structure of Lutheranism,* pp. 55—56.
[38] Gerhard, *Loci Theologici,* III, 69. Cf. Baier-Walther, II, 14.
[39] *Systema,* II, 178-91.

to Calov. It means that God is all-knowing; He knows all things in one all-embracing act (Acts 15:18 KJV). It means that He possesses a good and gracious will (Ps. 119:3; Dan. 4:17; James 1:18). It means that He cannot be limited or caught by any anthropomorphism, He has no parts or human form. Spirit denotes therefore the divine, triune essence of God. The term is necessarily marked by infinitude which means that there is no quantitative extension of God, but His essence is perfect in every respect (Ps. 145:3; Job 11:7-8), unlimited and absolutely immense (Bar. 3:27), dependent upon nothing outside Himself.

Such a description of God with the term "Spirit" is by no means academic to Calov, but very practical. The descriptive term "Spirit" actually enables us to know God as He really is in His divine nature and as He differs from all that is not God; and consequently it enables us to worship Him in spirit and in truth, that is to say, our spirit rests in Him as Savior. Our response to Him as Spirit is with corresponding spiritual thoughts (Rom. 8:5; 1 Cor. 2:14), spiritual actions (Rom. 8:13), spiritual words and songs (Col. 3:16; Eph. 5:19), spiritual sacrifices (1 Peter 2:5), spiritual prayers (John 4:24) and spiritual unity (Eph. 4:3). Thus also we are filled with the Spirit (Eph. 5:18), renewed in our minds by the Spirit (Eph. 4:23), ruled by the Spirit (Gal. 5:18), we walk by the Spirit (Rom. 8:6), and we are planted in the Spirit. (Gal. 6:8)

The spiritual essence of God cannot be comprehended, according to Calov. God cannot be examined by any sort of human investigation. This is both humbling (Law: Is. 40:15, 17) and comforting (Gospel). For the paradoxically infinite Deity has condescended to approach us so that we become participants and sharers *(participes et consortes)* in His goodness and majesty, so that we have our rest in Him, in the joy and comfort and bliss which are had only in Him. Yes, we may be said to possess the infinite God. For what after all, asks Calov, is the nature of God? It is eternal truth, righteousness, wisdom, eternal life, peace, joy, and pleasure, and every good that can be named. And he who shares in the divine nature has all these things: he lives forever, he has peace and joy and pleasure forever, he becomes clean and righteous and powerful against the devil and death. And nothing in all the world can harm him. All this is known and acquired (to know God is to have Him) when one knows and has the infinite God. And for this reason the proper description of God is never something academic but of highest practical importance to the church.

It is quite clear from the foregoing that the old Lutheran theologians, although discussing a number of philosophical questions and using a good deal of philosophical vocabulary, do not see God as some sort of neuter First Cause, but as the Lord of history who is also Creator of all. Theirs is a Biblical rather than a philosophical notion of God. This will be seen more clearly as we observe their concentration on the *creatio continua* in another chapter. But the nagging philosophical questions arise, and the old Lutheran theologians often feel bound to give an answer — though at times half hearted — of some kind. The problem for them is that apologetics often gets quite mixed up with the straightforward Biblical picture which they intend to present; and this at times will tend to blur the Biblical picture.

God's Attributes

CHAPTER THREE

The doctrine of God is the most difficult *locus* in Christian dogmatics. This fact is brought out clearly as we study the history and development of Lutheran dogmatics after the Reformation. How does one approach this article and speak adequately and systematically about the transcendent God? One cannot. There is complete agreement in Lutheran theology on this point. One can speak only inadequately of Him who is absolutely sublime, and of the Eternal One who has no beginning or end, no past or future, one can speak only according to an arbitrary, conceptual, human order and arrangement. The fact that God in His grace has emerged, as it were, from the inner abode of His majesty and made Himself known through cognitive words and through the Word made flesh makes, of course, the doctrine of God a possibility. But God's revelation has not been total — we do not see Him face to face — but only fragmentarily and piecemeal; and so our doctrine of God can present only a partial, incomplete, imperfect, and paradoxical picture of Him.

How does one begin methodologically to present the doctrine of God? Four possible starting points presented themselves to the old Lutheran theologians. One could begin with the names of God, and Gerhard and others began their presentation with fruitful studies of the divine names. One could begin with the attributes of God, and this is the real starting point of most of the later dogmaticians. One could begin with the works of God. This possibility, which is the most Biblical, presented itself to the Lutheran teachers, and some gave brief attention to the works of God in their *locus de Deo*. But they all preferred to treat such an all-embracing theme as the works of God under the following *loci:* Christology, soteriology, ecclesiology, etc. Finally one could begin like the ancient creeds and the *Augsburg Confession* with the doctrine of the Trinity. This was the approach of Chemnitz, as it had been for Melanchthon, Selnecker, Heerbrand, Hafenreffer, and all the Lutheran dogmaticians until Gerhard.[1] In a sense this made all dogmatics a sort of commentary on the creeds. None of these earlier theologians offer any discussion of the attributes of God, except in passing, as they expound their Trinitarian description of God.

It remained for John Gerhard,[2] the innovator, to offer the first extended and detailed discourse on the divine attributes in Lutheran dogmatics. This had to be done sooner or later. The systematic theology of the Lutherans had left a real gap at this point, and it had to be filled. But there is a real risk in what Gerhard attempts to do. Can the attributes of God be considered prior to (and apart from) His works? Does not all of Scripture and experience teach us that God is known a posteriori through His works of judgment and grace? And surely the doctrine of the Trinity, which introduces God as Creator, Redeemer, and Comforter, should precede and lead to an enumeration and discussion of the divine attributes? Unquestionably aware of these and other objections to his procedure, Gerhard nevertheless elects to begin his discussion of God with the divine attributes. Why? He offers no reason. It is probably due to his concern for logical order.

Quenstedt,[3] however, defends Gerhard's procedure, which he and all

---

[1] Martin Chemnitz, *Loci Theologici* (Wittenberg, 1653), p. 17 ff.; Jacob Heerbrand, *Compendium Theologiae* (Tübingen, 1573), p. 9 ff.; Nicolaus Selnecker, *Institutiones Christianae Religionis* (Frankfurt, 1573), p. 73 ff.; Matthias Hafenreffer, *Loci Theologici* (Tübingen, 1611), p. 27 passim: also Leonard Hutter, *Loci Communes Theologici* (Wittenberg, 1619), p. 98 ff.; Balthazar Mentzer, *Exegesis Augustanae Confessionis* (in *Opera Latina*, Frankfurt, 1669), I, 306 ff. Of the later Lutherans only Friedmann Bechmann follows this procedure and omits any discussion of the attributes — and this because he follows Hutter. See *Annotationes Uberiores in Compendium Theologicum Leonhardi Hutteri* (Frankfurt and Leipzig, 1690), p. 55. Cundisius, even though writing comments on Hutter's earlier compendium, adapts himself to the latter mode of presentation. See Gottfried Cundisius, *Notae et Observationes quibus Compendium Theologicum Dn. D. Leonhardi Hutteri Illustratur* (Leipzig, 1705), L. 2, q. 2, p. 68 ff.

[2] *Loci Theologici*, III, 84 ff.

[3] *Systema*, P.I, C.8, S.1 (I, 284 ff.). See also Baier-Walther, II, 11 ff.

the later dogmaticians follow. He begins with a distinction: God can be viewed in an absolute sense according to His essence without regard to the Three Persons, or relatively as being Three Persons. Viewed in the first manner we speak of God's essence and essential attributes; we speak of what He is. Viewed relatively we consider the essence of God according to the Trinity of Persons and the characteristics of the divine Persons; we consider who God is. Quenstedt is arguing against Chemnitz's [4] more direct and simple procedure.

To Chemnitz all articles of faith center in this article of the Trinity. We know what God is by knowing who He is. And in his discussion Chemnitz chose to distinguish only between God's essence (His unity and trinity) and His will as it works its way out in creation, preservation, and particularly in all His gifts to the church. According to this procedure any discussion of divine attributes is subsumed under the *locus* on the Trinity or the works of God, which include the whole of dogmatics. To Chemnitz revealed theology should begin with the doctrine of the Trinity, which tells us who the true God is and leads directly to what God has done.

Quenstedt disagrees with this method of procedure [5] and says that although the doctrine of the Trinity is fundamental and necessary to know for salvation, it is also a matter of revelation that God is good, wise, just, etc. This is true, but Quenstedt has hardly proved thereby that his method is preferable; and as a matter of fact Chemnitz's approach gets to the subject of the works of God (redemption, the Gospel) much sooner than Quenstedt's. Quenstedt's approach is unquestionably more logical and allows for more discussion of the attributes which had not been given sufficient attention by the earlier teachers. But it is based on a questionable distinction and tends to abstract God from His works which are always the works of the triune God. It is interesting and rather ironic that Quenstedt as a matter of fact gives rather perfunctory attention to the divine attributes when he finally gets down to it — much less than Gerhard had done.

What are divine attributes? What is their function? What is the relation of the divine attributes to the essence of God? Are the divine attributes real? Perhaps the best beginning answer to these several ques-

---

[4] *Loci Theologici,* I, 23 ff.

[5] *Systema,* P.I, C.8, S.1, Th.2, nota 2 (I, 284).

tions is supplied by Quenstedt.[6] "Attributes," he says, "are nothing else than inadequate [7] conceptions of the divine essence . . . . Since our finite intellect cannot adequately conceive of the infinite and absolutely simple essence of God by a single adequate conception, it therefore apprehends the same by distinct and inadequate conceptions which represent only inadequately the divine essence. These inadequate conceptions are called the properties and attributes of God, properties because they have to do with the divine essence and denote it, attributes because they are attributed to the same by our intellect." It is clear that Quenstedt's point of departure for this statement lies in the absolute unity and simplicity of God, that God is *ohne Stücke, Deus impartibilis,* as the Augsburg Confession, Art. I, had put it. This fact must never be overlooked. And yet God has attributes which we can grasp with our understanding and to which we can cling with our faith.

But how can a number of different attributes be reconciled with the infinite and undivided essence of God? The attributes of God, although they are considered separately, are actually all one with the divine essence. In this way the immutability of God is safeguarded.[8] Since there is neither composition nor accidents in God, this must be the case: the attributes cannot actually *(realiter)* differ from the divine essence, but are distinguished from God's essence only according to our way of thinking.

It would be a mistake, however, to assume that, because the divine attributes are one with the divine essence, they are therefore only phenomenal or nominal or illusory. The attributes are real and they are in God prior to any conceptualization of ours.[9]

It would be a further mistake to assume that the attributes which are all one in God are therefore confused and not to be distinguished from each other. Such a mistake would conflict with all that Scripture says about God and would caricature God utterly.[10] For instance, it is necessary to say that God's love redeems and His wrath condemns. But is it

---

[6] *Systema,* P.I, C.8, S.1, Th.2, nota 1 (I, 284).

[7] The term *inadaequatus* in this context means partial or imperfect, never faulty or misleading.

[8] Calov, *Systema,* II, 231.

[9] Quenstedt, *Systema,* P.I, C.8, S.2, q.2, (I, 296): "Attributa divina ante omnem intellectus nostri operationem revera & proprie sunt in Deo."

[10] Hollaz, *Examen Theologicum Acroamaticum* (Rostock and Leipzig, 1741), P. I, C.1, q.21 (p. 249).

possible not to confuse the divine attributes when they are all identified with God Himself and therefore cannot be distinguished from each other *realiter?* [11] How can we speak of different divine attributes, if they are all identical with the same thing?

Hollaz attempts to extricate us from this apparent contradiction. He says,[12] "When we assert that the mercy and justice, the wisdom and goodness of God do not differ *realiter* in the Creator in the same way as they do in His creatures, but differ only formally, the foundation of our assertion lies in the supreme simplicity of God and His perfection according to which the divine attributes cannot be distinguished ontologically from the divine essence or even from each other. For although certain attributes actually produce distinct operations and perform different effects, still these attributes themselves remain simply one." Hollaz is saying that the attributes can and must be distinguished by their effects, which are quite different. And he means to say that, although they are all one with the divine nature, there is a foundation within the divine nature for the distinctions we make on the basis of Scripture.

Quenstedt [13] attacks the same problem with his usual meticulosity and perhaps helps us a bit to understand better the Lutheran solution. He points out that we often think of properties as being distinct from their subjects. And this is perfectly in order. Not so in the case of God, however. There are no divine properties or perfections which in reality are distinct from God Himself. What happens is that we are forced to conceptualize God in terms of properties. But strictly speaking God has no properties *(proprietates)* but is an absolutely undivided essence which is without diversity or composition of any kind. We, however, are incapable of taking in the essence of God in one sweep, as it were, we cannot get at this undivided essence with any one adequate conception.

"Therefore," says Quenstedt, "we apprehend it with conceptions which are inadequate and distinct from each other, conceptions which only inadequately represent the divine essence. These inadequate conceptions, which are identified with the reality of the divine essence itself, are appre-

---

[11] John Dorsch, for example, says unabashedly, "Ontologically the divine essence is not distinguished from the attributes, nor are the attributes distinguished from each other in this sense *(realissime)*, but they are in this simple ontological sense the same."

[12] Loc. cit., p. 249.

[13] *Systema,* P.I, C.8, S.2, q.2, ekthesis 3 (I, 296-7).

hended by us in terms of properties which we call attributes. And so with our intellect we distinguish things which in reality are not distinct, and we conceive of the divine essence at one time as a transcendent Spirit, at another time as omnipotent, at still another time as all knowing, etc." The divine attributes do not denote anything superadded to the divine essence, Quenstedt says, but are only inadequate conceptions of the infinitely perfect essence. The essence itself is like a vast ocean of all infinite divine perfections. We cannot exhaust this ocean with any unitary conception, and so by means of various conceptions we draw drop by drop something, as it were, from that infinity.

But if God's essence is free of all composition, if each attribute (such as infinity, omnipotence, eternity) is said to be the very essence of God apprehended differently by us,[14] and if therefore the distinction between the attributes is only conceptual and not real,[15] have we any right to ascribe attributes to God at all? And have we the right to ascribe any reality to the attributes? This is the nagging question which haunts the old Lutherans as they struggle to affirm both the reality of God's attributes and the total perfection of the divine essence.

No adequate reply can be given the question except to say that Scripture, which is God's revelation of Himself, speaks of His perfect Godhead and of His attributes, and does so not just metaphorically but literally. Quenstedt also warns us not to create difficulties unnecessarily. That God is without composition does not imply that He is without attributes. And the simplicity of God is quite compatible with His being one and true and good. Quenstedt also says,[16] "Although the divine attributes are considered to be in God according to our mode of thinking, this mode of thinking is not without all foundation in reality. Nor are the attributes predicated of God only loosely and anthropopathically. But they truly and actually correspond to Him. Thus, when God is said to have life in Himself (John 5:26), what can be more certain than that God truly has life, and this means life not according to some anthropopathism, but truly and actually."

One might wonder if the intricate and scholastic discussions of Hollaz and Quenstedt concerning the essence and attributes of God have

---

[14] Quenstedt, ibid., q.3 ekthesis 7.

[15] Ibid., thesis.

[16] Ibid., fontes solutionum 5 (I, 298).

really helped us to know God better. Perhaps a more Biblical approach such as one finds in the earlier dogmaticians would be preferable — certainly more winsome. But we must in all fairness to these two scholastic theologians recognize that they were speaking to a problem which was very real in their day and has not gone away to this day.[17] As evangelical Christians they thought it possible and incumbent upon them to speak cognitively of the absolutely transcendent God, to affirm His uniqueness and *simplicitas,* but also to mention the other attributes which seemed to conflict with His transcendence and *simplicitas.* What they tried to do was to penetrate (inadequately of course) and give a description (inadequate) of the transcendent and simple Deity in the light of the Biblical attributes. This seemed the only possible course open to them, a course which could end in mystery and paradox, but also in knowledge and true worship.

If there is difficulty in reconciling the attributes of God with His perfect essence, there is equal difficulty reconciling the divine attributes with each other. In what order does a theologian arrange the divine attributes? How many attributes are there? How does one classify them? Since the attributes are not distinguishable from the divine essence *realiter,* there can be no order among them; one attribute does not precede or follow the other except conceptually.[18] Therefore all the questions above are really quite open. And in fact there is almost no agreement among the Lutheran dogmaticians as they go about the arbitrary business of arranging, numbering, and classifying the attributes.

Concerning the number of attributes Baier lists 15, Gerhard 19, Hollaz 24, and Quenstedt no less than 31. Calov treats 10 attributes (a perfect number) in his *Apodixis Articulorum Fidei*[19]; in his *Syste-*

---

[17] The very point of the essays in the highly significant book edited by Anthony Flew and Alesdaire MacIntyre (*New Essays in Philosophical Theology* [London: SCM Press, 1955]) is whether attributes can be cognitively ascribed to a God who is transcendent, without making theology nonsense. Cf. Frederick Ferre, *Language, Logic and God* (New York: Harper, 1961). The negative answer to this question lies behind much of the "God is dead" theology which emerged in the United States not long ago. See Paul M. van Buren, *The Secular Meaning of the Gospel* (New York: The Macmillan Company, 1963). Cf. also John Warwick Montgomery, *The 'Is God Dead?' Controversy* (Grand Rapids: Zondervan, 1966).

[18] Quenstedt, *Systema,* P.I, C.8, S.1, Thesis 6 (I, 285).

[19] Abraham Calov, *Apodixis Articulorum Fidei* (Lüneburg, 1684), p. 62 ff.

ma [20] he gives consideration to 22, ranked within four different classifications. This great diversity in the number of attributes was due to three obvious factors. (1) In the nature of the case the numbering and listing of divine attributes is an arbitrary business. The dogmaticians all recognize this and, for the most part, spend little time defending their particular list and order. (2) There is not always agreement on which were actually divine attributes. None of the old Lutherans thought of the Trinity as an attribute of God. Gerhard does not include unity as an attribute either, but treats the theme prior to his discussion of attributes. The same is done by him with respect to the life of God. All the later teachers consider unity and life to be attributes of God. (3) It is always possible to subsume one or two or three attributes under one basic theme. For instance, Quenstedt and Hollaz list incomprehensibility as a divine attribute, Gerhard and Baier do not, obviously subsuming this concept under such other attributes as infinity and simplicity. Again Gerhard and Quenstedt consider perfection as an attribute of God; Hollaz subsumes the idea under other attributes which he treats. Quenstedt includes the will and the freedom of God as attributes; Hollaz only the will. But Baier does not consider the divine will an attribute, but an act of the divine intellect and power. [21] Examples of such differences could be multiplied.

In the matter of classification of attributes the Lutherans realized that they were again dealing with an open question, and for this reason we find no unanimity among them. By far the most complex list of classifications is presented by Gerhard. [22] He begins with the usual warning that the attributes are all one with the divine essence and that there is no disagreement *(contrarietas)* between them, since there is no opposition in the divine essence itself.

---

[20] *Systema,* III, 223 ff.

[21] Baier-Walther, II, 32. In the end it makes little difference whether one calls the will of God an attribute or a divine work as long as one is Scriptural in his treatment. And Baier understands this. But like all the dogmaticians he considers it necessary to distinguish God's attributes from His works *(opera).* See Calov, *Apodixis,* 62. The attributes of God are necessary; the works are free. For instance, the goodness of God which is necessary ought to be distinguished from His sending His Son to save the world, which is a free act. Hollaz feels that the will of God falls better into the category of a work of God than of an attribute. But as we study the other dogmaticians we will see that they have some valid arguments for the contrary opinion. This difference of opinion just points up the extreme difficulty of classifying divine attributes and works.

[22] *Loci Theologici,* III, 84—89.

No doubt feeling the difficulty of the problem, Gerhard lists no less than nine different classifications. (1) Certain attributes are predicated of both God and man. However, they are only accidents [unessential qualities, predicates] in men, whereas they are essential in God (for example, God is good and wise). Other attributes can be ascribed only to God (eternity, infinity). (2) Certain things are said of God absolutely without relation to His creation (for example, God is eternal and immense). Other things are said of God relative to His creation (example, God is Creator, King, Judge). (3) Some things are said of God only in a negative way (He is invisible, immortal, incorporeal). Other things are said of God affirmatively (He is good, righteous). (4) Some attributes are predicated of God in a strict sense: He is good, wise, etc. Other things are said of God in a loose or figurative sense, as when by anthropopathism human feelings and members are attributed to Him. (5) Some things are said of God in the abstract (God is life, truth, goodness). They are also said of God concretely (God is living, true, good). (6) Certain attributes are ascribed simply to the Divinity apart from any external operations (God is a spiritual essence, invisible, eternal, immutable, immortal, and infinite). Other attributes are ascribed to God as He deals with His creatures (God is powerful, good, righteous, wise, free, true). Perfection, majesty, glory, and goodness are ascribed to God in both cases. (7) Some attributes are internal, such as infinity and eternity. Others are external, such as omnipotence and omnipresence. Only some of the external attributes are imitable, such as goodness and righteousness. (8) Some attributes apply to God from all eternity (God is infinite, immense). Other attributes apply to God in time as the Creator and Conservator of all things. (9) A distinction is made between attributes which are common to the entire Trinity and those which are characteristic only of the individual Persons such as the fatherhood of the Father, the eternal generation of the Son.

One can perhaps find justification for each of these classifications listed by Gerhard. And they all serve to illustrate the variety of ways in which the attributes may be viewed — and incidentally the arbitrariness of the whole enterprise. Gerhard is clearly intent upon presenting as complete a picture of God as possible by his discussion of the divine attributes. And with this prime interest of his in mind we note that he felt compelled to treat the names and works of God along with his discussion of the attributes.

But the structure of Gerhard's system of classification was too complicated, too cumbersome to follow. And so almost without exception [23] the later dogmaticians treat the divine attributes according to a very general twofold classification which can be traced back to Gerhard. They distinguish between absolute, sometimes called negative or immanent attributes (ἀνενέργητα), and relative, sometimes called positive or external attributes (ἐνεργητικά).

With such a twofold classification they ordinarily begin with such attributes as unity, immutability, eternity, and infinity, and conclude with the goodness of God. The first set of attributes seeks to describe God as He is in Himself apart from His creation. The second are *extra se* and seek to describe God as He acts in relation to creation and especially to men. The distinction is, of course, not in any sense to be considered ontological, but is only in respect to our way of thinking, "since all things are the same in the divine essence, and nothing is in God which is not God Himself." [24]

The inadequacy of this most popular classification or of any classification of attributes is readily recognized by the Lutheran dogmaticians. Calov and the others waste no time defending their particular arrangement. They insist merely that we are forced to speak of God in terms of attributes because Scripture does so and because our finite understanding cannot grasp in one adequate conception what the essence of God is. And so we do the best we can. But actually a simple listing of attributes as Calov does in his *Apodixis* would have probably been preferable to the arrangement which finally won out; for there are some real flaws in it.

What are these shortcomings? First is the intrinsic difficulty of the project which makes any rigid classification a severe hardship to follow consistently. For instance, certain attributes such as God's presence must be discussed twice, first as an absolute attribute (immensity) and then

---

[23] Dannhauer is the exception. He lists and discusses all the attributes under four headings: (1) the name Yahweh implies the attributes of uniqueness, majesty, unity, and life. (2) That God is Spirit implies that He is infinite, incorporeal, powerful, and omnipresent. (3) God is *light* means that He is pure and holy and omniscient. (4) God is *love* means that He is merciful and good. See *Hodosophia Christiana* (Strasbourg, 1649), pp. 144 ff.

[24] Calov, *Systema,* II, 223.

as an operative attribute (presence). Hollaz *(Examen)* feels compelled to discuss the truthfulness of God twice. Considered as an absolute attribute, God as truth *(veritas)* is the conformity of the divine essence with the divine understanding, which means that God in Himself is the true God (αὐταλήθεια) and the source of all moral truth and truth within the created order. Viewed as a relative attribute God's truthfulness *(veracitas)* means that He keeps His promises (Num. 23:19; Heb. 6:18). But can truth *(veritas)* in God possibly be one of the ἀνενέργητα, especially when the two Bible passages brought to illustrate this attribute (Jer. 10:10; 1 John 5:20-21) refer to God's relation to creatures?

Second, it is highly questionable whether one should ever speak of ἀνενέργητα in the living God, of attributes *sine ulla relatione ad creaturas.*[25] God is as He has revealed Himself to us,[26] and He has revealed Himself as the living, speaking, acting God. This brings up the question posed above whether it is wise, as the Lutherans after Gerhard attempt to do, to speak of the nature of God in terms of attributes before speaking to some extent of God's works. This approach of the later Lutherans does display a certain simple logic, but there is also the peril of failing to see God's attributes in the light of His works. For instance, His justice and wrath must be seen in the light of His judgments in history; and His love in the light of His acts of redemption and salvation through Christ. It is true that the acts and attributes of God are not separated by Protestant theology as they seem to be for Thomas Aquinas. *Proprietates Dei essentiales sunt actus.*[27] The divine attributes belong to the living, acting God. The *vita Dei* is always considered an ἐνεργητικόν, and God is said to be *semper actuosus.* But why should the so-called absolute attributes not be related to God's creatures, as they are in Scripture?

---

[25] Gerhard, *Loci Theologici,* III, ch. 7, pp. 85—90. Werner Elert faults Gerhard and Quenstedt at this point. See *Der Christliche Glaube* (Berlin: Furche Verlag, 1941) p. 279; 5th ed. (Hamburg, 1956) pp. 230—31. "Es gibt keine ἀνεργητικά [sic] in Gott," he says. The point is well taken: here was a case where the dogmaticians took over too readily the older mode of speaking of Aquinas (*Summa Theologica,* P.1, q. 3-26). This is perfectly understandable. Gerhard had to draw from some source as he sought to cover ground not previously traversed by the older Lutheran theologians. For Thomas had touched many Biblical themes which deserved to be considered in a Lutheran dogmatics.

[26] Calov, *Apodixis,* p. 74; Giles Hunnius, *Opera Latina,* I. 89.

[27] This aphorism probably coined by Amandus Polanus could have been echoed by any Lutheran theologian of the day. See Polanus, *Institutiones Theologicae* (Geneva, 1609), L.11, C.7 (I, 386).

A third shortcoming we notice is the serious lack of balance in many presentations of the divine attributes. This results not so much from the division into absolute and relative attributes as again from the intrinsic difficulty of the enterprise. Just how does one thoroughly treat the doctrine of God from the point of view of His attributes without thereby writing an entire dogmatics?

For instance, Quenstedt gives rather thorough attention to the goodness of God under five themes, but Hollaz offers nothing but a brief unenlightening discussion of the grace of God. As a whole Hollaz had not neglected the subject of God's grace; in fact his entire doctrine of soteriology is subsumed under the theme of God's grace in Christ.[28] He just cannot see any advantage in the redundancy of discussing God's grace (which he considers an attribute) twice.

Gerhard, on the other hand, does not treat the grace of God as an attribute but discusses the theme under the *locus* on justification. The result is that in the case of Hollaz and Gerhard the theme of a gracious God probably does not receive the emphasis and attention under theology proper that it deserves in Lutheran dogmatics.

The lack of balance in classical Lutheran theology as it treats the divine attributes will become apparent as we now proceed to discuss the attributes one by one. Some attributes are treated in an unoriginal and almost completely scholastic form; others are merely mentioned in passing; in the case of others a good deal of deep thought and Biblical study has been expended.

Since there is no unanimity among the old Lutherans as they arrange and treat the divine attributes, we will try to be fair to what is the general trend in arrangement. At the same time, for the sake of clarity, we will in our survey subsume attributes under as few main headings as possible. And we will try to dwell at length only on those contributions of the old Lutheran theologians which seem to be unique or of high importance to them.

1. THE UNITY OF GOD

The unity of God means that God is one and undivided in essence. A correlate of this fundamental truth is the uniqueness of God (mono-

28 *Examen*, P.III, S.1, C.4-12 (pp. 787—975).

theism), that He alone is God, and there are no other gods beside Him. The one truth involves the other, and the Lutheran theologians do not separate the two notions in their discussions.[29]

The unity of God is the very foundation stone of Christianity. It is one God who has created the world and sustains it. It is one God who has revealed Himself to Adam, Abraham, the prophets, and in the New Covenant through His Son. The schema of the Old Testament Israelites brings out the unity of God. The term Yahweh in this schema denotes the infinite, indivisible, and immutable essence of God, an essence which is an absolute and simple unity.[30] This deity in its unity and glory cannot be communicated or likened to anything apart from God. (Deut. 5: 6, 7; Is. 42:8; 48:11)

It is not possible to examine the vast Biblical evidence offered by the old Lutheran theology for the unity and uniqueness of God. The evidence is usually marshalled under several classifications. (1) Passages where God is said to be uniquely and singularly one (Ex. 3:14; John 4: 24; Mal. 2:10). (2) Passages where the negative is stated (Deut. 4:35, 39; 32:39). (3) Passages which exclude other deities (2 Kings 19:15; Is. 37:16; Ps. 83:18). (4) Passages which are both negative and exclusive (Is. 45:14). (5) Passages which ask the question of the existence of other gods and imply the negative response (2 Sam. 22:32). (6) Passages in which God is compared to other gods, the implication being that nothing and no one is God but Yahweh (1 Kings 8:23; Ps. 86:8; Neh. 9:6; Dan. 3:29). (7) The entire New Testament testimony (e. g. Mark 12:29; 1 Cor. 8:6; Gal. 3:20; Eph. 4:6). (8) The terrible examples of God's wrath against all idolatry.[31]

Is there any conflict between the Christology of the New Testament and the unity of God? Not at all, reply the Lutherans. Jesus presents Himself in the New Testament as having come from God and being

[29] See, for instance, Chemnitz, *Loci Theologici*, I, 30. Chemnitz uses passages expressing God's uniqueness in pressing for His unity (e. g. Deut. 32:39; Is. 44:8; 1 Cor. 8:4).

[30] Calov, *Apodixis Articulorum Fidei*, p. 64.

[31] The orthodox Lutheran theologians were well aware that a different construction might be placed on the evidence of category 6. The Socinians (Socinus, Schmalz, Völkel) maintained that such passages implied a monolatry or henotheism in the theology of the Old Testament by allowing for the existence of lesser deities than the one Yahweh. Such interpretations were rejected by the Lutherans. See ibid. Cf. Calov, *Theologia Naturalis et Revelata*, p. 553.

one with God. But He also speaks of one God and repeats the Old Testament schema (Mark 12:29, 32). There is no conflict between the deity of Christ and the unity of God; but there is mystery. Against the charge that the unity of God and the Trinity of Persons cannot be reconciled Lutheran theology offers no clever answer. We can only respond in Christian simplicity, Gerhard says,[32] that both of these facts are true and Scriptural, and then take our reason captive to this mystery of faith. The entire *regula fidei* must be accepted, and the rule states that God is one, but also Father, Son, and Holy Spirit. The charge of tritheism leveled by the Socinians can be made only when interpreters of Scripture refuse to accept all the Biblical evidence in its native sense. Gerhard says, "To the question whether the Persons of the Trinity militate against the simplicity of God we reply in the following manner: (1) Different articles of faith are not to be opposed to each other. Both the simplicity of the divine essence and the Trinity of Persons are set forth in the Word for our benefit. Hence we ought to accept both with the obedience of faith. (2) We do not contend that the divine essence must be distinguished from the Persons in reality . . . but we assert that the divine essence and the Three Persons of the Deity are one in the most real and simple sense. And therefore there is nothing composite in the Godhead. (3) The personal characteristics (of the Persons) do not multiply or compound the divine essence, since one and the same divine essence is in the Father ἀγενήτως, in the Son γενήτως, and in the Holy Spirit ἐκπορεύτως." Gerhard is no doubt reflecting the statement of the Augsburg Confession at this point: the confession states, "We unanimously hold and teach, in accordance with the decree of the Council of Nicaea, that there is one

---

[32] *Loci Theologici,* III, 76—84. Giles Hunnius (*Opera Latina,* I, 89) warns against thinking of God as a species. Father, Son, and Holy Spirit are not God in the same sense as Peter, Paul, and John are man. For the latter are three men, not one man. Hunnius then cautions against making God over; rather we are to hold to Him just as He has revealed Himself, for so He is. "God has not revealed Himself to us according to any man's way of thinking, but as He really is." Applying this rule to the unity of God, Hunnius goes on to say, "Furthermore, the evidence adduced from Scripture clearly shows that God is one in essence and in number. Indeed, when Moses says, Hear, O Israel, the Lord thy God is one God, it is the same as if he should say, Your God is one in essence. The term Yahweh is an expression for the absolutely pure essence of God. Likewise Paul opposes the unity of the true God to the multitude of heathen gods in 1 Cor. 8:5-6 in order to show clearly this contrast that we must recognize and confess God to be one in number." And this unity, says Hunnius, must be maintained along with the fact that God is Father, Son, and Holy Spirit.

divine essence *{una essentia divina}* which is called and which is God."
The confession then continues by saying that all Three Persons "are one
divine essence, eternal, without division, without end, of infinite power,
wisdom, and goodness, one creator and preserver of all things visible and
invisible." (German text)

The orthodox Lutheran teachers labor to explain what may be meant
by the unity of the divine essence. Gerhard resorts to the terms used in
Ex. 3:14 ("I am that I am") and in John 4:24 ("God is a spirit"). Essence and spirit in these passages are not universal terms which may be
applied to God and to angels. Rather they signify something absolutely
infinite and simple and one in number. If such terms are applied to angels or other created things it is neither in an analogical or univocal
sense; but these phrases are singular phrases for the one God. For infinite and finite essence, uncreated and created spirits, are of a totally different nature. This is brought out in three ways by Scripture, Gerhard
observes: (1) from the simple affirmation that God is one and unique
(unus et solus), (2) from the negation that there are many gods, and
(3) from the exclusion of any God prior or posterior to the one true God
(Deut. 6:4). Thus God is one according to the highest unity *(unitate
summa)*, and this unity is not accidental but natural and essential.

Gerhard is speaking of the oneness of God in the absolute sense.
Taken in a *relative* sense oneness in number is merely one among many
of a similar kind. The Lutheran teachers said there were two kinds of
unity: (1) arithmetic or quantitative, and (2) essential or transcendental.
Numerical unity in the *relative* or *quantitative* sense cannot be predicated
of God, but in the *absolute* and *transcendental* sense unity can be predicated of God. Whether this verbal gymnastics helps Gerhard in presenting his position is questionable. But at least it is clear what he is trying
to safeguard with it all. He is concerned to uphold the absolute transcendence of God against any ideas of unity which would undermine
this. And he is concerned to show that the doctrine of the Trinity in
no way vitiates the unity of God. At the same time he is emphasizing
God's unity as the foundation of the Christian faith.

Do the attributes of God militate against His perfect and absolute
unity? Again the answer is no. And the reason is that the attributes,
considered in and through themselves, are actually one with the divine
essence. Gerhard points out, "If the attributes really differed from the

essence of God, and if God then were composed of essence and accidents, then the divine essence would not be one and undivided."[33] Nothing can be added to God nor can He add to Himself. Therefore He is good and wise according to His very essence. And hence goodness, power, wisdom, etc. must be called attributes, not qualities or accidents. Here the old rule applies: *Nihil est in Deo, quod non est ipse Deus.* The divine essence is identical with everything which is in the Deity. This is brought out by the statements in Scripture which call God love, life, light, etc., and by the personifications of many of His attributes. (Cf. Ps. 25:6)

Quenstedt supports Gerhard's point as follows: "Whatever creatures do, they accomplish by their own diverse and distinct powers and qualities; God however does and performs everything through His own essence. We are men according to our essence, we are good and wise men according to our condition or state; we are just according to one virtue, generous according to another; but God is and does everything according to His essence. Therefore we cannot conclude that things in God really differ just because their effects are different or even contrary."[34]

This statement, which seeks to preserve the majesty and immutability of God, while maintaining the distinction of attributes, shows clearly that for Lutheran theology there are no relative or amissible attributes (such as omnipotence, omnipresence, omniscience) in God. This position, which has been apparent throughout our survey, becomes more forcibly articulate in the Lutheran Christology which taught consistently that the humiliation of Christ pertained only to His human nature.[35]

The unity of God has definite practical doxological and cultic implications.[36] The unity of God separates Christianity from all other religions; and it implies and demands unity of worship and doctrine. Furthermore, with a knowledge of this unity we are enabled to consecrate all that we have and are to Him alone; our hearts, minds, and members

---

[33] *Loci Theologici,* III, 108.

[34] *Systema,* P.I, C.8, S.2, q.2, *fons solutionum* 9 (I, 305). Cf. also *fons solutionum* 8.

[35] Chemnitz, *De Duabus Naturis in Christo* (Wittenberg, 1653), p. 108; — *Two Natures in Christ,* trans. J. A. O. Preus (St. Louis, 1971), pp. 279—80; 487—94. Friedemann Bechmann, *Annotationes Uberiores in Compendium Theologicum Leonhardi Hutteri* (Frankfurt and Leipzig, 1703), p. 174. Cort Aslakssøn, *De Statu Christi* θεανθρώπου (Copenhagen, 1622), Abr. Calov, *Apodixis,* p. 242.

[36] Calov, *Systema,* II, 290.

are not to be led astray (Phil. 3:19). God's unity *(unitas)* is to be used to bring about unity *(concordia)* in the church, and this alone can bring about such unity in worship (Eph. 4:3, 6), since it is the basis of such unity.

Commenting on Eph. 4:3, 6, Calov says, "If the one God is above us all, then all of us who live under the power of this one God and are children of this one Father ought to worship in response to this unity. If the one God by His benevolent care is present among us all, then it is incumbent upon us to be one with all, since He desires to embrace all with equal care and providence. If the one God is in us all and wishes to dwell in us all as in one temple, then we should all be of one heart and mind (Acts 4:32). If the one God dwells in us all, then whatever would rend our unity would by that very act seek to tear apart the one God. The apostle heaps up many arguments for unity and harmony of worship among the faithful, but he traces all the arguments back to the wonderful and glorious unity which we worship and praise in God. . . . In the end he recalls our attention to the one God and Father of all, by whom we were all created and adopted as His children, who by His majesty is above all, by His providence is through all, and by His grace is spread abroad in all, so that under, through, and in Him we all move and possess true blessedness." This statement is typical of the Lutheran attempt, sometimes successful and sometimes not, to make the discussion of the divine attributes practical for the life of the Christian and of the church.

2. GOD IS SPIRIT

The first thing to be said about God after His unity is that He is Spirit (John 4:24; 2 Cor. 3:17). This means that He is without a body, illocal, not confined to one place.[37] He is the incomparable One (Is. 46:5).

---

[37] For the following (below) see Gerhard, *Loci Theologici,* III, 89—90, and Calov, *Apodixis,* p. 62. Bechmann (*Annotationes,* p. 57) insists that when God is called a spiritual substance, this implies no philosophical connotation but merely means that God is free of matter and form in the Aristotelian sense and is uniquely Spirit. But Gerhard advances some highly speculative and questionable philosophical arguments for God as Spirit being incorporeal and immaterial.

The spiritual essence of God, he says, can be inferred from His unity and simplicity. Every body is composite and can be somehow acted upon and divided. This is not true of God who is a being absolutely without composition *(ens simplicissimum)* and therefore cannot be corporeal.

As Spirit God is contrasted to all idols which are often fabricated from material things (Is. 40:18; Ps. 106:20; Jer. 2:11). And for this reason God prohibited even material images of Himself. As Spirit God is invisible and incomprehensible (1 Tim. 6:16; Col. 1:15), dwelling in an unapproachable light. The φῶς ἀπρόσιτον of 1 Tim. 6:16 is not a place, but rather the invisible and incomprehensible nature of God.[38] But invisibility is an attribute of the *Deus absconditus*. When God says, "There shall no man see Me and live," He does not mean that the man who sees Him must die, but that no living man can see Him. The hidden God, however, has come forth from the hidden seat of His majesty and made Himself known through apparitions and mighty acts and finally by sending His own Son — and in the word of preaching. The link between theology and life is clear again at this point where

Gerhard also argues from the fact that God is called life. "The highest being cannot be a body. For a body is either living or not living. A living body is superior to a body which has no life, inasmuch as that which lives is superior to a being which does not. However, a living body does not live by virtue of the fact that it is a body, or every body would be alive. That through which the body lives is superior to the body. Now since God is the most noble living being, He cannot have a body." This is Thomistic thought. (*Summa Theologica*, P.I, Q.3, a.3)

But it is clear from this bit of philosophical reasoning why Gerhard is so adamant in his insistence on the incorporeity of God: it is to maintain the absolute transcendence of God against every theory of immanence and pantheism, as he later points out. And there is also a practical reason for Gerhard's insistence that God is pure Spirit: as Spirit and life God gives to man the spirit of life (Gen. 2:7). Thus in faith and love our created spirit clings to Him, the uncreated Spirit. (P. 96)

Arguing from the same metaphysical premise, Gerhard says, "Nothing which is corporeal and visible can satisfy and fill the desires of our spirit, for our spirit is above and superior to all corporeal things. Nothing which is mortal, corruptible, and transitory can grant peace to the spirit, for our spirit has been created for eternity and seeks its peace in that eternal and therefore incorporeal and uncreated Spirit. Thus the apostle correctly describes the viewpoint of the righteous when he says (2 Cor. 4:18) that they look not at the things which are seen, but at the things which are not seen, for the things which are seen are temporary, but the things unseen are eternal .... After forming men God rested, because He wished to take His rest in man and make His abode in man. Therefore man too looks to the purpose of all his desires and seeks rest for his soul in the one God. He, the highest Spirit, is the creator of our spirit, its source and goal; and our spirit therefore will not rest except in its source." (P. 96)

One hardly knows whether such remarks are meant to represent dogmatic theology or a homiletical application of the truth that God is Spirit. Gerhard in his dogmatics indulges in both. But at least we see that it is no mere academic concern which prompts Gerhard to stress his point. The other Lutherans of the day do not follow these philosophico-theological reflections of Gerhard's.

[38] Calov, *Apodixis*, p. 62.

God is called Spirit. It was of immense practical importance, for instance, to the Samaritan woman that God was not a corporeal, local God, confined to Jerusalem or some other spot, but was Spirit. He who does not dwell in temples made with hands, whom the heaven of heavens cannot contain, is accessible to all. Men everywhere may pray to Him without wrath or doubting (1 Tim. 2:8), whatever the place or external circumstances may be.

3. THE SIMPLICITY OF GOD

As the Lutheran dogmaticians seek to delineate and divide concepts which are not clearly separated in Scripture and thus portray God according to a series of attributes, it is to be expected that their efforts will result in a good bit of overlap. This fact is seen as they discuss the simplicity of God which follows from the notion of God's unity and is derived from it. The term *simplicitas*, which in its modern derivative seems hardly appropriate to ascribe to the living God, is used to denote the single and unsupported nature of God. It means that He is without parts or composition, without division or mixture. "The absolute simplicity of God's essence means that it is entirely free of all composition; therefore nothing accidental can happen to it." [39] God who is infinite, eternal, perfect, and unchangeable cannot be enmeshed within the categories of matter and form, genus and differences, subject and accident, act and potency, etc.[40] Simplicity was a philosophical notion, derived from the medieval scholastics, to safeguard God's unity and uniqueness and transcendence. Any idea of composition in God would imply something more elementary or prior to Him, a clear denial of His perfection (Thomas Aquinas, *Summa Theologica,* P. I, Q. 3, a. 3); and the immutability and eternity of God would also be placed in question.

Put somewhat differently, simplicity means that there is nothing in God except being, and God is His own being.[41] One might almost say that to call God Spirit or to call Him simple or to call Him one is to say the same thing in different ways, and is merely an attempt to summarize

---

[39] Calov, *Systema,* II, 305.

[40] Gerhard, *Loci Theologici,* III, 99.

[41] Calov, *Systema,* II, 305: "Nihil in Deo est, nisi esse, et Deus est ipsum esse suum."

what long before had been expressed by the prophet Isaiah in his inimitable 40th chapter. But whereas the prophet was seeking to set God apart from all fetishes and idols made with hands, the Lutheran divines are attempting to affirm not only God's ontological transcendence but also His transcendence above all human thought and philosophy.

That God is simple should be of great comfort to the child of God and ought to be put to practical use. It means that He knows what He is doing; God is not whimsical but keeps His Word and treats all men the same (James 1:5). In practice, then, the simplicity of God assures us of His honesty and faithfulness (Ps. 25:21; 12:6) toward us, of what Paul calls the εἰλικρινεία θεοῦ (2 Cor. 1:12) that is, a simplicity and singleness in God which we are called upon to emulate. (Eph. 6:5)

The simplicity of God raises the same question for the Christian as the unity of God. Can such a notion be harmonized with the distinction between the Three Persons of the Trinity? Calov answers,[42] "This distinction does not imply any multiplication but it is in perfect agreement with the highest simplicity of the divine essence. For since the divine Persons are identical with the essence of God, each one of the Persons is consistent with the absolutely simple divine essence; and there is no multiplication among them, but the divine essence remains one and indivisible." Calov is saying that the essence of God, the Godhead, is communicable to all three Persons and therefore common to all three and totally and entirely in each Person. Actually Calov has not solved the problem of reconciling the simplicity of God and the Trinity of Persons, no more than one can reconcile the unity of God and the Trinity. He is merely stating the paradox in such a way that he avoids all error; for instance, the error that the distinction among the Persons in the Trinity implies quaternity or tritheism, an error which would imply multiplication within the Deity. Ultimately the mystery remains: the Three Persons differ from each other *realiter* as persons yet remain one simple and undivided essence.[43]

Another question discussed by Calov and others at this point is the problem of reconciling the simplicity of God with His decrees. According to classical Lutheran theology the decrees of God are represented in Scripture as taking place in time; but at bottom they are eternal thoughts of

---

[42] Ibid.

[43] See Hutter, *Loci Communes Theologici,* p. 98; Chemnitz, *Loci Theologici,* I, 38 ff.

the divine mind. For God's thoughts and will are in no sense conditioned by time. "All things which take place in time are carried out according to divine foreknowledge. Thus these things are known from eternity by the divine mind. Also the will of God which is perfectly wise determines in eternity concerning all these events. No divine word in God is transitory; no divine decision is bound by time." [44] Therefore God's decision, for instance, to redeem mankind, was known and determined from eternity and is therefore eternal and immutable. Ultimately the decrees of God are nothing else than God willing something from eternity, and in this sense are identical with the divine essence itself. [45] Therefore no essential change takes place in God as He makes His decrees toward us.

But what about the diversity among the decrees? How can this be reconciled with the simplicity of God? Calov offers a lengthy answer to this question and it is worthwhile to quote him in full. [46] "Diversity among the decrees of God implies nothing else than the different acts of the one and same divine essence as it makes decisions. To be sure the distinctions are there, as far as the objects of the acts are concerned, but to the subject they are the same. In the sense that they remain in the mind and will of God they introduce no diversity in respect to Him. Decrees then can be considered *either* in reference to the created objects in which they find their goal *or* as they are acts of the divine will. In the first sense there are many decrees, but in the latter sense there are not. For God did not decree to create the world by one act of the will and then to redeem man by another act of the will, but in God it is all one simple act. Likewise there are not many conditions whereby God knows or many acts of comprehension in God, although there are different conditions whereby God knows and different acts of understanding in God in the sense that there are different knowable objects — but God always comprehends everything in one absolutely simple action. We must not think that God brings about in Himself new acts of the intellect and will, acts which are accidents distinct from His substance. But what happens is that certain external things occur in time, and according to our way of thinking

[44] Dorsch, *Synopsis Theologiae Zacharianae,* II, 170.

[45] Calov, *Systema,* II, 286: "At decreta Dei, quae actus Dei sunt immanentes, non sunt realiter ab essentia Dei distincta, nedum per morem accidentium." Ibid., p. 307: "Decreta Dei a parte rei nihil aliud sunt, quam *Deus ipse aliquid* decernens."

[46] Ibid., II, 307.

God is related to His creatures as one who knows and loves and makes decisions. Furthermore, the decrees are likewise free insofar as they have their free terminus in created objects, but they are not free as they have their existence in God. For although God makes His decisions freely and although He freely deals with His creatures, nevertheless, as we all know, these decrees as they relate to the divine essence are in the divine essence and remain in it; and they are necessary, since God does not know or determine anything fortuitously, but directly through His own substance."

4. THE MAJESTY OF GOD

The term majesty or perfection is used by classical Lutheran theology to denote many closely related perfections which are ascribed to God in Scripture: glory, holiness, transcendence, and sometimes even goodness (Baier). The importance and comfort to be found in such themes are not given their due in the dogmatics of the old Lutheran theology; and one will need to repair to the exegetical works of the old theologians to gain an adequate picture of their mature thinking on such topics. Not to omit the subject entirely we offer a résumé of Calov's discussion, which is one of the more complete.[47]

Taken positively, God's perfection denotes that complete divine transcendence which extends in every direction (Matt. 5:48; Job 37:14-15), including perfect holiness, knowledge, wisdom, and eternity. At times the attribute points up God's complete lordship over all which might oppose Him (Job 23:16; Is. 13:16 passim), at times God's goodness which is almighty. Perfection, or majesty, is also a term for God as the Almighty One (παντοκράτωρ). In the negative sense the perfection of God is His incomparability. Nothing exists or has power apart from Him, and all depends on Him (Rom. 11:35-36). God is above all, transcendent, providing everything for all that is not Himself *(omnisufficientissimus)*. In an active sense perfection means that all God's actions are perfect and therefore our sufficiency is in Him (2 Cor. 3:5), who is all good and our highest good (Ex. 33:19) and our all in all (1 Cor. 15:28). In short, the majesty or perfection of God consists of all His perfections in His essence and works. His majesty is essential to Him — dependent on nothing but His good will; and it is active, since what He wills always takes place.

[47] *Systema*, II, 225 ff.

5. THE INFINITY OF GOD

The infinity of God is His greatness in the simple and absolute sense. Ps. 145:3 sums up the basic concept of infinity for the Lutheran theologians: "Great is the Lord, and greatly to be praised; and His greatness is unsearchable." Scripture most eloquently describes the infinity of God as it compares Him with created things (Is. 40:15, 17; 44:6): His infinity is seen through the works of His great wisdom and power and in His revelation of Himself (Ex. 3:14; Rev. 1:8). It is an infinity which is not merely phenomenal but is essential to God, or God would not be infinite at all *(absolute magnus)*. But His unlimited wisdom and power and glory cannot be investigated by any human thought. (Job 11:8)[48]

We see that the infinity of God is quite closely related to the concept of perfection and majesty, and sums up in superlatives, as it were, all the perfections of God. God is infinitely great, good, powerful, wise, holy, and the like. For this reason Quenstedt does not see any necessity of including infinity as a divine attribute. And Baier gives it only the most perfunctory attention as an introduction to his statements on the eternity and immensity of God.[49]

But in general the idea of infinity was ascribed to God as a way of summarizing or introducing two very important attributes, both suggested by the notion of infinity, namely, God's eternity and immensity. That God is infinite means that He is not bound by time or space. These two attributes, eternity and immensity, were for several reasons, some of them polemical, discussed in much greater detail and with far deeper Biblical penetration than any of the other divine attributes. The discussion of these two attributes represents the only really original and significant contribution to the entire subject of the divine attributes advanced by classical Lutheran theology, and even on this subject they owe much to their forerunners, especially Luther and Brenz.[50] Therefore I shall try to present a more comprehensive study of the Lutheran doctrine on these points.

[48] The foregoing is based on Calov, *Apodixis*, p. 63.

[49] Baier-Walther, II, 20.

[50] The older Lutheran discussions concerning God's presence and the modes of His presence were usually in the setting of the controversy with Zwingli on Christology and the Lord's Supper. Their thinking was carried over into the theology of the later Lutherans. See John Brenz, *De Majestate Domini Nostri Jesu Christi ad Dextram Dei Patris et vera Praesentia Corporis & Sanguinis ejus in Coena* (Frankfurt, 1562), p. 14 ff. See also Nicolaus Selnecker, *Recitationes*

6. THE ETERNITY OF GOD

Eternity and immensity are attributes of transcendence — eternity pointing to God's transcendence over time and immensity to His transcendence over space.[51] Duration and ubiety are states of God's being *(affectiones entis)* not mere appearances *(species):* God really endures and is present infinitely.

Eternity in God is understood as the unending duration or continuance of the divine essence,[52] a duration which is indivisible and independent, excluding all succession of time, all imperfection and change.[53] For God there is no before or after; no past, present, or future; but all exists at once in an eternal now *(tota simul).*[54] He is unending, enduring being *(interminabilis permanentia),* and there is nothing temporal in Him. Eternity in God does not mean a long continuance of time, but absolute duration, a continuous now, an eternity which is fixed and not moving or passing away *(fixum non fluxum),* a perfect and unfailing *(indefectibilis)* eternity which actively resists temptation or failure.

The intrinsic eternity of God is taught in those Scripture passages which say that there is no succession or change in Him (Ps. 102:27), so that He can truly say of Himself, "I am that I am" (Ex. 3:14). God is always the same (וְאַתָּה־הוּא). "And He who remains forever the same will continue into eternity as He was from eternity; moreover, in whatever He does there can be no change or succession of time." [55] Often Scripture contrasts God with His creation which has had a beginning and is time bound. But God has no source or beginning (Heb. 1:3, 10; 11:7). He is the author of time and its passage, and in Him are no periods of time or years. God's creation therefore shouts forth His eternity. So also the decrees of the everlasting God which are to be understood as eternal. (2 Tim. 1:9)

Gerhard presents a rather comprehensive survey of the Biblical phrase-

---

Aliquot (Leipzig, 1581), p. 142 passim. For Luther's position see Franz Pieper, *Christian Dogmatics* (St. Louis: Concordia Publishing House, 1950) I, 442—45.

[51] Calov, *Systema,* II, 379.

[52] Ibid., 384.

[53] Gerhard, *Loci Theologici,* III, 103.

[54] Calov, *Systema,* II, 426; *Apodixis,* p. 72.

[55] Calov, *Apodixis,* p. 72.

ology for the eternity of God.[56] He points out that although the term עוֹלָם often indicates a long duration of time (Gen. 17:13; Ex. 21:6), when applied to God it means that He has neither beginning nor succession nor end, no before or after, but is a Being who always is (Gen. 21:33; Ps. 55: 19; Is. 40:28; 57:15). For God is above all time and cannot be measured by it (Job 36:26; Is. 43:10; Ps. 90:4). His attributes and His counsels and even His actions are eternal: He is eternal power, eternal glory, eternal rule (Ps. 103:17; 33:11; Ex. 15:18; Dan. 6:26; 1 Peter 5:11). He is the Ancient of Days (Dan. 7:9, 22), who inhabits eternity and whose years have no end (Ps. 102:28; Is. 57:15); His days are not as men's days (Job 10:5). All these metaphorical expressions describe the eternity of God, according to Gerhard. Similarly Christ is called the eternal Son (Heb. 1:5; 5:5), who is always the same (Heb. 13:8), and possesses eternal glory with the Father. (John 17:5)

When Lutheran theologians called the eternity of God *simul tota,* they meant that eternity in God was not merely an endless succession of time: past, present, and future, but was a totally different dimension from time, a dimension belonging only to God.[57] Eternity may be called a duration in God but not outside of God; in God it is an immutable continuance *(duratio immutabilis)* without any temporal connotation and utterly beyond our experience. Time, on the other hand, is an ongoing continuance *(duratio successiva)* with one part following the other. Does this mean that there can be no relation or coexistence between God, the eternal One, and His creatures who are subject to time? Not at all. But the coexistence or relation is different for God than for His creatures. In this relation there is no change or progression for God, whereas for us creatures there is.[58]

The Arminian Conrad Vorst,[59] no doubt in the interest of emphasizing the closeness of God to the created order, had taught that God's eternity was a realm coextensive with all time but infinite. The Lutheran theologians were wary of such a position, which tended to deny, they thought, that eternity is a totally different category from time and to enmesh God

[56] Loc. cit.

[57] Jacob Martini, *De Tribus Elohim* (Wittenberg, 1619), p. 467.

[58] Ibid., p. 471.

[59] Conrad Vorst, *Tractatus Theologicus de Deo* (Steinfurt, 1606).

within the realm of time with its past, present, and future.[60] Of course God is intimately and directly related to the world and to time, and for this reason the eternity of God may be said to coexist with all periods of time. But this fact must not be allowed to blur the distinction between time and eternity or to deny the reality of either.

"The whole of today," Bechmann says,[61] "exists today, the whole of tomorrow exists tomorrow, etc. But this does not imply that God's eternity, although it coexists with time, is of successive duration. Our defectible duration may be broken down into tenses *(partes)*, but not the duration of our indefectible God." It is clear what is at stake as the dogmaticians take issue with the apparently innocuous view of Vorst: in terms also of His eternity they wish to uphold the absolute transcendence of God over His creation.[62]

There is a definite *usus practicus* in the notion of God's eternity. *First,* it helps us in our worship.[63] We must realize that eternity *a parte rei* is the divine essence itself, which does not vary with time and is not subject to change. In the nature of the case time passes and in a sense is no more — the present always becoming past. But God's eternity, which Scripture calls God's days or God's time (Job 10:5; Ps. 90:4; 2 Peter 3:8), is perfect and does not pass away. With such understanding we worship God rightly.

Second, to know God as the eternal One is a source of great comfort. The promises of Him who is above the laws of speed and time will not be delayed (2 Peter 3:8-15). Gerhard makes much of this comfort,[64] "Our hope rests in an eternal God whose truth and mercy abide forever (Ps. 117:2), who keeps His truth forever (Ps. 146:6). Such a hope will not disappoint us (Rom. 5:5). 'For the mountains shall depart, and the hills be removed; but My kindness shall not depart from thee, neither shall the covenant of My peace be removed, saith the Lord that hath mercy on thee.' (Is. 54:10). His is an eternal mercy and an everlasting covenant of peace."

Third, The eternity of God is used to exhort the believer to cultivate

---

[60] Calov, *Systema,* II, 426.

[61] *Annotationes,* p. 57.

[62] Martini, *De Tribus Elohim,* p. 494.

[63] Calov, *Systema,* II, 427.

[64] *Loci Theologici,* III, 109.

a heavenly viewpoint. Gerhard waxes eloquent on this theme: "O, my soul, which has been made for eternity, cast off the love of earthly and transitory things, and seek those things which are heavenly, since they alone are eternal. Nothing which is temporal and passes away can bring rest to the soul and fill its desires, for the soul has been fashioned by God for eternity. Therefore let us cling with all our affection to our eternal God who is the goal of all our desires. 'For we are but of yesterday, and know nothing, because our days upon the earth are but a shadow' (Job 8:9). Let us therefore press on to the eternal, lest with the passing world we pass away. For the world passes away, the earth perishes and all therein, particularly he who sets his heart on earthly and transitory things. God has deigned that the visible and earthly things happen with the greatest variation and inconsistency, in order that we might lift our hearts from these fleeting things to those things which are above and eternal and say with David (Ps. 142:5): 'Thou art my refuge and my portion in the land of the living,' and (Ps. 73:25, 26), 'Whom have I in heaven but Thee? and there is none upon earth that I desire beside Thee. My flesh and my heart faileth; but God is the strength of my heart, and my portion forever.' " [65]

7. THE IMMENSITY OF GOD

The doctrine of God's immensity and the doctrine of divine omnipresence attained great prominence in the theology of classical Lutheranism. Although many of the divine attributes were discussed superficially and almost carelessly, much careful attention was given to the discussion of God's presence. The reason for this is not primarily the controversies with the Reformed on the somewhat related subjects of Christology and

[65] Loc. cit. The eschatological application of the eternity of God is very strong and pronounced in Lutheran theology and illustrates the preoccupation with eschatology. Cf. Calov, *Systema*, II, 394: "He who loves things transitory and secular and the things of this world perishes with the passing things of this world, but he who clings to the eternal God becomes one spirit with Him and lives with Him forever. Our life here is brief, frail, fleeting, and filled with all kinds of troubles (John 14:1). Therefore let us fly away with our thoughts and carry ourselves to eternity. We are of yesterday and we do not know that our days are shadows on the earth (Job 8:9). Therefore let us draw near to Him who alone inhabits eternity (Is. 57:15), let us ascend from earth to heaven, from shadows to the truth, from time to eternity, from created things to God, the eternal Creator and King (1 Tim. 1:17)."

the Lord's Supper (*Formula of Concord,* VII, VIII), but the importance and the inherent difficulty of the subject itself, as we shall see.

We have observed above that the eternity of God, which was infinite, was portrayed in such a way in the old Lutheran theology that God's immanent relation and involvement with the world of time was neither lost sight of nor minimized. — So also with the attributes of immensity and omnipresence, which in no way modified or undermined God's transcendence. These were presented in such a way that His personal and mighty involvement with His creatures was given the greatest stress.

The earlier dogmaticians discussed the immensity and omnipresence of God together, though never confusing the two ideas. Although they all held to the immensity of God in the strict Lutheran sense, their chief concern was to emphasize God's presence within the created order and especially within His church and to make use of the practical comfort to be derived from this. Some of the later Lutherans (Calov and Hollaz) consider the two concepts separately, and this results in their giving more attention to the immensity of God than was previously done. By far the longest and best of the treatments on God's immensity was given by Calov, and we shall follow his presentation in our résumé.[66]

What precisely is meant by immensity? The definition is somewhat diffuse and involved. Immensity or ubiquity in God should be distinguished from His presence or omnipresence. For immensity means not merely to be present, but to be incapable of not being everywhere present. It is an absolute attribute, essential to God (ἀνενέργητον), whereas omnipresence is usually thought of as being extrinsic and relative and operative (ἐνεργητικόν). Immensity is defined as uninterrupted and unending thereness (*ubietas interminabilis*) or as the direct and simple limitlessness of being present with no expansion or diffusion or mixture or local inclusion, a simple and direct presence to and for and in all things. In such a sense God is absolutely unending.[67]

---

[66] Calov, *Systema,* II, 380 ff. See also Quenstedt, *Systema,* P.I, C.8, S.1, Thesis 19 (I, 290).

[67] Unlike Calov, the earlier Lutherans subsume the notion of immensity under the attribute of God's omnipresence, as one aspect of it. Gerhard (*Loci Theologici,* III, 122) speaks of immensity as the *"essentialis Dei omnipraesentia"* and understands it as follows: "God is present not only according to His power and efficacy, not only by His seeing and knowing all things; but also His total and undivided essence is present to all things. For not only His power and knowledge are immense and infinite, but His essence as well." Cf. Thomas Aquinas, *Summa*

The Lutherans firmly believed that such a description which was Scriptural was meaningful and had its referent in the God who had acted and revealed Himself really and empirically in history. At the same time they believed that the description of God at this particular point had the merit of showing that He transcended any world picture; God cannot be comprehended within the concepts derived from even the profoundest knowledge of the created order. The following statement is important in bringing out this point. "Now although God, when He is thought of as being everywhere is said to be present in all places, still He is not present συνεκτῶς in the sense that He is comprehended, but συνεκτικῶς in the sense that He comprehends all places, not as one who is contained and circumscribed, but as the One who contains all things, according to a presence which is illocal and not local. This is what the scholars meant when they said: God is everywhere and God is nowhere — everywhere inasmuch as His presence comprehends *(continet)* all things, nowhere inasmuch as He is inclosed in nothing. God is in all things but not included; He is outside all things but not excluded. It must be added that God by the power of His immensity is present everywhere in such a way that it is impossible for Him not to be everywhere. Now immensity must not be described as the negation of the possibility of existing adequately in finite space and the capacity of existing in infinite space, as some think. No, immensity involves not so much the capacity of being present as the actual uninterrupted presence itself. By His almighty power God not only can be everywhere, but He is everywhere in the sense that it is not possible for Him not to be present everywhere — just as eternity involves not only the capacity to continue but an absolutely unending continuance." [68]

Two observations may be made in the light of this statement. First, Calov is attempting to portray a doctrine of divine immensity which transcends any world picture and at the same time to affirm a real and not merely conceptual or potential immensity. Second, his statement clearly excludes any notion of pantheism or of a limited God.

Theologica, P.I, Q.8, a.3. When Gerhard later describes "the immensity and essential omnipresence of God" as "efficax et operosa" he is clearly departing from Calov's more strict distinction between immensity and omnipresence. Baier (Baier-Walther, II, 21-27) does the very opposite of Gerhard, beginning with the notion of immensity and under this heading then discussing the various modes and aspects of God's presence in creation and among His people.

[68] Calov, *Systema,* II, 380—81.

The Biblical evidence for the immensity of God lies in those passages and pericopes which speak of God's presence at the same time in heaven and on earth (Josh. 2:11; Ps. 139:1-14; Amos 9:2-3), which say that He fills all things (Jer. 23:23) and is never absent, that He cannot be contained even in the heavens (Acts 7:48-50; 17:24; 1 Kings 8:27), and which describe Him as infinite (Is. 40:12, 15, 17). God is represented in Scripture as never absent but always actively *(in actu)* present (Acts 17:27), sustaining all things (Acts 17:28). "For God does not do anything as one absent," says Calov, "but as one who is directly present, present according to an immediacy not only of power but by an hypostatic immediacy, as they say, since the power of God cannot be separated from His essence." This statement of Calov's together with the Biblical evidence he employs to support his doctrine indicates clearly that the notion of immensity cannot be separated from God's omnipresence and personal activity in the created order. It would almost seem that the conceptual distinction between immensity and omnipresence breaks down, and immensity like omnipresence becomes an ἐνεργητικόν. But why then should Calov retain the distinction which was not generally made and even stress the idea of God's immensity as he does? Baier,[69] for instance, seems to be much more in accord with the Biblical data when he joins the two notions as negative and positive aspects of the same attribute, and after a very brief definition of immensity proceeds to a long discussion of God's omnipresence and its *usus practicus.*

Calov's strong emphasis upon God's immensity is to safeguard the transcendence of God, the fact that He is incomprehensible.[70] Specifically this means that God cannot be comprehended or bound within any world picture.[71] Baier's brief definition of immensity also made this point clear: "The immensity of God consists in this, that the divine essence cannot be measured by or included within any limitations of place." But Calov has something more specific in mind. God is simply outside the universe,

---

[69] Baier-Walther, II, 21—27.

[70] *Systema,* II, 618: "Manet immensa Dei omnipraesentia, ut omni creaturae, ita rationi humanae immensurabilis, & incomprehensibilis." Unlike many of the dogmaticians (for example, Quenstedt and Hollaz) Calov did not treat incomprehensibility as a divine attribute.

[71] Calov, *Apodixis,* p. 71. The implication of 1 Kings 8:27 is that He whom the heaven of heavens cannot contain must be present in every conceivable space *(spatium imaginarium).*

he said.[72] This was the point of 1 Kings 8:27, Is. 40:12, and Job 11:9, which in poetic imagery speak of God as higher than the heavens and deeper than hell. Calov believed, like those of his day, in the finitude and reality of space and the created order. But he would not allow his doctrine of God to be conditioned by this opinion.

It was a couple of Arminian theologians who forced Calov to discuss his position more thoroughly and to clarify it as he did. Conrad Vorst[73] held that God's infinity was an infinite magnitude. But at the same time Vorst denied that the immensity of God could be conceived of as outside the creation. This view brought down upon him the charge that his position after all made God finite in the sense of having magnitude like the created order.

Simon Episcopius[74] was more outspoken but more convincing than Vorst. It is necessary for salvation, he maintained, to believe that God is everywhere; for otherwise His providence would be denied and not all men would be compelled to worship Him. However, this was a presence only according to God's power *(ratione potentiae)* in that He had made and now rules over all things, only according to His providence *(ratione providentiae)* in that He sees and cares for all things, and only according to His knowledge *(ratione scientiae)* in that He directly knows and sees even the most hidden things. But that God is present and fills all things by the very immensity of His being — Episcopius employs the loaded terminology: *"omnia loca et spatia hujus mundi"* — is quite absurd. Such a presence, he feels, is too subtle and difficult to understand and it implies that God could be present in filthy and vile things, which would

---

[72] Calov has borrowed his terminology here from Gabriel Vazquez (Vasquez). See *Commentariorum ac Disputationum in Primam Partem S. Thomas Liber I* (Alcolá, 1597), Q.8, A.2, Disp. 28, C.5 (I, 219 ff.). Although many of the scholastics held that God was not *extra coelum*, Vazquez, leaning on Cajetan, taught that God must have existed in some "conceptual and infinite space" before the creation of all things and also now. He recognized fully the limitations of his terminology. This means that God was "outside" the universe *(extra coelum)* and His presence fills a sort of "infinite space," as it were. But Vazquez held also that the immensity of God was only an aptitude: "It is not consistent to say that God from eternity was actually everywhere; in fact He was not anywhere, since from eternity there was nothing where He could be." Immensity to him, like omnipotence, had to be considered always in respect to the created order.

[73] Conrad Vorst, *Epitome Exegeseos Apologeticae* (Steinfurt, 1611).

[74] Simon Episcopius, *Institutiones Theologicae in Quatuor Libros Distinctae,* L.4, S.2, C.13. See *Opera Theologica* (Amsterdam, 1650), I, 293.

be unworthy of His majesty. Thus we would eat, vomit, and excrete the divine essence. Arguing against the position that God is "outside this world" Episcopius contends that there can be no presence in nothing. "To say that God has an intrinsic presence according to which He actually exists in Himself is to invent a presence without relation or specific connection to that to which something is supposed to be present, and this involves a contradiction." His conclusion is: "Nothing can be present to itself." Therefore immensity is not an attribute of God at all, but an aptitude.

It is clear that Episcopius has restricted himself in his conversations to a three-dimensional notion of space and presence and is therefore talking past Calov. In general Calov [75] replies to such objections by saying that he is always speaking of an immensity and presence of God which is not confined within the categories of any human conception of space and place *(praesentia atopica)* and never of a presence which divides the Deity into parts or sections *(praesentia atomica);* for where God is present He is totally present. To him the divine majesty and power of God demand His eternity and immensity; in other words, to speak of the immensity of God's power, but not of the immensity of God, would be absurd. Likewise providence and omnipresence are never merely potential — never mere aptitudes.

The strength of Calov's position against Episcopius lies in the fact that he exposed the metaphysical assumptions which lay behind the latter's speculations regarding God's presence and which tended to force limitations on God's presence. But there is a weakness in Calov's position which never would have satisfied Episcopius. Calov portrays the immensity of God with no serious reference to God's activity — again the fault inherent in speaking of ἀνενέργητα in God.[76] The earlier Lutherans were not guilty of this fault. The distinction between the immensity and the presence of God was of course an old one. It was clearly expressed in the *Decisio Saxonica* of 1624.[77] But the *Decisio Saxonica* carefully joined

---

[75] *Systema,* II, 406.

[76] Calov does not always commit this fault, however. In his *Apodixis,* p. 70, he represents God's immensity as meaning not merely that He fills heaven and earth (Jer. 23:23-24; Amos 9:2, 3), but that He is near to each one of us. And then Calov applies the notion of divine immensity in terms of Law and Gospel.

[77] *Solida, Verboque Dei & Libro Concordiae Christianae Congrua Decisio Quatuor Illorum Inter Aliquos Theologos Augustanae Confessionis Nuperrime*

the notions of immensity and divine presence, relating both notions to God's creatures and insisting that God is with His creatures both with His presence *(adessentia)* and His activity *(operatio)*. In the Biblical sense there can be no modified presence of God, separated from His activity. Almost every page of the *Decisio Saxonica* is directed against any notion of divine presence as *nuda propinquitas*.[78] True, it was taught there that God's presence is also likened according to Scripture with God's free, merciful, and omnipotent rule over all things (Ps. 30:8; Luke 12:32; 1 Cor. 1:21; Col. 1:17; Heb. 1:3; Eph. 1:9, 19 passim) and depends on it.[79] The idea of God's immensity being ἀνενέργητος is quite absent from the *Decisio Saxonica*.[80]

With the exception of Calov the orthodox Lutheran teachers speak much more of an operational divine omnipresence than of God's immensity. In contrast to immensity God's omnipresence is described as follows:[81] "The omnipresence of God is an attribute which is related to creation, an attribute whereby God is present to all creatures, present not only by the nearness of His substance but also effectively and operatively." Such a presence is not merely a "being there" (ἀδιαστασία, *indistantia*),

Controversorum Capitum Principaliorum, de Vera Descriptione & Fundamento Praesentiae Dei. Ejusque Filii Jesu Christi apud Creaturas (Leipzig, 1624). See p. 2: "Duo ad plenam definitionem praesentiae Dei requiri: Primo adessentiam infiniti & immensi Dei: secundo praesentis Dei operationem."

[78] See, for example, p. 11: "Si in Scriptura Sacra non reperitur ullus praesentiae divinae modus sine inclusa operatione definitus, utique nec praesentia Dei sensu Biblico per solam adessentiam complete definire potest: Sed necessario simul per operationem definiri debet." The "Our Father who art in heaven," for instance, implies more than mere presence; it implies divine lordship, power, and help. Even Job 11:8, 9 does not refer to a *nuda adessentia,* but speaks of the infinite and incomprehensible divine wisdom of God.

[79] Ibid., p. 21: "Quoad universalem vero praesentiam Dei, duo accurate pensitanda veniunt. Primo, adessentia Dei ipsa, quae ab immensitate, & infinitate essentiae ac potentiae divinae oritur. Nisi enim infinitus, immensus ac omnipotens esset Deus, creaturis omnibus adesse non posset: quia vero immensus, infinitus ac omnipotens est, hujus ipsius immensitatis & omnipotentiae ratione a creaturis abesse non potest. Deinde in hac universali praesentia Dei considerandum est regamen mundi, quod utique a liberrimo Dei arbitrio unice dependet: si enim ita visum fuisset Deo, a gubernatione coeli & terrae prorsus abstinere potuisset."

[80] The closest the writers of the *Decisio Saxonica* get to Calov's manner of presentation is to say, p. 17: "Heterodoxum est, quod Dei immensitas, pro praesentia ejus apud creaturas nonnunquam sumatur. Infinitus enim & immensus fuit Deus ab omni aeternitate, antequam ulli creaturae praesentiam se exhibuit."

[81] This is Calov's description (*Systema*, II, 612), and it is significant that the same passages are used to support God's omnipresence as His immensity.

but an activity whereby God actually upholds and affects His creation. What is being emphasized at this point is God's active presence, His activity, in creation and especially among His people, a presence which may assume many modes: for example, a spiritual presence among the worshiping community, a sacramental presence, a mystical indwelling in believers, etc. Such active presence is more than immensity, mere "thereness" — it is an activity, a profound, dynamic, creative, and redemptive presence.[82]

The omnipresence of God is something manifold and varied. He is present in His creation according to different modes of operation. To distinguish between modes of presence is the only way Lutheran theology feels it can be faithful to the diverse Biblical data describing God's presence. One recalls how the Lutheran *Formula of Concord,* following Luther,[83] had spoken of three modes of Christ's presence. In a similar way the Lutherans of the late 16th century speak of modes of God's presence in the world and among His saints. There is no agreement, however, on the number or nature of the modes. This should not surprise us. Since God is transcendent and infinite, any list or description of His modes of presence represents only a stammering human attempt to reflect the Biblical data which talks of His presence.

In general the earlier Lutherans follow the example of Selnecker and list four different modes of God's presence,[84] and they expatiate with a

---

[82] It is, according to Calov (*Systema,* II, 622), not a mere *adessentia* in the strict sense, *distincta ab operatione,* but a *praesentia plena, sive complexa,* which denotes a divine activity. See p. 628: "Non, *Ecce ego vobiscum sum,* non notat tantum adessentiam, sive propinquitatem, sed simul etiam paternum favorem, & gubernationem."

[83] Luther listed three modes (*WA* 26, 335 ff.) of Christ's presence: a comprehensible, corporeal mode of presence as when He walked on earth; an incomprehensible, spiritual mode as when He left the closed grave or is present in the Lord's Supper; a divine, heavenly mode whereby according to His divine nature He both transcends and is present in all creatures. And Luther says there could be more modes. See *Formula of Concord,* SD, VII, 98—103 passim.

[84] Nicolaus Selnecker, *Institutiones,* III, 244: "How many modes of presence does God have?" asks Selnecker. "Four. The first is a universal presence by which God fills all things. The second is a manner by which God is present and dwells also visibly and inseparably among angels and saints in heaven as though in temples and dwelling places. The third is a mode by which God is present in the lives of the regenerate. Thus He is present in the entire ministry of the Word and also in the Sacrament in a manner which He Himself has determined. The fourth mode is unique to the Son of God who in His person and once and for all assumed a human nature and in this nature ascended to the right hand of almighty God,

good deal of practical application on these different modes of His presence. The *first* mode hinted at in Scripture pertains to God's work of creation and providence. It is a universal and general presence whereby He is present to all creatures, preserving and governing them. It is a repletive presence *(repletio coeli & terrae)* whereby God rules over all creation and "comprehends it in himself." [85] This mode of presence is considered by the Lutheran theologians to be an *activity,* and is sometimes almost equated with providence. God is never a mere passive onlooker. Balthasar Mentzer puts it as follows: [86] "The divine presence is portrayed in Holy Writ and in our theological schools as a mighty activity of the God who is present. It is never depicted as a mere presence of God, an empty and inactive presence. And so from Scripture we learn that God cannot be found without His mighty deeds, nor can His deeds be found without God." Again Mentzer says,[87] "God does not exist inactively among His creatures but is freely ruling the entire universe. This is the explanation and reason why the divine Presence among creatures is always defined by means of divine works." Mentzer is carelessly equating God's being and presence with His works; but he is saying that God's mode of presence is determined by His activity (as we shall see more clearly later) and must be viewed and appreciated in the light of His activity.

The *second* mode of God's presence listed by the earlier Lutheran dogmaticians Mentzer calls God's *praesentia gratiosa.* God is present in the church, speaking, forgiving, comforting, protecting, saving His people, and building up their faith through the means of grace (cf. Ps. 23:4; 91:15; 124:2-3; Is. 43:2; Jer. 1:8; 2 Tim. 4:17). Such a presence involves the presence of Christ, the God-man and Savior. "It is Christ Himself who preaches the Gospel, He baptizes, He administers the Lord's Supper, not through angels but through ordinary ministers of the church (Matt. 10:20; Luke 10:16)." [88]

and together with the Father and the Holy Spirit and with equal power reigns as God and man."

[85] Calov, *Systema,* II, 622.

[86] Balthasar Mentzer, *Opera Latina* (Frankfurt, 1669), II, 358. See also ibid., II, 1328. Mentzer does not talk of immensity and rarely uses the term omnipresence in his discussions. To him all the modes of God's presence are modes of operation.

[87] *Opera Latina,* II, 410.

[88] Ibid., II, 358.

The *third* mode of divine presence is a glorious, eschatological presence among the saints and angels of heaven and pertains to the doctrine of eternal life.

The *fourth* mode of presence of God mentioned by the earlier dogmaticians was the presence of the Son of God who assumed human flesh and in His state of exaltation rules all things according to an almighty presence of both His divine and human natures. This mode of presence was not discussed by the later dogmaticians at such an early point in dogmatics, but only later under Christology.[89] For the sake of completeness we must merely mention at this point what was involved in this mode of presence.

The Lutheran theologians held that Christ, who was exalted to the right hand of God, enjoyed a mode of presence which was subject to neither time nor place but was a glorious and majestic rule over all. Like the throne of God, the right hand of God is a figurative expression in Scripture denoting God's power and majesty.[90] Therefore one could say "the divinity is the right hand of God itself." [91] At His exaltation, which took place in time, Christ was raised to this state of power and glory and presence according to His human nature.

What are the implications of this exaltation in terms of Christ's presence? Mentzer answers,[92] "In a bodily manner and in agreement with human nature we grant that Christ is in time and place. But insofar as He sits at the right hand of God He is King and Lord of all creatures and thus also of space and time, because all things are in His hand and all things are put under His feet. If you make an exception of place, space, interval, or time, then I can only infer that Christ was not given all power in heaven and in earth and that He who is on the right hand of the throne of God does not rule and have dominion over place and time, but rather place and time rule Christ and hold Him in check." True, Scripture calls heaven a place and dwelling of God, but in only a

[89] Hollaz, *Examen,* P.III, S.1, C.9, q.2; Calov, *Systema,* II, 622.

[90] Sebastian Schmidt, *In Epistolam ad Hebraeos* (Strasbourg, 1680), p. 51. See also p. 869. Cf. also Jesper Brochmand, *Commentarius in Epistolam ad Hebraeos* (Copenhagen, 1706), p. 31: "Dextra enim Dei & dextra μεγαλωσύνης sunt ταῦτο; Deus enim, quantus quantus est, mera μεγαλωσύνη seu majestas est."

[91] Brochmand, ibid., p. 31. Also p. 32: "According to His divine nature Christ does not sit at the right hand of God, but is the very right hand of God."

[92] *Opera Latina,* II, 909.

modified sense, not in a strict local sense. The right hand of God, then, is everywhere; and in no sense is it subject to place or space. It is a state of being, a majesty, and it is an activity, a rule; but it is also a presence, an omnipresence.

Brochmand puts it as follows:[93] "He who rules in person *(praesens)* and powerfully over all things, must be considered to be all powerful and everywhere present. For what else, I ask, is it to be omnipotent and omnipresent than to uphold all things and govern all things according to one's good pleasure, and this with a most present power and a most powerful presence. Paul himself explains the sitting at the right hand of God as a reigning." We notice in Brochmand and Meisner the refusal to enter upon any metaphysical speculation about ubiquity, but at the same time there is an insistence upon the inseparable connection between Christ's omnipresence and His ruling activity.[94]

The later Lutherans of the 17th century do not discuss the presence of Christ at the right hand of God in their treatment of God's presence, but restrict themselves to the first three modes of presence mentioned by Selnecker and Mentzer.[95] Like their predecessors, the later Lutherans center

[93] Brochmand, p. 32.

[94] It was at this point that the Calvinists could not accept the Lutheran position concerning Christ's presence. That Christ ruled all things according to His human nature was one thing; that His was an omnipresent rule was quite another. William Bucan, for instance, does not question the Lutheran understanding of the right hand of God as a metaphorical phrase for Christ's exalted rule, but his rejection of the *genus majestaticum* of the communication of attributes prevents him from going all the way with the Lutherans. See *Institutiones Theologicae* (Geneva, 1609), p. 263. Bucan says, "In respect to the divine nature which is infinite, Christ sits at the right hand of the Father everywhere, but in respect to His human nature which is finite He sits where He is with His body which after His ascension is in heaven and not on earth (Col. 3:1; Heb. 1:3; 8:1). For the glorious state of Christ is one thing; place is another thing. And therefore the apostle distinguishes both in Eph. 1:20: 'He sitteth at the right hand of God in the heavenly places.' To sit at the right hand of God signifies a state or condition, but 'in heavenly places' signifies a place." Bucan then says that Christ, like any king, may rule everywhere, or in several places, without being in several places.

[95] An exception is Theodore Thumm who offers a rather unique list of modes of God's presence, or *communio,* in respect to His creation. (1) A *general* presence by which God fills all things. (2) A *special* presence by which God dwells in His saints as in His organs (John 15:5). (3) A *very special presence,* called spiritual or sacramental. Here is a unique spiritual fellowship *(conjunctio)* of God and the believer, an intimate and close communion of God and those who embrace the Gospel, a communion of such a nature that He is in them and they in Him and He fills them with new life. See *Impietas Weigliana* (Tübingen, 1622), p. 139. With this list of Thumm's we have the beginning of a new emphasis and

their discussions entirely upon God's *praesentia gratiosa* and its practical application. Here was a divine presence in which the poor sinner could take comfort, not a mere nearness of God's being, but a power and activity *(efficacia et operatio).*[96] Here was a presence whereby the God of all grace dwells among His people, works in them, blesses them, defends, comforts, justifies, and renews them (Gen. 31:42; 39:21; Ps. 139:10; 145: 18, 19; Is. 8:10; Jer. 1:8; Matt. 18:10). This gracious presence is peculiar to God's people, His church; and it happens in time and is related to our time (John 14:23; James 4:8). But it endures; it is God's presence in the church until the end of time (Matt. 28:20), when God's *praesentia gloriosa* is ushered in.

There is something new in the later dogmaticians' treatment of God's gracious presence among His people, namely a vigorous emphasis upon the mystical presence of God in the believer *(unio mystica).* The mystical presence had of course always been taught among Lutherans, as Werner Elert has shown.[97] But prior to the time of Calov the doctrine was associated primarily with the doctrines of the Lord's Supper and the church. Among the later Lutherans the *unio mystica* was mentioned specifically as a mode of God's presence in His people[98] and was emphasized at that early point in dogmatics. When it was later taken up as a part of the *ordo*

approach to the *unio mystica,* as Otto Ritschl has pointed out. See *Dogmenge-schichte des Protestantismus* (Leipzig: J. C. Hinrichs'sche Buchhandlung, and Göttingen: Vandenhoeck & Ruprecht, 1908—27), IV, 208 passim.

[96] Calov, *Systema,* II, 612. See also ibid., II, 622.

[97] *The Structure of Lutheranism,* pp. 154—76. Elert's evidence for Luther's teaching concerning an *unio mystica* is far better and more conclusive than for a specific and conscious teaching of the doctrine among his successors. It is curious that Elert, in his lengthy delineation of the Lutheran doctrine of the *unio mystica,* does not even mention Otto Ritschl's long discussion of the doctrine and its development in Lutheran theology (op. cit., IV, 192 ff.), since he was well acquainted with Ritschl's work. Ritschl remarks that although there was a connection between the Lutheran doctrine of ubiquity and the *unio mystica,* the dwelling of Christ or of the Holy Spirit or of the Trinity in the believer as taught in the orthodox period was due to the "fundamental biblicism" of the orthodox Lutherans. They simply took seriously such passages as 1 Cor. 6:19, Gal. 2:20, and others and accepted the fact of such an indwelling as a mystery which no power of human comprehension could fathom. This judgment is correct. In the standard and massive exposition of the doctrine by Quenstedt no connection is made with Christology, but a simple exposition of such passages as Eph. 3:17 and John 14:23 is offered. See *Systema,* P, III, C. 10, S.1 (III, 614 ff.). But in this and other later treatments of the doctrine the mystical presence of God in the believer is clearly related to God's immensity, as we shall see.

[98] Calov, *Systema,* II, 620.

salutis and thus achieved a certain prominence in Lutheran theology, it was again discussed specifically as a gracious presence of God in His people. What was the mystical presence of God in the believer? It was a gracious indwelling. And since God is infinite and immense this indwelling is a mystery, just as Christ's being Head of the church is a mystery. "God dwells in those who are reborn and justified, who love Christ and keep His Word. For God has been reconciled to men, so that He might attach Himself as a friend and have fellowship with him in an intimate and familiar way. Thus God Himself called Abraham אֹהֲבִי, 'My friend' (Is. 41:8)." [99]

The Biblical images for this union are many: the marriage bond (Hos. 2:19; John 3:29); the Vine and the branches (John 15:1); the Head and the body (Eph. 5:23). It is an intrinsic union, a presence of the very substance of the Holy Trinity with the believer whereby we become partakers of the divine nature (2 Peter 1:4; 1 Cor. 3:16). There are two aspects of this mystical union. First, a gracious personal indwelling, what Hollaz calls a real ἀδιαστασία, a continuity and nearness of God to the believer (John 14:23). Second, a gracious ἐνέργεια by which God comes to us and dwells in us and fills us with all the fullness of His wisdom, holiness, power, and other divine gifts (Eph. 3:18). So intimate and close is this presence of God that the dogmaticians call it a περιχώρησις, the very term employed for the intimate interpenetration of the persons of the Trinity and of the personal union of the two natures of Christ. Of course, the presence of God in the believer is not some sort of hypostatic union with God. Both God's substance and man's retain their identity in this fellowship. But neither is the presence merely an operational one. God Himself is present in the believer. God's presence is always operative — but never merely operative.[100]

Since the divine presence in the *unio mystica* is not merely operational or a mere communication of divine gifts, but the presence of the very Godhead *(substantia totius SS. Trinitatis)* and of the human nature of Christ, the God-man, the question arose: what is the difference between the general presence of the Godhead for all creatures and this special personal presence? Is there somehow more presence involved in the lat-

---

[99] Hollaz, *Examen*, P.III, S.1, C.9, q.2. I follow mainly Hollaz in the succeeding discussion.

[100] Calov, *Systema*, II, 615, 623, 638. Cf. also *Systema*, X, 506.

ter? Is there any explanation or real meaning in the distinction? And if not, why retain the distinction? Such queries were considered at some length by Quenstedt,[101] and by way of response he cites a very significant letter of Balthasar Meisner's which admirably sets forth the Lutheran view and gives insight into the old Lutheran conception of God's modes of presence.

Meisner says, "Our mind is able to differentiate between a divine operation and divine presence, but the Holy Scripture does not usually do this. Besides, this very intimate union according to which believers are implanted in Christ as in their Head is not the same thing as God's immensity or His nearness to all creatures or His general presence; nor is it merely a gracious operation. What is it then? I cannot define it, but I firmly believe it. It is Christ's dwelling in us so that we become one body with Him. It is a personal relationship and tie and union, and nothing in this life can be considered more dear and sweet, nothing more full of comfort." The refusal here to differentiate between God's activity and His presence, which we have noted before, is significant. Just as the right hand of God, a local designation, means a state of being or power or activity in Lutheran theology, so also in the present case — as God's works differ (as in judgment and grace), so His presence differs in mode or manner. The idea of God's presence being confined to locale or even being conceived in terms of locality is simply absent from Lutheran theology. God's presence is conditioned by His operation. But at the same time this presence is in every case ontological, *substantialis*.

The notion of *Werturteil* is unknown in classical Lutheran theology. This fact is made very clear in a subsequent statement by Meisner. He insists that the presence of God cannot be judged by local categories. The omnipresent God is always present in His very substance (*substantialiter*), even when He withdraws His gracious presence from the wicked. Such a position may appear like a hopeless contradiction; but only if God's presence is viewed according to local or logical categories and not in the light of His works.

Meisner says, "If God's gracious presence involves a certain kind of substantial and personal nearness, then it would seem to follow that in the same time and manner as God leaves people He withdraws from them in respect to His substance. For what else is a withdrawal of personal

[101] *Systema,* P.III, C.10, S.2, Obj. 3 (II, 629).

nearness than a withdrawal not only according to grace but according to substance itself?" This is the problem, as Meisner poses it. "But this cannot happen," answers Meisner, "for the infinite which completely fills all things can in no sense be withdrawn from His creatures and separated from them." Meisner then distinguishes between a divine immensity or nearness to all things, which always obtains, and God's gracious or evangelical presence for and in His people. He says, "When God comes to men in a form which He has assumed, then He is said to come and to go in the true and strict sense, yet without any change of the divine nature or of its immensity or of His nearness to all things *(communis indistantia)*. Thus, when the Holy Spirit is given to certain persons, they are not said to be merely the temple of the Holy Spirit's gifts. And when the Spirit is grieved or driven out by sins against conscience, we must not say merely that the gifts of the Holy Spirit have been lost, but the Holy Spirit Himself. And yet neither His immensity nor nearness to all things nor His general presence is thereby denied. The presence of God among His creatures as described by the sacred Scriptures is as follows. (1) It is not the same thing as God's immensity according to which God from eternity is absolutely and universally immense. (2) It is not a nearness to things flowing simply and alone from God's immensity, a nearness which itself is immutable and does not permit any negation. Rather it is the immense and infinite God's true and personal act of being present *(assistentia)* among His creatures. According to this act of being present He rules them with wisdom and power." In very brief Meisner is saying that a mode of God's presence (for example, *praesentia gratiosa*) may not obtain under all conditions and among all people, but God is still present everywhere. This is the only way he thinks he can be true to both the omnipresence of God and the Biblical picture of God's coming and going in terms of acts of judgment and grace. The *Decisio Saxonica* had expressed the same conviction when it said,[102] "There can be no doubt that

---

[102] *Decisio Saxonica*, p. 4. See also Calov, *Systema*, II, 628 ff. Cf. also Baier-Walther, II, 24: "Quod autem aliquando Deus dicitur *accedere* ad homines et ab illis *recedere*, non intelligendum est, quasi secundum essentiam suam aliquo loco circumscribi incipiat aut desinat, sed tanquam per ἀνθρωποπάθειαν dictum . . . Nam et, quod Scripturae *specialem* quandam Dei in sanctis *habitationem* et *propinquitatem* tradunt, etsi praesentiam Dei indistantem quoad substantiam (sive ἀδιάστασιν) supponat, formaliter tamen significat certum aliquem *modum* praesentiae *modificatae,* seu talis, qua Deus praesens esse dicitur, ubi se praesentem esse per certas operationes manifestat, nempe quod hominibus *renatis* dona spiritualia praestantiora praesens confert atque auget, aut alias providentiae suae signa edit;

God with His grace is far from the wicked. But He is still with them according to His nearness and His effective activity. He still protects them by His power as He does other creatures."

8. THE GOODNESS OF GOD
(HOLINESS, MERCY, GRACE, RIGHTEOUSNESS)

The discussion of the goodness of God and of related themes within the *locus de Deo* in classical Lutheran dogmatics is quite incomplete, lacking in balance, and disappointing. There is an explanation for this: the themes are often considered in great depth elsewhere in dogmatics, usually within the *locus* on justification or the *locus* on Christ's work. But undoubtedly more should have been made of these themes within the discussions of the doctrine of God so that a fuller picture of God could be given at this early point. We cannot trace here all that Lutheran theology taught about the goodness of God, but we shall mention only how this was discussed as a divine attribute.

God's goodness is expressed by the term αὐταγαθός. God is intrinsically good and the source and measure of everything good. From His goodness proceed all His deeds of kindness, grace, and mercy (Ps. 25:8, 10; 86:8). This means that all that God does is good and nothing is tainted with injustice (James 1:13). He is never the author of evil [103] nor a party to it. He who hates the workers of iniquity (Ps. 5:4, 5) cannot be the cause of evil. "God is the avenger of sin; and God is not the author of that which He punishes."

Closely related to His goodness is God's mercy which always has respect to God's creatures, to men after the Fall.[104] Before the Fall God loved His creatures; now in love He beholds man's misery, sends His Son in the fullness of time to redeem the world and to offer all men eternal blessings in Word and sacrament. This is mercy. Gerhard seems to include

impiis cum accedere dicitur, iram suam declarat etc. . . . Ecce adventus Dei ad credentes in casu recto est ipsa exhibitio gratiae et beneficentiae! operatio, inquam, gratiosa et benefica, et ex adverso, respectu impiorum, operatio irae et justitiae vindicativae."

[103] Calov, *Apodixis*, p. 69; *Systema*, II, 354 ff. Calov takes up the problem of evil at this point and spends too much time on it here. We shall touch upon the problem in our discussion of providence where it is treated by most of the dogmaticians.

[104] Gerhard, *Loci Theologici*, III, 164.

God's love and patience and longsuffering all under the theme mercy. And he reserves the more thorough discussion of these attributes for his *locus* on Christology and soteriology. Like grace, God's mercy and love are absolutely gratuitous and free, *propter Christum*. There is nothing in us to deserve such mercy. And it is infinite mercy, transcending all our sins and guilt (Ps. 51:1; 103:8 ff.). Therefore we never need to be uncertain of His disposition toward us. (Ps. 117)

The holiness of God is the absolute goodness and righteousness and purity which dwell in Him alone.[105] It is something fearful, but it is also something marvelous and comforting by which God mightily reaches out and makes His claim on us. As we learn to know God's holiness we learn also to avoid every evil and flee from it and in all adversity to lean on His goodness alone. Righteousness and holiness are essential to God, but must be seen as a *vis,* as something active and effective. Righteousness, like holiness, may be viewed either *in malam partem* or *in bonam partem,* but unfortunately at this point it is usually considered as the divine justice which punishes sin. Neither the justice nor the mercy of God which forgives sins are to be regarded as mere effects of God's will; nor are they to be regarded as simply identical with God's actions; but they are real divine attributes. But neither are they opposed to each other but are in harmony. God's justice (wrath against sin) is manifested in acts of judgment, and His mercy is manifested in deeds of redemption and forgiveness. This fact is merely stated in a sort of Law-Gospel dialectic by the Lutheran teachers, and no effort at any reconciliation between God's justice and His mercy is usually attempted.[106]

Ultimately any reconciliation of God's justice and mercy must center in Christ's work of atonement and be found in it; His work of redemption was carried out in response to both God's mercy and justice.[107] God's mercy and goodness are not of such a sort that they ignore sin, but they deal with it in a righteous fashion. God's grace which pardons and saves sinners is not absolute, but is in Christ; and in Christ this divine grace does not violate God's justice but satisfies it. (Rom. 5:10)[108]

---

[105] Calov, *Systema,* II, 340 ff.

[106] Baier-Walther, I, 18.41; II, 283.

[107] See Quenstedt, *Systema,* P.III, C.3, Memb. 2, S.2, q.7, Obj. dial 21, (III, 310).

[108] Jerome Kromayer, *Theologia Positivo-Polemica* (Frankfurt and Leipzig,

The Lutheran teachers urge that goodness and holiness and mercy must be very seriously preached and applied in the church. For one must respond to divine goodness and mercy. How does one respond? With joy and glory in the Lord and with songs of praise to Him (Ps. 106:1; Luke 1:47); with love toward Him by whom we have been loved abundantly; with the earnest desire to imitate His mercy in our intercourse with all men (Luke 6:36; 1 Peter 1:16), and by clinging to divine mercy even in the most severe afflictions (Joel 2:13; Ps. 51:1; 77:8 ff.). In brief, our response is love — love for God and for all men (1 John 4:11). "If we love God, surely we will also love him whom God has placed before us to love." [109]

9. THE WILL OF GOD

God's will is that by which He alone, consistently and by an absolutely free act, wills all the good which He knows.[110] A fundamental characteristic of God's will is freedom.[111] All things which God wills outside of Himself He wills freely in the sense that He is able not to will them.[112] As God wills things in Himself *(ad intra)* His will is according to His nature *(naturalis)* and is necessary — otherwise there would be a contradiction in God and He would be mutable. God wills only what is good, and this not by any pretense, but in truth. He does not, indeed He cannot, will evil (Ps. 5:4; Deut. 32:4). God's will is not some faculty somehow added to His essence and distinct from it, but it is the essence of God Himself as He is inclined to carry out what is good. Therefore the will of God is good and righteous and unchangeable.

Of course there is in God only one will which is in no sense complex. But to catch all the Biblical nuances which speak of the divine will and to offer a whole picture, as it were, of God's will, several distinctions were thought useful because of the different things which God wills and the

1687), I, 140 ff. See also Quenstedt, *Systema,* P.I, C.8, S.2, q.3, Font. Sol. 10 (I, 303).

[109] Gerhard, *Loci Theologici,* III, 170.

[110] Quenstedt, *Systema,* P.I, C.8, S.1, thesis 17 (I, 290).

[111] Gerhard, *Loci Theologici,* III, 198: "Deus est essentia liberrime agens."

[112] Quenstedt, *Systema,* P.I, C.8, S.1, thesis 28 (I, 292). See also Bechmann, *Annotationes,* p. 64.

different ways in which He wills. We mention here only those distinctions which are the most commonly used and which seem most important.

a) One may distinguish between God's hidden and revealed will. Often the judgments of God are so deep that we can never understand His will (Rom. 11:33), and it is hidden from us. But in those matters which pertain to our salvation God's good and gracious will is known in His Word, and we can be certain of it and depend on it.

b) One may distinguish between God's absolute and His conditional will. God's will is said to be absolute in the sense that He wills certain things without conditions. Is. 46:10 and Rom. 9:19 speak of this. In this sense the will of God is always executed. God's will is said to be conditional when He wills something to happen according to certain conditions. Matt. 23:37 presents a classical example of this: God does not will to gather His children according to some inexorable, irresistible force, but according to certain conditions and means which can be resisted by men (Luke 7:30; Acts 7:51). At this point Gerhard is debating with Amandus Polanus and other Calvinists who held that both the salvation and the damnation of men were the result of God's absolute will. Gerhard held that such a position rules out faith as something which God looks to (*ad fidei perseverantiam intuitu*) as He chose to save some.[113]

c) One may distinguish between God's antecedent and consequent will. God's will is called antecedent when it is viewed as preceding any faith or unbelief in men. His will is called consequent when viewed as taking into account man's response to the Gospel. This distinction does not imply any change or whim in God. The consequent will is not contrary but subordinate to the antecedent will of God. To explain the distinction more clearly Gerhard employs the analogy of a father who loves all his

---

[113] Amandus Polanus (*Systema Theologiae Christianae* [Geneva, 1612], L.2, C.19 [I, 442]) speaks of the antecedent and consequent will in God as the Lutherans do, but at the same time he speaks of the absolute will of God which predestinates one to life and another to death. And God wills nothing today which He did not will in eternity. A somewhat milder statement of the position is voiced by Bartholomew Keckermann (*Systema Sacrae Theologiae* [Hanover, 1602], p. 296), who says that, strictly speaking, predestination does not include a reprobation of any kind, but signifies only an election to eternal life; and he condemns the statement that God has predestinated some men to damnation. But in dealing with the decree of reprobation he says later that it is God's "absolute act depending only on God's absolute will." This would never have satisfied Gerhard. To him "neither the cause of election nor the cause of reprobation is to be sought in or fixed in the absolute will of God" (*Loci Theologici*, IV, 200), but election took place in view of (*intuitu*) Christ and His merits and in view of faith in Christ.

98 The Theology of Post-Reformation Lutheranism

children equally and shows no favoritism, wishing all to become heirs
of his possessions. But because of the persistent abuse and degeneracy
of one son, he must exclude the son from the inheritance. Likewise, a
gardener who seeks to cultivate his plants must, if a plant withers, cut it
down. In like manner a physician whose patient dies has neither desired
nor caused that death.

It is interesting that the later Lutheran doctrine of predestination
intuitu fidei taught by Gerhard and all the Lutheran teachers who followed
him has practically identified election as a part of God's *voluntas consequens* and shows that he and the other Lutherans of his age have deviated
from the doctrine of the Lutheran Formula of Concord (Art. XI) on this
point. Actually Giles Hunnius was the first to employ the *intuitu fidei*
formula and to use the distinction between the *voluntas antecedens* and
voluntas consequens in connection with the doctrine of election.[114]

The question arises: Why should God will something which He knew
would not transpire? The reply was that God wills the salvation of all
according to definite means.[115] To use an analogy, God wills that a horse
reproduce a horse. However, if, due to some impediment, a horse produces a monster of some sort, God still intended a horse to be born, although this did not happen because of some defect *ex parte causae secundae.* Lutheran theology is quite willing to speak of a frustrated or ineffectual will of God, but with certain reservations. An ineffective will is
simply God's pleasure *(complacentia)* and not to be confused with His
antecedent will. Actually, God's antecedent will is efficacious "even if He
does not in fact grant salvation to all."

One can detect a definite Lutheran dialectic at this point. Two things
are taught with utmost seriousness. *First,* God's will concerning any object is invariable and fixed. Moreover, there is an immutable harmony
between God's will and His revelation of it.[116] God is utterly serious
as He wills and as He reveals that will. If the revelation of God's will did
not correspond to the will itself, then it is no revelation, but simple decep-
tion. "Could we ever say that God deals with us insincerely," asks Calov,

114 See *Articulus de Providentia Dei et Aeterna Praedestinatione Filiorum
Dei ad Salutem* (Frankfurt, 1596), pp. d2v, a3r, a5v.

115 Bechmann, *Annotationes,* p. 66.

116 Calov, *Apodixis,* p. 74: "Si immutabile est Dei concilium, etiam immutabilis revelatio de consilio Dei."

"when in the matter of salvation He makes known to us His whole counsel?" [117] But along with the unity, certainty, and immovable nature of God's will it must be taught *second* and with equal seriousness that God's will can be thwarted.[118] This is the clear implication of Is. 5:1, 2, Calov insists. In this parable we observe in God a desire and expectation which is not attained. "The conclusion can only be that the will of God is not always carried out. God's zeal and endeavor *(studium)*, toward His vineyard is by no means a mere low degree of volition which does not really prompt any action; for He actually cultivates the vineyard. And He protests, 'What could I have done.' And so there is a frustration of the counsel of God." It is the emphatic and consistent teaching of Lutheran theology that man has the frightening capacity to resist God's will (Calov lists such proof passages as Ps. 81:13 ff.; Prov. 1:24, 25; Matt. 23:37; Luke 7:30; Acts 7:51). If this cannot be harmonized with the single and immutable nature of God's will, Lutheran theology can only let the matter rest and remain silent before this mystery.

d) One may distinguish between God's legal or nomistic will and God's gracious and evangelical will which is centered in all that He has done through Christ.[119] For the Gospel which tells us what God wills and has done to save us does not do away with the Law which God wills to be obeyed. Here we encounter another fundamental dialectic for historic Lutheranism, namely that God has revealed His will in terms of Law and Gospel. But the revelation of the Gospel is infinitely higher than the revelation of the Law; and therefore we should cling always to the revelation in Christ of God's evangelical will, even though His will in the Law is never relaxed.[120]

e) One may distinguish between God's *voluntas efficiens* and *permittens.* According to the first, God wills and does what is according to the counsel of His own will (Eph. 1:11). But the will of God also permits evil to be done and does not stop evil, although God could do so. This does not imply that God wills sin as such or approves of it. But in His infinite wisdom God chooses to use sin for purposes of good. Meanwhile sin is always done against God's will.

[117] Ibid., p. 75.
[118] Ibid.
[119] Heerbrand, *Compendium Theologiae,* p. 45.
[120] Chemnitz, *Loci Theologici,* II, 210.

As we mentioned, a marked characteristic of God's will is freedom. All God's works toward us are done in complete freedom. The old Lutherans find real comfort in this fact. It means that God cannot be bound within any concatenation of causes. This is not a new theme, but one which recurs in Lutheran theology, as we have seen. Gerhard applies this comfort in the following way: [121] "The author of nature is not restricted by the laws of nature. 'Our God is in the heavens' (Ps. 115:3); that is, He is not subject to the laws of nature or earthly things. 'Whatever He has willed He has done.' " This freedom of God is a great comfort to us in affliction, Gerhard says. Moreover, in temptation the believer knows that Paul's question in Rom. 7:24 is answered; God who works in absolute freedom will renew us perfectly unto eternal life and will impart to us perfect freedom. The freedom of God also assures us in adversity that His will will be done; nothing can hinder it (Is. 45:9; 1 Sam. 3:18; 2 Sam. 15:26). In Him we find true freedom. "True freedom is to serve God and to follow after Him. The desire to be free to do evil is a miserable servitude."

10. The Immutability of God

The immutability of God means that He is free of accidents, whims *(affectus)*, composition, and change. In this sense it is closely related to God's unity and simplicity and indicates "that God is not of such a nature that He knows something today but not tomorrow — wills something today but not tomorrow." [122] We must never think of God as some sort of whimsical ruler whose decrees may or may not take place. [123]

Viewed positively, God's immutability is generally linked with His truthfulness *(veritas essentialis)* and considered by the old Lutheran theologians in connection with His grace and promises which cannot be thwarted and which He will always keep. God will keep His Word, says Calov, [124] and this is the basis for all exhortation and consultation in the church. For God's faithfulness and truthfulness continue unchangeable throughout history.

[121] *Loci Theologici,* III, 207.

[122] Calov, *Apodixis,* p. 67.

[123] Abraham Calov, *Socinismus Profligatus, hoc est. Errorum Socinianorum Loculenta Confutatio,* editio secunda (Wittenberg, 1668), p. 158.

[124] Calov, *Systema,* II, 318.

The Lutheran dogmaticians are at their best as they treat the attribute of divine immutability. They stick to their simple purpose of applying the doctrine in an edifying way, they avoid needless scholastic discussion, and they present a good amount of comment on the Biblical evidence for their teaching. Calov has an interesting comment on Mal. 3:6 ("I am the Lord, I change not; therefore ye sons of Jacob are not consumed.").[125] The implication of this passage for Calov is that the name of God, given to Moses (Ex. 3:6), denotes God's unchangeable nature in time and eternity. "If God were to change, He would not be. He is Yahweh, and therefore He says that He cannot change. It is because of the very stability of His nature and will that He is called Yahweh."

James 1:17 is the *sedes doctrinae* for God's immutability and is discussed at great length by the dogmaticians. In brief the exposition goes something like this. James is speaking not of the Father alone, but of the Trinity. The title πατὴρ φώτων denotes God as the source of light and all holiness (1 John 1:5). God is called the Father of lights because of the singleness, holiness, and immutability of His essence. The negation of variableness in Him is added for emphasis; alteration and change are impossible for God.

In his comments Calov reasons from the immutability of God to the certainty of His decrees which cannot be rescinded or revoked. James uses the strongest possible analogy: everyone recognizes the stability of the sun; and yet it turns, it rises and sets, and gives more light at some times than at others. But all this is absent from the Sun of righteousness and Father of lights: there is no shadow of turning in Him, but He is simply unchanging (*Deus simpliciter ἀπαράλλακτος est*), unchangeably good, unchanging in His grace; and all His dealings with us are invariably good. And the comfort we derive from this can never be altered or threatened (Ex. 3:14; Ps. 103:17; Mal. 3:6). So the immutability of God is the immutability of the God who acts graciously.[126] God's immutability must be seen in its evangelical center: His immutability should always comfort us so that we can trust His "unchanging and unfailing Word and oath to us."[127]

[125] Ibid., II, 326.

[126] Ibid.

[127] Sebastian Schmidt, *In Epistolam D. Pauli ad Hebraeos Commentarius,* (Strasbourg, 1705), p. 681.

The fact that God's decrees and actions were considered immutable, as we have seen, introduced two questions which were given a certain amount of attention in the post-Reformation Lutheran theology. First, does not the Incarnation deny God's immutability? The answer was that the Incarnation involved no change in God, no more than change is implied in the fact that God is Creator and Preserver and Lord of all. The incarnate Logos remained the Logos. "The divine nature did not change, but rather assumed a human nature. The union took place in an unchangeable manner and without any confusion of the two natures (ἀτρέπτως καὶ ἀσυγχύτως) and did not introduce any trace of change in the divine essence."[128]

More attention was devoted to the difficulties introduced by the many anthropopathisms applied to God in the Scriptures. Moods such as desire, hope, pain, or joy cannot be attributed to God absolutely; that is to say, such moods cannot be attributed to Him in such a way that they limit God or imply change or caprice in Him (Job 35:6,7; 1 Cor. 15:28; 1 John 1:5). Anthropopathisms must not be pushed to the point of denying God's continuous love, justice, grace, and other attributes. Brochmand[129] deals specifically with the problem introduced by those Biblical passages which speak of God repenting that He made the world or that He made Saul king of Israel. How can such statements be reconciled with God's immutability? In his exposition of James 1:17 Brochmand grapples with the problem. He says, "In order to resolve this difficulty we must point out briefly a couple of facts. The first is that, strictly speaking, there cannot be true repentance in God. In the strict sense repentance is an inner anguish of the soul and anxiety in the will which dislikes something that was done and desires that what was done might be undone. The reason for this is either ignorance of the past, present, or future; or it is an error of judgment or it is the instability of the will. Now repentance of this kind cannot occur in God, because His knowledge is infinite and neither present or past nor future can escape Him (Ps. 139:1,2; Acts 15:18; Heb. 4:13), because He is of unlimited wisdom and cannot err in judgment (Is. 40:13, 14; Rom. 11:33, 34; Eph. 1:11), and finally because His essence is such that His will is utterly unchangeable (Mal. 3:6). Hence

---

[128] Calov, *Systema,* II, 328.

[129] Jesper Brochmand, *In Canonicam et Catholicam Jacobi Epistolam Commentarius* (Copenhagen, 1640), p. 66.

the words of the Holy Spirit speaking in Scripture: 'God is not a man, that He should lie; neither the son of man, that He should repent' (Num. 23:19), and, 'The Strength of Israel will not lie nor repent: for He is not a man, that He should repent' (1 Sam. 15:29). Now since repentance, strictly speaking, cannot obtain in God, we are driven to the second point which is to explain in what sense repentance which is a sort of change can be attributed to God.

"The accepted answer is that repentance is ascribed to God as an anthropopathism. Actually, two things concur in true repentance, namely, the inner anguish of the soul arising out of error which we have committed and the results which follow this anguish, which burns inside the soul and which seeks to undo and destroy as much as possible the things which have been done. God is said to repent, then, when by reason of some monstrous wickedness He destroys and lays waste the work of His hands or when He offers His grace and renews His gifts; He is said to repent because the same effects are observed which usually are noticed in the repentance of men. There is all the while a general change in created things, but in God no change at all, since in Him there is neither παραλλαγή, nor τροπῆς ἀποσκίασμα."

From this statement we observe that Brochmand has not really resolved the difficulty at all, except by reminding us that moods ascribed to God are anthropopathisms. But it is clear too how strong his desire is not to go beyond Scripture as he grapples with the old problem of harmonizing God's immutability with His actions *ad extra.*

11. THE TRUTHFULNESS OF GOD

The truthfulness of God is closely related to His immutability and is often treated as an adjunct to it or application of it (Calov). At other times it is linked with God's goodness and is discussed prior to the attribute of divine goodness (Brochmand). As we mentioned before, some of the later dogmaticians (Quenstedt, Hollaz) discuss the truthfulness of God at two points: first referring to His *veritas essentiae* and then to His *veritas promissionis.* The distinction between truth as it applied to God and as it applied to statements and promises and the relation between these two ideas was a common point of discussion among the old Lutheran theologians. Giles Hunnius[130] mentions that truth which usually pertains to assertions is given a new meaning when applied to Christ and to the Spirit of God. When Christ or the Holy Spirit are called truth in Scripture, the term designates their Godhead. Truth is an absolute quality in God (God is true *per essentiam*). Men at times may be truthful, but God is truth itself, just as He is light itself, righteousness itself, and wisdom itself.

The significance of the close relationship between God's being the truth and His speaking the truth is quite apparent. As Jörg Baur has pointed out,[131] the relationship points to the fact that the true God has made Himself known truthfully and reliably. This means that God is not only knowable, but objectively describable, and this on the basis of Scripture which is His Word and bears His authority, His *veritas moralis*.

In what sense is the speaking and acting God truthful? In the sense that He is faithful to all His words and promises (2 Sam. 7:28; John 17:17; Heb. 6:18), and in all His activities and deeds (Deut. 32:4; Ps. 25:10).[132] Baier says,[133] "Because of the infinite perfection of His understanding and knowledge God cannot be led astray *(falli non potest);* in like manner because of the infinite perfection of His will He is unable to lead others astray *(non potest fallere).*" This was the common parlance of the Lutheran theologians in speaking of the truthfulness of God and of Scripture,[134] and was based upon a plain correspondence idea of truth as the *adaequatio conceptuum cum ipsa re* (Thomas Aquinas, *Summa*

[130] *Opera Latina*, I, 118: "It is one thing when the abstract term truth is predicated of a theological proposition or statement; in this case one easily realizes that this is said of an utterance because of God who made it. It is quite another thing to say of a person, or of a living intelligent nature, that He is truth. In this latter case truth fits no person or nature except God. Therefore, since the Holy Spirit (whom we have shown above to be a person) is according to the testimony of John the truth itself, this is a definite declaration that He is God."

[131] *Baur,* op. cit., pp. 182—83.

[132] Quenstedt, *Systema,* P.I., C.8, S.1, Thesis 37 (I, 293). See also Gerhard, *Loci Theologici,* III, 208. God must be true in all His works and ways, according to Gerhard. And he points out how often truth and life are attributed to God in the same Biblical context (1 Thess. 1:9; 1 John 5:20, 21). It is the living, acting God who is true in all His works (Deut. 32:4; Ps. 25:10) and words. (John 17:17; 2 Sam. 7:28; Heb. 6:18; Num. 23:19)

[133] Baier-Walther, II, 41.

[134] Robert Preus, *Theology of Post-Reformation Lutheranism* [I] (St. Louis, 1970), pp. 339—40.

Contra Gentiles, I, 59).[135] Bechmann, for instance, describes God's truth-fulness in the following scholastic manner:[136] "The truthfulness of God has to do with God's thoughts and signs by which He manifests something, these signs agreeing with the thing they manifest. And so God is true in the sense that He thinks and manifests that it is so."

The practical comfort to be found in God's truthfulness is the knowl-edge that He will not deceive us, that He is completely reliable (Baier speaks of the *rectitudo* of God's *voluntas* toward all His creatures), and that He keeps His promises to us. Brochmand[137] waxes eloquent on this theme. God, he says, does not invite many to His wedding feast unless He wishes all to come. He does not say things to us in His Word which He does not mean or intend. He is, in other words, absolutely faithful. But what about God's warning that the Day of Judgment is at hand (1 Thess. 5:2-10; 2 Peter 3:12) — and the other problems of this nature? Brochmand replies that in such passages God is urging us to prepare for judgment and attain an eschatological perspective, and He truly wills this; and there is no dishonesty involved in such cases. But ultimately the faith-fulness and truthfulness of God must be accepted on faith.

12. THE OMNIPOTENCE OF GOD

The power of God is one of those attributes which is discussed through-out dogmatics (for example in the *loci* on creation and providence, but also on redemption, ecclesiology, and eschatology) and is therefore given rather scant attention within the *locus* on God. One of the better treat-ments of the subject is presented by Calov in his short dogmatics text, *Apodixis Articulorum Fidei,* and we shall summarize this presentation.[138] The power of God is an act of the divine will and understanding. It is an infinite power which for this very reason often does not grasp the omnipo-tence of God in the birth of Christ (Luke 1:37,38), but faith accepts the miracle of the Virgin Birth, knowing that with God nothing is impossible.

[135] Ibid., p. 343.

[136] *Annotationes,* p. 63.

[137] Jesper Brochmand, *Definitiones Articulorum Fidei* (Copenhagen, 1628), p. 62, et passim. See also Mentzer (*Opera Latina,* II, 1209), where he stresses that the certainty of faith as God's gift is the certainty, among other things, that God will not deceive us. Faith in Christ involves such assurance, he says.

[138] *Apodixis,* p. 77.

It is the judgment of faith that divine power cannot be judged by reason (Mark 9:23; Gen. 18:14), for God is אֵל־שַׁדַּי and παντοκράτωρ. (Gen. 17:1; Rev. 1:8)

The infinite power of God is not only creative but redemptive (Eph. 3:20), working in us more than we could ever ask or think. This redemptive power is known in its breadth and length and depth and height only by knowing the love of Christ which passes knowledge; such an oxymoron is meant to emphasize that, although we are recipients of God's almighty grace and saving power, we never grasp it in all its dimensions. This gracious power of God is indeed incomprehensible, infinite, and immeasurable *(immensa)*.

Calov feels that great evangelical comfort is to be found in the infinity and immeasurability of God's creative and saving power, and he stresses this fact. But in His grace God often does what seems impossible or foolish to us (Zech. 4:6), and with acts which seem marked by weakness He accomplishes His saving will. For instance, we are bound by measurement, quantity, size, space. A camel does not pass through the eye of a needle (Matt. 19:24). But God is in no sense bound by any laws of space and measurement (Matt. 19:26). *Potentiae Dei non obstabit dimensionum penetratio.* Christ can pass instantaneously through one place to another (John 20:19). All this has significant implications for Calov's understanding of God. He has no trouble accepting what might seem contrary to fact when Scripture describes the actions of God. What may seem to be an error or contradiction to us is not so to God, and therefore is not so in fact. One can perceive that the same comfort which Calov sought to derive from God's infinite presence he now seeks to draw from the thought of God's infinite power.

Although the power of God is always one and the same infinite power, the orthodox dogmaticians sometimes distinguish between His ordinate and absolute power *(potentia ordinata et absoluta)*.[139] God's power is said to be ordinate when He is seen to work according to the laws and decrees which He Himself has established. This pertains to His providence, but also to His activity of regenerating and saving sinners through definite means which He has established, namely, the Gospel and baptism. God's power is said to be absolute when He works apart from the usual *causae*

[139] Baier-Walther, II, 43.

secundae. An example of such power is the creation of all things, but also God's preparing a virgin, His raising the dead, etc. It must be understood in regard to this distinction that God's laws and means are His, and He is not bound by them. "He who has freely established the laws of nature does not bind Himself by the laws and order of nature." [140] God has freely established in nature the laws that fire burns, virgins do not bear children, water seeks its own level, bodies heavier than water sink, bodies of the dead stay dead, and the heavenly bodies remain in their orbits; yet as He pleases, God freely reverses these laws (Dan. 3:27-28; Matt. 1:23, 25; Ex. 14:22; 2 Kings 6:6; John 11:43; Is. 38:8). God's power therefore is absolutely without limits and infinite.

There are of course things that God cannot do: He cannot contradict Himself, He cannot lie or sin or die. But this fact does not vitiate God's power; it only shows that His will and power are one, and it draws attention to the perfection and righteousness of His power.[141]

[140] Kromayer, *Theologia Positivo-Polemica,* II, 122.

[141] The orthodox dogmaticians give a surprising amount of serious attention to the old objection that the omnipotence of God is somehow denied unless God can lie, die, etc. Quenstedt dismisses the argument by saying that "to be able to do such things is an argument not for power, but for impotence" (*Systema,* P.I., C.8, S.1. Thesis 36 [I, 292]). This is exactly the argument used by St. Anselm. See Anselm de Cantorbéry, *Pourquoi Dieu s'est Fait Homme,* trad. de René Roques (Paris: Les Editions du Cerf, 1963), II, 17 (p. 430). Gerhard (*Loci Theologici,* III, 154) replies to the objection as follows: "Just as we speak of knowledge in reference to the things which are knowable, we speak of power in reference to things which are possible. Impossibilities therefore do not fall under the province of power, and hence neither limit nor restrict the infinity of (God's) power. If they fell under the province of power, they would not be impossibilities." Gerhard is attempting to show that the objection is based on an absurdity (See Thomas Aquinas, *Summa Theologica,* P.I, Q.24, a.3. Cf. Aristotle, *Metaphysica,* V, 17). With the same seriousness Bechmann (*Annotationes,* p. 66) replies in the same vein. God's omnipotence carries a threefold qualification, he says. (1) God can do all things which can possibly be done, but not all possibilities in any sense at all. For instance, God cannot be subsumed under His own omnipotence. (2) At the same time we can speak of absolute possibilities being in accord with God's omnipotence. For instance, to make children of Abraham out of rocks is not possible under conditions of creation, but is possible absolutely for God. (3) However, certain absolute possibilities are not compatible with God's omnipotence. For instance, to sin is absolutely possible, but it is not compatible with God's omnipotence. John A. Schertzer (*Systema Theologiae* [Leipzig and Frankfurt, 1698], p. 55) is merely sarcastic to the objection: "God cannot deny Himself, or die or sin or give a creature an infinite perfection so that he lacks nothing. He cannot make yesterday so that it has not passed or tomorrow today. Such things would involve a contradiction either in God or in the things themselves. If God were to lie or die or sin, He would not be God. If yesterday had not passed away, it would be no yesterday. If tomorrow existed today, there would be no today."

13. GOD'S LIFE AND IMMORTALITY

The Biblical doctrine of the living God is given scant attention in the old Lutheran theology, and the notions of life and immortality in God which are considered only by some of the later dogmaticians are usually brought up to introduce the subjects of God's knowledge and will.[142]

According to Lutheran theology life and immortality in God is the necessity of living (1 Tim. 6:16). God lives, not as the result of His will, but He is in His very essence the living God. And yet life must be considered an ἐνεργητικόν of God: He lives perfectly and actively, and He lives directly through His own essence. Scripture ascribes life to God as His very essence when it calls Him true and living (Deut. 5:6; Heb. 10: 31); it indicates the activity of His life when it says that He lives (Deut. 32:40). God's "I live" is God Himself, for He swears by Himself and His life, and this life is eternal. (Rev. 4:8)

Viewed as His very nature and essence (in actu primo), God's life ought to be distinguished from His living actions and operations. But it is also possible (in actu secundo) to view God's life as an activity which proceeds from His divine nature (operatio vitalis et immanens). In either case God's living is not an impersonal or vegetable-like existence, not an evolution, but a life of knowing, willing, and doing. As perfect life (vita perfectissima), God is the source of all life and all life exists in Him (Gen. 2:7; Ps. 34:10; Acts 17:28). For this reason He is distinguished infinitely from all idols and all that is not God. Thus the Lutheran theologians attribute life to God essentially (οὐσιωδῶς) since He alone has life in Himself, uniquely (ἀντιθετικῶς) because He is opposed to all idols and created things, and especially (ἐξαιρέτως) because, contrary to all creatures, God not only lives but is life and alone can say, "I live." (Deut. 32:40; John 11:24,25; 14:6; 1 John 1:2,5; 5:20)

14. GOD'S KNOWLEDGE (OMNISCIENCE)

The life of God expresses itself in knowledge and will and power. Since God's knowing (intellectus Dei, scientia Dei), like the other divine attributes, is not really different from His essence, it cannot be a quality or accident in God. It is rather an immeasurable and infinite knowledge with which all things are known to God directly and from eternity. Past,

[142] Calov, Systema, II, 434; Baier-Walther, II, 28; Hollaz, Examen, P.I, C.1, q.39; Quenstedt, Systema, P.I, C.8, S.1, Thesis 21 (I, 266—89).

present, and future things; things contingent (Matt. 11:21) and not decreed by Him; as well as things which He has decreed (Is. 47:7-9) are all known to Him.[143] This being the case, God's knowledge is absolute, it is an omniscience; for if God knows my thoughts which are contingent (Ps. 139:2), then He must know all things absolutely. God's absolute knowledge is shown by His prophecies, particularly of those things which happen contrary to His law (for example, Judas' betrayal, Peter's denial).[144] God's knowledge is never partial or piecemeal or imperfect, but is a *cognitio perfectissima* which extends over everything completely and grasps totally all that is known with absolute clarity and distinctness.[145] It is true and certain and infallible and can in no sense be likened to mere opinion. It is an eternal and unchangeable knowledge which is one single, immediate act, an act which has no steps in it and is not discursive.[146] God does not acquire knowledge like men; all things are simply known to Him, all at once and totally; all things are eternally present *(praesentissima)* to Him, even possibilities. (Is. 41:22)

15. CONCLUSION

Although we have made some comment throughout our resume of the old classical Lutheran treatment of the divine attributes, a few final remarks might be in order. We said in the beginning of this chapter that the doctrine of God is the most difficult in Christian dogmatics. We think the Lutheran dogmaticians have now fairly well proved this point. It is one of their weakest *loci,* and this for several reasons.

First, any discussion of the divine attributes should lead to a definite evangelical knowledge of God. One should learn that the revealed knowl-

[143] Calov, *Apodixis,* p. 78.

[144] Bechmann, *Annotationes,* p. 64.

[145] Calov, *Systema,* II, 438. Although the orthodox Lutheran terminology in regard to God's knowledge at this point leans heavily on the older scholasticism (Thomas Aquinas, *Summa Theologica,* P.I, Q.14, a.7-16), a good deal of Biblical study is also brought to bear on the discussion of God's omniscience; and it is clear that the dogmaticians make a strong effort to show the Biblical basis for their doctrine (for example, from the implications of 1 Sam. 2:3; Rom. 11:33; Col. 2:3). The scholastic jargon was calculated merely to set forth systematically the Biblical basis for God's omniscience (1 Tim. 1:17; Job 12:13; Dan. 2:20). It was thought that a glimpse of the depth of divine knowledge was in a special way to be seen in God's knowledge of us. See Calov, ibid., II, 439; Dorsch, *Synopsis Theologica Zacharianae,* II, 150.

[146] Baier-Walther, II, 30.

edge of God which the *locus* on the divine attributes introduces presents a God of grace who has acted redemptively through His Son and now acts mightily to bring sinners to repentance and faith. This was surely the intent of the Lutheran teachers as they introduced their study of the revealed knowledge of God with the *locus de attributis divinis*. But such a picture of God does not come through with the clarity and impact which an evangelical Lutheran might desire. In this regard it would be better to read the old Lutheran dogmaticians in almost any other *locus;* for there we would be introduced more quickly to the *sola gratia* and *solus Christus* and learn that these post-Reformation Lutherans were indeed evangelical Lutherans in the tradition of the Reformation.[147] The doctrine of creation, for instance, as treated by the old dogmaticians, shows very clearly the evangelical center of the Post-Reformation Lutheran theology.

Second, the *locus* on the divine attributes is perhaps the least Biblical and most scholastic *locus* in Lutheran dogmatics. It seems that the discussion was more or less forced upon Gerhard and those who followed him, if they were going to write a complete dogmatics; and they fulfill their duty with a lack of enthusiasm uncharacteristic of them. Since it was a new subject never before treated systematically in Lutheran theology, Gerhard understandably repaired to the works of Aquinas and others who had written on it. Although he and the other Lutherans supply much more Biblical basis for their doctrine than Thomas, still the stereotyped and tiresome scholastic terminology and presentation persists. What a marked contrast between this *locus* and their fresh and strongly exegetical approach to such subjects as soteriology and Christology! We could of course have made the Lutheran dogmaticians look much better at this point, if we had consulted more of their exegetical works which often treat certain divine attributes in greater detail and in the context of God's works. But such a procedure would have taken us far beyond the purpose of the present study, which was to survey the doctrine of God in its dogmatic setting.

[147] In this connection I might refer to two articles of mine which show that the doctrine of justification was central to the theology of Lutheran orthodoxy as it had been for the Reformers and that orthodoxy makes a definite effort to see and treat every article of faith in the light of this pivotal article. See "The Justification of a Sinner Before God," *Scottish Journal of Theology,* 13, 3 (Sept. 1960), pp. 262—77; "The Doctrine of Justification in the Theology of Classical Lutheran Orthodoxy" in *The Springfielder,* XXIX, 1 (Spring, 1965), pp. 24—39. The thesis of these articles is probably less clear from our present studies than anywhere else in the classical Lutheran theology.

Third, although the Lutheran teachers do some deep thinking and provide some valuable discussion on certain divine attributes such as immutability and omnipresence, there are some Biblical themes belonging within their discussions which receive only the scantiest attention. Can they, for instance, be possibly justified in not treating love as a divine attribute? And is it proper or even possible to discuss the life of God apart from the articles of creation, soteriology, and the gift of eternal life? This leads us again to the criticism which has already been expressed: is it wise to begin dogmatic theology with the doctrine of the essence and attributes of God and not rather to allow the attributes of God to arise out of His works? Lutheran dogmatic theology elected to treat the essence and attributes of God before treating His works, just as it chose to treat the person of Christ prior to His work of redemption. Scripture, on the other hand, teaches us who God is by introducing us first of all to His works.

Fourth, although the Lutheran theologians make every effort to make the divine attributes meaningful and a source of practical comfort, their *usus practici* sometimes appear a bit strained. And this is because the reader has not yet the background in the works of God to make sufficient application of the divine attributes to practical life. All in all, however, Lutheran theology did quite well in making the divine attributes relevant to the Christian life of faith, considering the limitations imposed upon them by their methodology. Discussions which sometimes appear sterile and purely academic often take on a new aspect and become relevant when seen in the light of their *usus practicus*.[148] In these recurring sections called *usus practicus* we perceive the practical and evangelical concern of the post-Reformation Lutheran theologians.

---

[148] A good example of this is found in Gerhard's section on the practical application of all the divine attributes (*Loci Theologici,* III, 89). It may be a question whether Lutheran dogmatics, especially in the case of the large works of Gerhard, Quenstedt, Calov, and others, was written to be read from beginning to end, or whether these large works were constructed as source books in dogmatics to be read at any point. If the latter is the case, then some of our criticism above may appear somewhat out of place. One thing is certain in the old Lutheran dogmatics: all theology was seen as one connected entity *(una copulativa),* like a human body *(corpus),* with many parts or members *(articuli).* See Calov, *Systema,* I, 773; cf. Luther, *WA* 24, 402, 46 ff. Therefore it would never do to read only one or two *loci* in dogmatics and leave it at that. And in reading any *locus* one is expected to bring with one a definite theological *habitus* (aptitude) which includes both faith and an understanding of the principles of the Christian faith.

The Triune God

CHAPTER FOUR

The doctrine of the Trinity as taught by post-Reformation Lutheran theology manifests little that is original or novel. The theologians of the era, following the Formula of Concord, remain very close to the theology and even the terminology of the ancient creeds, just as the Reformers had done before them. In fact they shun all novelty as they treat this great mystery of the Christian faith.[1] This does not mean that they took the doctrine for granted or took it lightly.

In their treatment of the doctrine of the Trinity they reveal not only their acceptance of the ancient creeds, but also their conviction that their doctrine was firmly grounded in Scripture. In the controversies against the anti-Trinitarians of their day they were most active — and this almost exclusively in the presentation of Biblical proof. They saw any deviation from the doctrine of the Trinity as *eo ipso* a deviation from the Christian faith. The doctrine of the Trinity was considered by the Lutheran teachers to be not only a touchstone for Christian orthodoxy but a fundamental article of the Christian faith, an article necessary to know for salvation.[2]

[1] Werner Elert (*The Structure of Lutheranism*, p. 219—20) points out how the orthodox Lutherans after the Formula of Concord show a marked reticence toward the more philosophical and less Biblical treatment of the Trinitarian doctrine of Melanchthon and his school. And he claims that these later Lutherans were the first to offer a solid Biblical basis for the doctrine. According to Elert, the dogmaticians, unlike Luther, believed that the economy of divine revelation gives rise to the doctrine of the Trinity and not historical heresies.

[2] See Baier-Walther, I, 52 ff. for evidence of this fact.

For to know and worship God as triune means to know Him and worship Him aright as a gracious God who through His Spirit seeks and saves sinners for Christ's sake.

Here we see the reason Lutheran theology insisted so emphatically on the doctrine of the Trinity: not only because this doctrine presented the right teaching concerning God's nature, but because the doctrine, rightly taught and directed, focused attention on Christ the Savior. It is significant that the doctrine of the Trinity became in many cases a sort of preamble for a thorough treatment of the doctrine of Christ.[3]

Apart from the importance of the subject itself, there was a weighty historic reason for the Lutherans after the Reformation to deal very thoroughly with the doctrine of the Trinity, namely the rise of Socinianism with its neo-Arian doctrine of God. The Socinians held that the article of the Trinity was not taught expressly in the Scriptures and therefore could not be considered necessary for salvation; for everything necessary for salvation must be expressly taught in Scripture.[4] They insisted, in fact, that the doctrine of the Trinity was a false doctrine. They rejected all the traditional Old Testament proofs for the Trinity (plurality of names, divine appearances, *opera ad intra,* plural verb forms, and the like) or brushed them aside.[5] And the New Testament passages which supported the doctrine were usually taken in an adoptionist sense.[6] In some cases

---

[3] Both Selnecker (*Institutiones Christianae Religionis,* I, 93) and Heerbrand (*Compendium Theologiae,* pp. 23—38) include the doctrine of the personal union and the doctrine of the two natures of Christ in their treatment of the Trinity. The later dogmaticians, who do not do this, nevertheless give very thorough attention to the doctrine of the person of Christ in their treatment of the article of the Trinity.

[4] See Valentin Smaltz, *Refutatio Disputationis de Spiritu Sancto* (Cracow, 1613), p. 3. Also *Responsio ad Scriptum Hermani Ravenspergeri* (Cracow, 1613). A hermeneutic rule for the Socinians was that an article of faith could not be based on any inference drawn from a Scripture passage or number of passages, but only from the express words of Scripture without any consequences. See *Catechesis Racoviensis, seu Liber Socinianorum Primarius* (Frankfurt and Leipzig, 1739), *praefatio.*

[5] See Valentin Smaltz, *Refutatio Thesium de Sacrosancta Imitata Divinae Essentiae et in eadem Sacrosancta Personarum Trinitate a Jacobo Schappero Propositarum* (Cracow, 1614), p. 3 ff. At times Smaltz makes statements which sound very like the Trinitarian position, for example, p. 9: "Diximus ab initio, nos non negare, Patrem Filium & Spiritum Sanctum esse, & hanc Triadem appellari posse." But such a statement is a concession only in terminology when we view his entire position.

[6] Ibid., p. 3.

their treatment of the evidence was quite cavalier and fanciful as when they argued against the equality of the persons from John 5:33, 37, 39 (Father, Son, and John the Baptist). They maintained that only the Father is called God κατ' ἐξοχήν in Scripture and in the Apostles' Creed, which does not say, "I believe in one God . . ." but, "I believe in God the Father . . ." Their attack against the Trinity centered in a denial of the divinity of Christ. The fact that He grew in wisdom and professed not to know the Day of Judgment showed that He could not possess full deity with the Father.[7] And Christ admitted that the Father was greater than He. The very humility of Christ precludes His divinity, "for there can be no humility in God."[8] Christ may be called God as an honorary title but not eternal God. He is the firstborn among many creatures. He is born of the Father and therefore posterior to the Father.[9] Even 1 Tim. 2:5 was used against the Trinitarian position: the argument was that a mediator could not be one with the offended party who is God.

It was this kind of theology which the Lutherans were struggling against as they labored to defend and, if possible, clarify the traditional doctrine of the Trinity. There is no doubt that Socinianism occasioned deep concern among all the Lutheran theologians to restudy the doctrine of the Trinity in the light of the Biblical evidence used traditionally to support it, and then to present the old doctrine unchanged but on the basis of this evidence. Why this deep concern among the Lutherans? After all, Socinianism in its day represented only a small and ineffectual movement. It gained very little following among the masses or among the scholars of Europe during the 17th century. And it claimed few real scholars within its own ranks. Yet even the Scandinavian and Strasbourg theologians who had no direct contact with it felt compelled to deal thoroughly with its doctrines, and particularly in regard to its doctrine of God. The reason for this preoccupation with Socinianism and the detailed refutation of its errors was not merely to protest the orthodoxy of Lutheranism against certain Roman Catholic aspersions. Nor were the Lutheran dogmaticians merely using the Socinian error as a foil for presenting their Trinitarian doctrine. No, the only explanation for the deep Lutheran fear of Socinianism lies in the deep fear of all heterodoxy, par-

[7] Ibid., p. 22.
[8] Ibid., p. 24.
[9] Ibid., p. 38.

ticularly in the article of the Trinity, which was considered the touchstone for orthodoxy. This fact, I believe, will be brought out in the course of our studies.

The great bulk of attention devoted to the presentation of the doctrine of the Trinity lay in the amassing of Biblical evidence for the plurality within the Godhead and for the personal characteristics and deity of the Three Persons. A certain amount of groundwork, however, had to be laid for this dogmatico-exegetical presentation. In the main, three preliminary points were discussed, and we shall now consider them in order: (1) the necessity of believing in the Trinity, (2) the Trinity and reason, and (3) the terminology connected with the doctrine.

1. THE NECESSITY OF BELIEVING IN THE TRINITY

To be saved it is necessary to know that God is Father, Son, and Holy Spirit.[10] When the Lutherans insist on this principle, they are excluding not only those who deny the Trinity but those also who are ignorant of it. Not to know the Trinity is not to know God. Of course, there are great differences of understanding among Christians, and many have only an obscure and partial knowledge. And in fact none of us will ever know this marvelous mystery in more than a fragmentary way (1 Cor. 13:9; Ex. 33:20). Still a distinct knowledge *(Non confusa & implicita)* and confession of the Three Persons is necessary for salvation.

A great amount of Biblical proof was marshalled to support this conviction, which was not then questioned except among Socinians and Jews. *First,* Gerhard contends, we are to believe in God as He has made Himself known to us, for so He is. "Whoever does not know the mystery of the Trinity does not know God as He has revealed Himself in His Word." And whoever does not know God as He has revealed Himself makes some sort of idol for himself in his heart. *Second,* Christ explicitly makes salvation dependent upon faith in Him as well as in the Father (Matt. 11:27; John 5:23; 1 John 2:23; 2 John 9). Furthermore, the Scriptures clearly

---

[10] Gerhard, *Loci Theologici,* III, 209. Gerhard's discussion is typical. Cf. Martin Geier, *Opuscula Philologica,* p. 147. The discoveries in the new world apparently incited speculation not only on the question of pre-Adamites and polygenism, but also whether God was somehow known to those who had not received the Christian revelation or whether, as in the case of the Jews, acknowledgment of God as Creator was sufficient for salvation.

state that those who are without Christ and therefore outside the church are without God (Eph. 2:12) and do not know Him (Rom. 10.14; Gal. 4:8; 1 John 5:12). They are children of wrath (Eph. 2:3), and the wrath of God abides on them. (John 3:36)

From Gerhard's routine discourse on the necessity of believing in the Trinity we learn that for Lutheran theology the doctrine of the Trinity is bound inextricably to the doctrine of Christ and salvation through faith in Him. This fact is brought out much more clearly in Quenstedt's statement of the issue.[11] Quenstedt takes pains to point out that when it is said that one must know the triune God to be saved, this knowledge is not mere intellectual assent to a dogma, but it involves a firm, immovable trust *(cordis fiducia)* in God and infers also a new obedience. It is therefore no mere theoretical knowledge which is required but a practical, living knowledge — not merely an acknowledgment of the Trinity as such, but an evangelical knowledge of God centered in the person and work of Christ.[12] In other words, every mention of the necessity of believing in the triune God must be set in a Christological context, in the context of justification through faith in Christ. This fact is apparent in Quenstedt's discussion of the subject, which scarcely mentions the Trinity at all but places all the stress on the necessity and importance of faith in Christ and the blessings which are gained through faith in Him. Commenting on 1 John 5:1, 12, Quenstedt says,[13] "Here we observe *first* that eternal life is in the Son in a threefold sense, (a) because faith and knowledge of Him lead to eternal life, (b) because by His death He has secured eternal life for us, and (c) because He offers that life to us by showing us Himself in whom eternal life and blessedness abide. *Second,* we observe that to have the Son means to embrace Him with true faith; and so he who believes in the Son has eternal life, he has it here in hope, he has it there in substance; he has it here in its beginning, he has it there in all its fullness (John 3:36)." To believe in the Trinity involves believing in Christ as Savior. If this fact does not always become as clear as it should, it is because the old Lutheran theology begins dogmatics with the doctrine of the Trinity, as had been done traditionally, and does not allow the doctrine to arise out of the doctrine of salvation.

[11] *Systema,* P.I, C.9, S.1, Thesis 4 (I, 319 ff.).
[12] Dorsch, *Synopsis Theologiae Zacharianae,* II, 236. Calov, *Apodixis,* p. 105.
[13] Loc cit., Thesis 4, nota 2.

2. THE TRINITY AND HUMAN REASON

Lutheran theology maintained that the doctrine of the Trinity is a mystery of faith which cannot be supported or even defended philosophically or with the aid of human reason. The principle is stated by Gerhard,[14] "The mystery of the Trinity cannot and ought not be proved aprioristically by natural reason." This principle does not rule out all illustration. The church fathers and even Luther had called forth imperfect analogies from nature to illustrate the Trinity. But Gerhard warns,[15] "Our reasonings which are taken from the light of nature and applied to the mystery of the Trinity must not be thought of as occupying the function of corroborating this mystery but only of illustrating it in various ways." In the nature of the case the doctrine of the Trinity is above the grasp of all human reason, and therefore we must realize that the principles of reason ought not be used to advance the doctrine (Matt. 11:27; 16:17; John 1:18; 1 Cor. 2:11). Quenstedt is even more cautious at this point. The doctrine cannot be demonstrated aprioristically or aposterioristically, he holds. He does not even like the idea of analogies being used to illustrate the doctrine. "Indeed," he says,[16] "there is not even the possibility of this mystery being supported by natural reason, for to reason, as it reflects on its own principles, it appears to be impossible and absurd."

[14] *Loci Theologici,* III, 220, 228 (Thesis V).

[15] *Loci Theologici,* III, 221. Cf. also I, 208—10; III, 228—29. Gerhard cites Luther generously at this point and wants to show his agreement with him. See Robert Preus, *The Theology of Post-Reformation Lutheranism* [I] (St. Louis: Concordia Publishing House, 1970) pp. 126—28.

[16] *Systema,* P.I, C.9, S.1, Thesis 2 (I, 318). Cf. also ibid., P.I, C.6, S.2, Q.3 (I, 265). Emil Brunner (*Revelation and Reason,* trans. Olive Wyon, Philadelphia, Westminster Press, 1946, p. 114) seems to have misunderstood Lutheran orthodoxy completely on this point. In a footnote he cites Melanchthon's well known statement from his 1521 *Loci Communes,* "Mysteria divinitatis rectius adoraverimus quam vestigaverimus" (*CR* 21,84), substituting the word "trinitatis" for "divinitatis" probably because he is speaking of the Trinity in the main body of the text. He then remarks that such a notion "characteristically . . . vanishes with the growth of orthodoxy." The implication is that later orthodoxy made "the mystery of the Trinity into an intellectual puzzle." It is obvious that, with their insistence upon the impossibility of reason probing the mystery of the Trinity and that the mystery of the Trinity is ὑπὲρ νοῦν, ὑπὲρ λόγον, καὶ ὑπὲρ κατὰ λῆψιν (Quenstedt, *Systema,* P.I, C.9, S.1, Thesis 1 [I,318]; cf. also ibid. P.1, C.5, S.I, thesis 1, notae 2,4,5,6,8 [I, 348—49, 1715 ed.]) the old Lutheran theologians are not in the slightest guilty of the charge Brunner levels against them. The usual verb associated with mysteries of the faith is "believe." The object of the term "adore" is usually God Himself or the Divinity, in the parlance of the later dogmaticians.

Quenstedt has indicated a very important aspect of the entire issue, namely that the Trinity is not only above human reason but contrary to the concrete reason of fallen man who is opposed to the mysteries of God. And Gerhard does not neglect this point either. Reason, he points out, can indeed know that God is and grasp some of His attributes, but the article of the Trinity tells us who God is in Himself, and here is a subject which human reason cannot penetrate. For all human reason is corrupt, darkened, utterly prejudiced against any evangelical knowledge of God and against God Himself. (Eccl. 8:17)

If human reason cannot support the doctrine of the Trinity, the obverse of the fact is also true; human reason cannot and should not be used to oppose the doctrine. There are two reasons for this. *First,* such a procedure would be logically impossible. Things which are believed cannot be judged by things which are within the sphere of understanding; if this were possible all articles of faith would automatically fall.[17] Gerhard argues as follows: "The judgment of our senses cannot and ought not to be urged against the judgment of reason. Therefore the judgment of reason cannot be urged against the judgment of faith." Gerhard is of the opinion that most rational judgment against the Trinity springs from the refusal to admit that there are special cases where valid axioms of a general nature do not apply. Such rational judgment against the Trinity would be therefore begging the question, since the article of faith and particularly the Trinity are *specialis,* which such negative judgment a priori denies.[18] He says, "All arguments which are brought by reason against the mystery of the Trinity assume in their major premise some axiom which holds true only within the sphere of created things and is therefore an axiom limited to one sphere. Then these arguments apply this axiom to the uncreated and infinite essence of God, that is, they assume that their axiom is useful in an absolute and unlimited sense, which is contrary to all logic."

Jacob Martini argues in much the same manner.[19] Why is it impossible, he asks, for the article of the Trinity to be opposed by any law of

---

[17] Gerhard, III, 229: "Quemadmodum τὰ νοητὰ non sunt judicanda ex αἰσθήσει, ita τὰ πιστὰ non sunt judicanda ex νοήσει." Cf. Quenstedt, *Systema,* P.I, C.9, S.1, Thesis 1 (I, 318).

[18] Gerhard, *Loci Theologici,* III, 229. See also ibid., I, 209. Cf. Hollaz, *Examen,* Prol I, Q.27; also ibid., Prol. III, Q.4.

[19] *De Tribus Elohim,* II, 402.

logic, such as the law of contradiction? It is because God who has given us our reason has also revealed Himself as triune. And He who is the source of all truth will not contradict Himself. This argument is a variation of the principle of the unity of all truth and of the agreement between the book of nature and the book of Scripture. Martini is most insistent that what God has said to us in nature and in all human experience He will not deny. But, to take another example, an accepted axiom of nature is that nothing can rise out of nothing. How can this axiom be harmonized with the Christian doctrine of creation *ex nihilo?* There is no contradiction here, says Martini. Within nature the axiom holds; but creation was a divine act prior to nature and utterly supernatural. Then, getting back to the subject, Martini concludes, "Therefore we say that the Three Persons in one essence is not contrary to any truth from nature, although it is indeed above all truths which are known from nature." And since it is above the light of nature it cannot be judged by nature or proved false syllogistically or logically.

There is a *second* and more important reason why human reason cannot oppose the doctrine of the Trinity. The reason is theological rather than logical. The tragic fact is that human nature is totally corrupt. And when corrupt human reason seeks to judge and criticize the articles of faith it wantonly misuses God's gift of reason and embarks upon a course which is not only hopeless and ridiculous but sinful and utterly reprehensible. Gerhard says, "Human reason not only labors under great weakness, but also under blindness, darkness, and errors when it presumes to judge in matters of faith (Rom. 1:21; 1 Cor. 1:19; Eph. 4:17). [Human reason] not only lacks the ability to understand divine things fully and completely, but with its inclination to the contrary it pursues only errors and vice. 1 Cor. 2:14: 'The natural man receiveth not the things of the Spirit of God: for they are foolishness to him; neither can he know them, because they are spiritually discerned.' The inference of the apostle is that spiritual things must be judged spiritually." This statement of Gerhard's shows that the solution to the problem persisting between the doctrine of the Trinity and human reason lies in repentance. But the theme of repentance as it pertains to faith is sounded much more clearly later in dogmatics.

The failure of sinful human reason to cope with the mystery of the Trinity leaves open only one avenue whereby we can know God as Father,

Son, and Holy Spirit; as Maker, Redeemer, and Comforter; namely, God's revelation in Scripture. "The mystery of the Trinity," Gerhard says,[20] "ought to be demonstrated not from the little brooks of the Fathers or from the muddy ditches of the Scholastics but from the clear fountains of Sacred Scripture; and this can be done."[21] He then proceeds to say in a subsequent statement that the mystery is to be supported not only by the New Testament but by the Old as well. Against the Socinians, Gerhard and all the Lutheran theologians are fully convinced that the doctrine of the Trinity did not develop merely as a response to historical heresies, but is the doctrine of Scripture itself. And with much labor and erudition — and also much optimism — they marshal their evidence and state their case. But before tracing all the Biblical evidence which they present on behalf of their doctrine, we must briefly summarize their Trinitarian terminology, which at times can become quite technical.

3. THE ORTHODOX TRINITARIAN TERMINOLOGY

Most of the Lutheran dogmaticians feel compelled to discuss the terms, both Biblical and ecclesiastical, used in presenting the doctrine of the Trinity, and to search the meaning of these terms and weigh their comparative merit. Very deliberately they retain the terminology of the ancient creeds and of those early Greek and Latin church fathers whose orthodoxy at this point was unimpeachable.[22] We now offer some defini-

[20] *Loci Theologici,* III, 214.

[21] See also Dannhauer, *Hodosophia Christiana,* p. 92. Calov (*Apodixis,* p. 87) treats the matter more Christologically. He too asserts that nothing can be said about the Trinity which is not drawn from God's revelation of Himself. This means (Matt. 11:27) that no one will know God except through the revelation of His Son. Nature and reason are impotent in the face of this mystery. The mystery of the Godhead is utterly inscrutable apart from Christ (John 1:18). Furthermore, God's nature is something hidden and terrifying, apart from the witness of the Spirit who alone can reveal to each of us the hidden things of the divine nature. (1 Cor. 2:11)

[22] See, for example, Gerhard, *Loci Theologici,* III, 238 ff.; Quenstedt, *Systema,* P.I, C.9, S.1, thesis 5 ff. (I, 320 ff.); Calov, *Systema,* III, 94 ff.; Chemnitz, *Loci Theologici,* I, 34 ff.; Hollaz, *Examen,* P. I, C.2, Q. 4 ff. We cannot here trace the dependence of the Lutherans upon the theology and terminology of the creeds and church fathers. We refer the reader to G. L. Prestige, *God in Patristic Thought* (London: S. P. C. K. Press, 1950; and *A Patristic Greek Lexicon,* ed. C. W. H. Lampe (Oxford: Clarendon Press, 1961—). One thing is quite certain: the Lutheran dogmaticians got their terminology and approach to the doctrine of the Trinity directly from the early fathers and not through Luther or especially

tion and discussion of the main terms and concepts used to present the mystery of the Trinity.

a. οὐσία *(essentia)* was a term indicating the being and essence of God. It was a term for the "I am" or "I will be" and the name of God (Ex. 3:14), sometimes identical with θειά φύσις (2 Peter 1:4) or θεότης (Col. 2:9) or even μορφή (Phil. 2:6). In the technical Christian sense Gerhard says,[23] "The term . . . used of God signifies the one (in number) and undivided essence common to the Three Persons of the deity which is not partly in the Three Persons in the sense that part is in the Father, part in the Son and part in the Holy Spirit; but the whole is in the Father, the whole is in the Son and the whole is in the Holy Spirit. . . ." At times Gerhard would say that God is above being (οὐσία ὑπερούσιος) in that He is not confined within the usual categories of being, nor does He possess features which pass away, but His attributes are His essence. Since God is His own essence and exists by and of Himself He is absolutely unique in essence.

b. ὁμοούσιος is the term used to express the unity of the essence which Christ possesses with the Father, although He is a distinct person. (John 10:30)

c. *Persona* was used by the Lutheran theologians interchangeably with ὑπόστασις, ὕπαρξις, and πρόσωπον. Technically the terms mean a subsisting individual, intelligent (conscious), incommunicable, and not subsisting in another *(substantia individua per se ultimato et immediate subsistens).*[24] Specifically, three things must be said about a divine Person in the Trinity. (1) A divine Person subsists in Himself and not in another subject (like a property or feature). (2) A divine Person is Himself a center of consciousness *(est intelligentis naturae).* (3) A divine Person is distinguished from another person by specific characteristics *(opera ad intra).*[25] For instance, the Son is not the Father. At this point we notice the great difference between human and divine persons. A human person always has his own incommunicable essence. But the divine Persons have

Melanchthon, who also dealt rather thoroughly with the doctrine. (See Michael Rogness, *Melanchthon, Reformer Without Honor* [Minneapolis: Augsburg Publishing House, 1969], pp. 78 ff.) In their studies on the Trinity they went more deeply into both Scripture and the fathers than did Luther or even Melanchthon.

23 *Loci Theologici,* III, 238.

24 Quenstedt, *Systema,* P.I, C.9, S.1, Thesis 12 (I, 321).

25 Chemnitz, *Loci Theologici,* I, 40.

one and the same communicable essence, and there is an intimate, intrinsic communication or interpenetration (περιχώρησις) between the Persons, a περιχώρησις which is essential to the Godhead and unique.

It is important to recognize this unique sense in which the term person is predicated of God.[26] The statement, God is a Person, is not a tautology, but means that God has His own distinctive mode of existence (ὑπάρξεως ἴδιος καὶ χαρακτηρίστικος τρόπος). But to call God a Person or to describe Him as a personal God does not mean that the Trinity or Deity itself is one Person; but the term Person as a τρόπος ὑπάρξεως is ascribed to the Father and to the Son and to the Holy Spirit. When I call myself a person, this means that my person and essence are identical. Not so in the case of the Persons of the Godhead, although, like me, they are individuals. When we consider that the Three Persons of the Godhead differ from each other as persons *realiter* and yet remain one undivided divine essence, we realize the inadequacy of our stammerings and of even the most careful terminology; for we are faced here with the ineffable and inscrutable mystery of the Trinity, and the church can only do the best she can in speaking of this on the basis of revelation and in avoiding all heresy.

d. *Trinity* (τριάς) includes the notion of unity and means simply three in one (Athanasian Creed). The "three" specifically applies to the Persons of the Godhead, but inferring in no sense anything else than the Three Persons (no quaternity). The term applies to God in a unique sense, since it does not imply any threefold composition, but the Three Persons of one essence. God is therefore not triple, composed in some way of three parts, but triune, having three modes of subsistence *(subsistendi modi)* in one essence. Gerhard puts it as follows:[27] "Therefore God is not three in respect to His essential attributes which are simply the same as the essence itself, nor in respect to genus or species, but in respect to the three ὑπάρξεως τρόποι which consist of ἀγεννησία in the Father, γέννησις in the Son and ἐκπόρευσις in the Holy Spirit."

Perhaps the most complete and precise definition of the Trinity was given by Quenstedt, and since all our subsequent discussion depends on a full understanding of exactly what the orthodox Lutherans meant by the term, we quote him in full. He says,[28] "The divine essence which is

26 Hutter, *Loci Communes Theologici*, p. 98.
27 *Loci Theologici*, III, 254.
28 *Systema*, P.I, C.9, S.2, Q.1, ekthesis (I, 344).

absolutely one and therefore absolutely single is also Three Persons: Father, Son, and Holy Spirit — Persons who are distinct from each other, each according to an incommunicable personal characteristic. And so the Father, Son, and Holy Spirit are (1) truly such Persons, (2) distinct Persons from each other, and (3) divine Persons who are in their essence the one true God in whom are ἄλλος καὶ ἄλλος, one Person and another Person, not ἄλλο καὶ ἄλλο, one thing and another thing.

"We must distinguish between the term 'God' and the term 'possessing divinity.' I can say correctly 'there are Three who possess divinity,' but I cannot say that there are three Gods. This is because 'God' is understood substantively, and 'possessing divinity' is understood predicatively. I can also say correctly: one who possesses divinity begets another who possesses divinity. But I cannot say: God begets another God. Also I do not say: there are three omnipotent Ones. But I say: there are Three who possess omnipotence. Or I say: the Three are one omnipotent One. This is in accordance with the Athanasian Creed which says there is one deity, one omnipotence, one eternity, one infinity, etc. in the Three Persons.

"God is not *divided* into three persons, but the Three Persons, distinct from each other, participate in the one essence which is unique, indivisible, but also infinite and therefore communicable to the several Persons.

"We say that the one essence is in the Three Persons, not as a whole consists of parts (for each Person possesses the whole essence), not as a genus consists of species (for the Persons are not species, but individuals) nor as a species consists of individuals (for the essence itself is one in number and cannot be divided into many essences), but the total essence is in each individual person in a unique manner which we can neither conceive with our mind nor express with words."

e. *Character hypostaticus* is the special characteristic *(proprietas characteristica)* which belongs to each individual Person of the Trinity and distinguishes Him. These "personal characteristics" can only be ascribed to each individual Person. What are these personal characteristics? It is the characteristic of the Father to *beget* the Son *(paternitas)* and to breathe the Spirit *(spiratio activa)*. It is the personal characteristics of the Son to be eternally begotten of the Father *(filiatio)* and to breathe the Spirit *(spiratio activa)*. It is the personal characteristic of the Holy Spirit that He proceeds from the Father and the Son *(spiratio passiva)*. These personal characteristics are eternal acts *(opera ad intra)* within the eternal

Godhead. Quenstedt offers a very concise explanation of this terminology, and again it is worth our while to quote him.[29] "Basil in his *Adversus Eunomium*, II, 20, teaches what the χαρακτὴρ ὑποστατικός is: according to him, the personal qualities *(proprietates personales)* are called individual or personal characteristics *(notae)* and distinctive marks *(characterea)*, which show the distinction of the Persons within the common identity of the essence. Augustine calls these personal qualities notions *(notiones)* through which a divine Person and His distinction from the other Persons becomes known. Thus the Father becomes known and is distinguished from the Son through fatherhood, the Son becomes known and is distinguished from the Father through filiation, both Persons become known and are distinguished from the Holy Spirit through their active procession, and He from them by His passive spiration, or procession. Others call these personal qualities relations *(relationes)*, because through paternity the Father regards the Son, by filiation the Son views the Father, and through procession the Holy Spirit has regard to the Father and the Son." [30] These personal characteristics not only describe each Person of the Godhead, but distinguish each Person from the other Persons. As we shall see, there are only analogies — and imperfect analogies at that — for the personal characteristics and the relation of the Persons to each other.

This fact poses some problems which have perennially confronted Christian theology and which we have already broached. Can one by using only analogy speak meaningfully and cognitively about God? To speak meaningfully and cognitively about the Trinity must we not employ some literal language from our sphere of experience and not resort to imperfect analogies? The same question arises in reference to the doctrine of the incarnation of Christ. What does it mean, for instance, when Quenstedt[31] says that the incarnation is unique (ἐξαίρετος, καὶ μονότροπος), not common to any other union and removed entirely from any other kind of union? Does such a concept have any meaning? For it appears that nothing from our sphere of experience can help us to understand just what the incarnation (or the Trinity) is.

[29] *Systema,* P.I, C.9, S.1, Thesis 9 (I, 321). Cf. Bechmann, p. 72.

[30] Cf. also Quenstedt, *Systema,* P.I, C.9, S.1, Thesis 24 ff. (I, 330 ff.); Calov, *Systema,* III, 119 ff.; 382 ff.; 803 ff. See also John of Damascus, *De Fide Orthodoxa,* I, 8 (MPG 94, 823); Basil, *Adversus Eunomium,* II, 20, (MPG 29, 636); also Basil, *Epis.* 38 (*MPG* 32, 326 ff.).

[31] *Systema,* P.III, C.3, S.1, Thesis 26 (III, 83).

The Lutheran dogmaticians do not meet this problem head on and at times seem unaware of it. The Trinity, like the incarnation, is simply called a mystery which transcends human understanding and conceptualization. This of course places such mysteries above rational analysis or criticism, as we have seen. But then can one discuss cognitively at all the mysteries, if they are supernatural and impenetrable? The answer to the problem, so far as it is given, runs as follows. The fact (ὅτι) of these mysteries may be conceived and spoken of cognitively, but not the why (διότι).[32] For instance, the expression "eternal generation" of the Son is not a figurative or metaphorical expression for something else; but a literal description of an event, namely the communication of the essence of the Father to the Son by generation. In this sense the event is like any other generation. But there are aspects of this event which differ from any birth within our world of experience. It is an eternal generation; there is no beginning or end to it, the Father eternally begets the Son and the Son exists from eternity as the begotten One. And so, although generation must be understood literally as an actual *opus ad intra* of the Trinity, nevertheless the *mode* of this generation *(modus generationis)*, because it is eternal and pertains to the Deity, is unknown and incapable of cognitive description *(incognitus et ineffabilis)*.[33] Actually there is no greater difficulty in speaking meaningfully of the Trinity and the *proprietates personales* than to talk of God at any point. If God has revealed Himself to man at man's level of comprehension and in terms of man's experience, He can also make known the fact of certain divine mysteries which transcend human comprehension.

Gerhard seeks to answer the problem, but he does not really face the issue as Quenstedt did.[34] It is true, he says, that the ordinary use of language is employed and accommodated to express the mystery of the Trin-

[32] John Adam Osiander, *Theologicum Systema seu Theologia Positiva Acroamatica* (Tübingen, 1679), p. 237 ff.; Scherzer, *Systema Theologiae*, p. 23 ff.; Friedemann Bechmann, *Theologia Polemica* (Jena, 1719), p. 95 ff.; Gerhard, *Loci Theologici*, I, 26—28. In this discussion I am drawing mainly from Quenstedt, *Systema*, P.I, C.9, S.2, Q.8 (I, 378 ff.).

[33] Quenstedt, *Systema*, P.I, C.9, S.2, Q.8, Ekthesis 5 (I, 379). See also ibid, fons solutionis 3: "Verae sunt in generatione temporali & physica, falsae in generatione divina et aeterna, quam Philosophus, qua talis non novit, adeoque ex proprietatibus generationis physicae. V.g. humanae, equinae, vaccinae, non est aestimanda et judicanda generatio Filii Dei, quod est πρῶτον φεῦδος in toto hoc negotio."

[34] Gerhard, *Loci Theologici*, III, 236.

ity, but terms from our ordinary discourse do not retain their usual signification in every case. What happens is that the church invests these ordinary words and language with a sort of new citizenship, as it were, and gives them new and deeper meaning, a unique meaning *(significatio peculiaris)*. The fault of heretics is to use these terms in their ordinary sense as they speak of the sublime mystery of the Trinity. But Gerhard has not really met the problem at all, since he has not shown how the "new" language of the church, which he insists is unassailable from the canons of human logic and experience, can be meaningful.

4. THE BIBLICAL PROOFS FOR THE DOCTRINE OF THE TRINITY

We have now reached the point where we can trace the kind of exegesis offered by the Lutheran dogmaticians to substantiate the doctrine of the Trinity. The Biblical evidence is vast, as we shall see, and the exegesis extremely lengthy; so we can only provide a sort of overview of their approach to the vital subject and trust that we shall thereby be fair to their concerns and their theology.

All discussion of the Trinity begins with the assumption that God is one. No Biblical datum regarding plurality in the Godhead or personal characteristics of the Persons may be allowed to vitiate or compromise the fact of God's unity. Thus the task of Christian theology in presenting the doctrine of the Trinity is simply to discover what is said in Scripture about plurality within the Deity and about the Three Persons and to allow these findings to stand with the unity of God.[35] The conclusion on the basis of such exegetical procedure will be that the Three: Father, Son, and Holy Spirit, are divine and possess individual personalities (three "I"s). From this conclusion the ecclesiastical doctrine of the Trinity results. In the disputes between the Lutheran theologians and the Socinians and a few Remonstrants there was not so much disagreement concerning the personality of the Son or the deity of the Holy Spirit as concerning the full deity of the Son and the personality of the Spirit. Therefore the chief efforts of the Lutheran teachers were spent in proving exegetically the deity of Christ and the personality of the Spirit. If the personality of the Holy Spirit could be proved, then His deity would follow and also the deity of the Son.

[35] Gerhard, *Loci Theologici,* III, 278 passim. Cornelius Martini, *Theologiae Compendium* (Wolfenbüttel, 1650), p. 93.

a. *New Testament Evidence for the Trinity*

The usual procedure among the dogmaticians in carrying out the task of proving the Trinity from the New Testament was to begin with the clear pericopes which referred to the three Divine Persons in the God-head and then to follow with direct and indirect Old Testament evidence which was not so clear and was interpreted in the light of the New Testament revelation. Curiously enough, little attention was given to the many bipartite and tripartite formulae in the New Testament. Most of the pericopes which were thought to support directly the Trinity of Persons were from the Gospels and touched upon Christ's life and ministry which were believed to reveal the Trinity.

(1) The first pericope to indicate the Trinity was the story of the Annunciation (Luke 1:32).[36] The reasoning goes as follows. The Father who sent Gabriel is certainly to be distinguished from the Son of the Highest who was to be born of Mary. The two are distinguished also according to their works. To assume flesh and blood involves a *personal action* which is proper only to the Son. But is He a divine Person? His deity is shown by the use of the term "highest," which occurs three times in the pericope and is a designation for God alone (Ps. 96:4; Titus 2:13). That He is called Savior also shows His deity. And the glory and eternity ascribed to His reign shows that it is a divine rule. The deity of the Third Person of the Trinity is also clearly revealed in this pericope: only God could cause the miraculous conception of Christ. Just as the Spirit of God was originally a cause of the creation of the world and of man, He is in this case seen to be a cause of man's restoration through Christ. This is typical of the kind of exegesis employed by Calov, Gerhard, and all the Lutherans as they deal with the pericopes which teach the Holy Trinity. This fact will become quite clear as we now proceed to trace this exegesis further.

(2) Next in the life of Christ we find testimony to the Trinity at His baptism (Matt. 3:16-17). Here three distinct names are mentioned. And three distinct signs are present and apparent: the Father's voice, the Son's flesh, and the Spirit's presence in the form of a dove. Three distinct actions are performed: the Father's speaking, the Son's baptism, and the Spirit's

---

[36] In the following, for the sake of brevity, I lean primarily on the clear and brief treatment of Calov (*Appendixis,* p. 90 ff.). But cf. Gerhard, *Loci Theologici,* III, 280 ff. The discussion is very similar among all the dogmaticians.

descent. Finally, three distinct blessings are manifest: the Father sends the Son, the Son obeys the Law for us, and the Spirit anoints Christ for His redemptive work. "Go to the Jordan," says Calov,[37] "and you will see the Trinity." Commenting further on the pericope, he says, "The story of this theophany teaches that the Son is distinguished from the Father. For the Father does not have flesh, but the Son stands in the flesh at the Jordan. And the Holy Spirit is also clearly distinguished from the Others. And so we reason as follows: He who first takes on a bodily form, then descends upon Christ in the same form, and third was observed visibly in that form, certainly must be an individual subject *(suppositum)*. For an influence does not take on a body. But the Holy Spirit assumed the bodily form of a dove." And there is other evidence, says Calov, for the Spirit directing the activity of Christ, evidence which shows that the Spirit is truly God. (John 3:34; Luke 4:1; Matt. 12:28)

(3) The formula Jesus used when He instituted Baptism supports the doctrine of the Trinity. The Lutheran teachers remark that only God has the authority to institute such a rite. For such a rite is a means of salvation, and salvation is the work of God alone. The mention of all Three Persons indicates that all Three are the author of the sacrament and that all Three are divine.

(4) By far the most important pericope supporting the doctrine of the Trinity from Christ's ministry is His valedictory address (John 14—16) where, according to Calov, "Christ especially instructs His apostles concerning this mystery." Actually every aspect of the doctrine of the Trinity is indicated in this pericope: the plurality of the Persons, the distinction of the Persons, the ὁμοούσια of the Persons (14:16, 20); the Son's mutual participation *(communio)* with the Father (16:15), His interpenetration *(circumincessio)* with the Father (14:10), His divine honor (14:23; 16: 23) and divine activity (giving peace [14:27]; answering prayer [14:13; 16:23]); the Spirit's divine names (Paraclete, Spirit of truth), His procession from the Father and the Son (15:26), His divine works (glorifying Christ, leading and directing the apostles, convincing the world of sin).

What we have observed in these comments of Calov's is clearly what would be called dogmatic exegesis. In the present context the Lutherans are reading the above pericopes only to see what light they shed on the doctrine of the Trinity. The doctrine as such is never questioned — and

---

[37] *Apodixis,* p. 92.

cannot be. And the Scriptures cannot therefore be studied merely inductively and without personal commitment, as though they might not present the doctrine of the Trinity. At the same time the polemical confrontation with the Socinians compelled the Lutherans to do inductive exegesis; it was the only possible way they could demonstrate that their doctrine was Biblical and not forced upon Scripture — a concern which was vital to their interests. And so in their discussions we have a curious mixture of a shallow use of *dicta probantia* and of serious and thorough exegesis. But the most serious and thorough exegesis, in their dogmatic works at least, was always carried on in the shadow of the Socinian menace — just as the Socinian exegesis on this point was not carried on without polemics.

This interesting combination is illustrated in a rather lengthy summary comment of Gerhard's on Jesus' valedictory address, a comment which reveals some solid exegetical skill, but at the same time obvious polemical interests. We mentioned how the deity of Christ and the personality of the Holy Spirit were the two pillars on which the Trinity stood in the controversy with the Socinians; and Gerhard's comments are geared to these concerns. He says,[38] commenting specifically on John 14:16-17, "We can very effectively use Christ's testimony here to demonstrate the personality of the Holy Spirit and the deity of the Son; and the Photinians [Socinians] admit that when both of these facts are legitimately proved, then the Trinity itself is proved. The personality of the Holy Spirit is clearly inferred in this passage, not only because He is distinguished from the Father and the Son but because He is called 'another Comforter.' Now we hold that anyone who is distinguished from the Father and the Son in such a way that He is called another Comforter is distinguished from them either in respect to His essence or His person. The Holy Spirit is here distinguished from the Father and the Son in just such a way that He is called another Comforter.

"And so it follows that He is distinguished from them either in respect to His essence or His person. The first alternative cannot be granted since in that case the Holy Spirit would be another God, which is impossible since Scripture testifies that there is only one God and denies that there is any God beside the Father or apart from the Father. Therefore the second alternative commends itself, that He is distinguished from the

---

[38] *Loci Theologici,* III, 280.

Father and the Son by reason of His person. From this it follows that the divine essence is One, but there are in it three distinct Persons.

"This fact can be brought out by consulting a parallel passage, John 14:26: 'The Comforter, which is the Holy Spirit whom the Father sends in My name, He will teach you all things.' In this verse (1) the Holy Spirit is distinguished from the Father and the Son, (2) the neuter τὸ πνεῦμα is later rendered by the masculine ἐκεῖνος, and this change of gender used in reference to personal actions always indicates a person (cf. Gen. 3:15; Eph. 1:14; Col. 2:19). (3) to the Holy Spirit is ascribed an action which is proper only to a person, for the apostle says that He will teach all things and bring all things to our memory which Christ has said. [This is brought out also in] John 15:26: 'When the Comforter comes whom I will send you from the Father, namely the Spirit of truth, He (ἐκεῖνος) will witness concerning Me.'

"In this passage there is expressed a distinction from the Father and the Son, there is a change of gender, there is the specific mention of a personal action which consists of testifying; but this passage also expressly mentions the personal attribute according to which the Holy Spirit is inwardly distinguished from the Father and the Son, namely eternal procession (ἐκπόρευσις). This proceeding is ascribed to the Spirit but not to the Father, for it is said that the Holy Spirit would come after the ascension of Christ, and this cannot be said of the Father. Moreover it is said that He proceeds from the Father — that He is sent by the Father; therefore He is distinct from the Father, though obviously not according to His essence. No, the distinction is according to His person.

"And so we have proved our first point, the personality of the Holy Spirit. And our second point, the deity of the Son, may be shown from this passage as follows: He who is not true God does not have the power to send the Spirit. But Christ sends the Holy Spirit, and therefore He is true God."

b. *Old Testament Evidence for the Doctrine of the Trinity*

Fully as much labor was exerted by the orthodox Lutheran theologians proving the Trinity from the Old Testament as from the New. Such a procedure was deliberate and should not surprise us. All these theologians believed in the continuity of truth: God does not change, and the same God who has revealed Himself in the life of Christ and in the

New Testament was the God of the Old Testament. Therefore it is quite in order to read the theology of the New Testament, which is Christ's theology, into the Old, or, more accurately, to read the Old Testament in the light of the New. For the New Testament was really a commentary on the Old in terms of fulfillment. Moreover, Lutheran theology believed in the unity of Scripture and believed this unity to be Christological.[39] Christ was and is the center of all Scripture, New and Old Testament alike, and all Scripture must be read and interpreted from a Christological perspective. This Christological unity of Scripture implies also a doctrinal unity, and this idea of unity becomes a hermeneutical norm as the old Lutherans interpret the Scriptures. It is therefore not at all surprising to find them ranging all over Scripture as they trace any theological motif, from the doctrine of God to eschatology. All this does not imply that the Old Testament will present a given article of faith with the same clarity or fullness as the New. The theology of the New Testament is often only prefigured in the Old in terms of shadows and types. And such differences due to time must not be overlooked by the exegete. But at bottom the theology of all Scripture is one, even as God is One. And so the Lutheran theologians felt free to go to every possible intimation of the Trinity in the Old Testament and draw out all its implications in terms of all the New and Old Testament parallel evidence.

There is another reason for such lengthy consideration of the Old Testament evidence for the doctrine of the Trinity. This was the Socinian threat. The Socinians had particularly attacked the Old Testament traditional arguments for the Trinity, and Lutheran theology was bent on meeting this challenge head on. Such a determination necessitated lengthy treatments of the Old Testament data which was thought to support the doctrine of the Trinity.[40] The Lutherans believed that the Old Testament

---

[39] Quenstedt, *Systema*, P.IV, C.2, S.2, Q.1 (IV, 61 ff.): Michael Walther, *Officina Biblica* (Wittenberg, 1703), p. 15; George Dedekenn, *Thesauri Consiliorum et Decisionum* (Jena, 1671), p. 332; Chemnitz, *Loci Theologici*, II, 202 ff.; John Conrad Dannhauer, *Christosophia seu Sapientiarum Sapientia, de Salvatore Christo, ejus Persona, Officio, Beneficiis, Explicita atque Variis Corruptelis Purgata* (Strasbourg, 1638), p. 1 ff.

[40] Perhaps the most detailed study of the Trinity in the Old Testament was Jacob Martini's *De Tribus Elohim* (Wittenberg, 1619). The entire first volume of over 400 pages carried on a violent debate with Socinian George Enyedim (†1597) and defended the traditional doctrine of the Trinity as taught in the

inferred the Trinity with sufficient clarity for a man (for instance, a Jew) to be convinced of the doctrine without the Scripture of the New Testament. They even went so far as to say on occasion that the knowledge of the Trinity was necessary for salvation also in the Old Testament.[41]

The first type of Old Testament evidence advanced by the old Lutherans for the doctrine of the Trinity consisted of the many hints of plurality in the Deity. Plurality in the Godhead was inferred, it was thought, in the plural pronouns which God uses of Himself (Gen. 3:22) and even from the prot-evangel which distinguishes the Seed from Yahweh and still attributes to Him divine power (Gen. 3:15). Throughout the Old Testament plurality is seen in the fact that the Promised One is distinguished from the Promiser. Furthermore, the very names for God are often plural. Many plural titles are ascribed to God in the Old Testament (Ps. 136:3; Mal. 1:6; see also Job 35:10-11; Is. 44:2; 54:5; Ps. 58:11).[42] *Opera ad intra* among the Persons are suggested as the Deity consults with Himself.[43] Again, many construct adjectives are found in the plural in the Old Testament (חַיִּים in 1 Sam. 17:26, 36; קְדֹשִׁים in Joshua 24:19; עֶלְיוֹנִין in Dan. 7:18, 22, 25, 27). Throughout the Old Testament the Angel of the Lord, sent by God but clearly a different person, indicates plurality in the Godhead (e. g. Gen. 19:17, 18; 21:17; 22:2; 48:16; Hos. 12:3, 4; Joshua 5:13; Judg. 2:1; 6:11; 13:8, 9; Ex. 9:3 ff.; Dan. 5:11). Finally plural verbs are often used in the Old Testament as it describes God's actions; and Calov says, "We must note here that verbs

---

Old Testament. Enyedim in a book entitled *Explicationes Locorum Scripturae, Veteris et Novi Testamenti, in quibus Dogma Trinitatis Stabiliri Solet* (second ed., Groningen, 1670) had systematically attacked the Trinitarian interpretation of all Old Testament passages used by Christians to prove their doctrine. Martini with just as much erudition and labor defended the Christian interpretation. The Lutheran defense of Old Testament proof for the Trinity was not merely an academic matter, however, but sprang from the conviction that there was at just this point a place of contact also with non-Christians. See, for instance, Abraham Calov, *Veritas Religionis Christianae per Praecipua Capita, adversus Judaeos ex Sacro Ebraeo Codica* (Wittenberg, 1679), where the author deals with the evidence for the Trinity in the Old Testament primarily to show the person and office of the Messiah.

41 Calov, *Apodixis,* 105; *Systema,* III, 149.

42 Martini, *De Tribus Elohim,* I, 5 ff.; Calov, *Apodixis,* p. 86; Heerbrand, *Compendium Theologiae,* p. 10; Giles Hunnius, *Opera Latina,* I, 90—91.

43 Calov, *Apodixis,* p. 60: "Ubi sunt diversi consultates, ibi est pluralitas personarum." Cf. Gerhard, *Loci Theologici,* III, 312.

using the plural of the First Person can be explained in no other way than that more than one person is designated." [44]

It was primarily from many divine actions and theophanies in the Old Testament and from certain pericopes that the Lutheran dogmaticians found vestiges of the Trinity. We cannot possibly trace all these references which number into the scores, but we will mention just a few which were most commonly advanced, and we do this to show the line of thought of the Lutheran theologians at this point.

(1) Many of the Lutheran teachers held that the various accounts of creation taught plurality in the Deity by ascribing creation to the Son of God, the hypostatic Word. Commenting on Ps. 33:6, Calov states his position, "He to whom the work of creation is ascribed is the true and mighty God. Now this work is ascribed not only to Yahweh, or God the Father, but also to the Word of the Lord (not the spoken but the hypostatic Word) and to the Spirit of His mouth. Hence we conclude that these are the great and true Yahweh Himself." The unity of the Godhead is in no sense denied by such a position, for creation in this context is clearly the work of one God. All the passages parallel to the Genesis account support this conclusion, according to Calov. Genesis 1 indicates plurality in the creator God *(plures ex aequo creantes).* In Is. 42:5 *plures Elohim* are introduced into the subject of creation. Prov. 8 speaks of the Word (wisdom) as the artificer of all things. Elihu confesses that the Holy Spirit and the breath of the Almighty gave him life (Job 33:4) and Job voices the same thought (Job 26:13; cf. Ps. 104:30; 2 Sam. 7:21 [Word]). In all these references the Word and the Spirit may be understood hypostatically, even as they sometimes were in the Targums. [45] Martini [46] holds that the divine speaking, whereby all things were made, did not have its beginning at the time when all things were made. The creative Word does not refer to a word or quality in God which passes away, but is the immutable God Himself in the person of the Son. It is clear that both Calov and Martini make very much of the

---

[44] *Apodixis,* p. 99.

[45] Calov's reference to Genesis 1 in his *Systema* (I, 702) gives a different interpretation, namely that God created through the spoken word.

[46] *De Tribus Elohim,* II, 503. Martini believed that *creatio per verbum* meant creation only through the hypostatic Word. See also Martin Geier, commenting on Ps. 33:6 (*Opera Omnia* [Amsterdam, 1695], I, 428); Giles Hunnius, *Opera Latina,* II, 642.

analogy of Scripture at this point, particularly of the New Testament evidence. (John 1:3; Col. 1:16)

(2) Is. 63:9-10 is seen as another pericope which makes definite reference to all Three Persons of the Godhead.[47] The Angel of God's Presence, who is said to redeem Israel, is a Person distinct from Yahweh, the Father. He is the Son; for neither the Father nor the Spirit of God is given such a designation (Gen. 48:16). He is the Angel of God's face (Ex. 23:23; Heb. 1:3), the personal גֹּאֵל of Gen. 48:16 and Job 19:25, who redeems with His blood according to Christ's interpretation. Clearly the prophet has in mind here the Angel who was the guest of Abraham (Genesis 18), the Deliverer of Isaac (Genesis 22), the Redeemer of Jacob (Gen. 48:3), the One who appeared to Moses (Exodus 3), and who went before the Israelites in the pillar of fire (1 Cor. 10:4, 9; Jude 5). All these allusions indicate the deity of the Angel of the Lord. The Spirit of God too is explicitly mentioned in this text and distinguished from the Father and the Son as the One who led the Israelites through the sea (Is. 63:11) and who is exasperated over the sins of the Israelites and therefore strives against them.

(3) According to Lutheran theology[48] the Three Persons of the Godhead are once again specifically mentioned in Is. 61:1. Here we are told that the Spirit of Yahweh, who is the Father, rests on the Messiah. The activities of the Messiah here recited are activities proper only to God: only God can bind up broken hearts and give beauty for ashes and oil of joy for mourning. And He who equips the Messiah for all this, namely the Spirit of God, is more surely also divine. "He who sends forth the Messiah equally with the Father is true God."[49] So again the distinctions between the Persons in the Godhead are discernible; the Son is *sent* by the Father; the Spirit of the Lord is *upon* Him; these are distinctly *(seorsum)* activities of persons. Yet they are activities pertaining directly to our redemption, which is a divine act.

There is no need to list and summarize more of the evidence and argumentation of the orthodox Lutheran theologians for their position concerning the Trinity in the Old Testament. The kind of evidence they

[47] Abraham Calov, *Biblia Testamenti Veteris Illustrata* (Dresden and Leipzig, 1719), II, 353; *Apodixis*, p. 102, *et passim*.

[48] Calov, *Biblia Testamenti Veteris Illustrata*, II, 328—37.

[49] Calov, *Apodixis*, p. 105.

feel supports their case and the kind of exegesis they employ to bring out their point is quite obvious. But a few comments might be in order. First, we notice again what appears at first to be a very noninductive dogmatic exegesis prevailing — an exegesis which rigidly adheres to a set of dogmatic conclusions before it even approaches a given text and tends to ignore the historical setting of the text. We must bear in mind, however, that such an approach was quite conscious and deliberate; and it was in keeping and consistent with a number of theological presuppositions and hermeneutical norms which the orthodox Lutherans considered to be both Christian and Biblical and necessary for the exegetical task: the unchangeableness of God and of theology which comes from God, the unity of Christian theology and of Scripture, and the divine origin of Scripture which is the Christian's *principium cognoscendi* for theology. The orthodox Lutherans were quite keenly aware of alternative approaches and conclusions to the texts which they brought forth to prove their point. The Socinians had kept them well aware of all that. But they were fully convinced that the Socinians had their own presuppositions for interpreting the Old Testament texts and that these presuppositions were sub-Christian and false. To the charge that they were reading the Old Testament texts out of their natural and historical context, they replied that it was the Socinians who had departed from the *sensus literalis* of the texts and not the Lutherans.[50] The Lutherans were not ignoring the context of the pertinent pericopes but viewing them in their widest theological and historical context, namely, the context of the New Testament fulfillment and commentary. The theology of the New Testament was the best possible light for understanding both the context and theology of the Old Testament, and thus getting at the *sensus literalis*. Against the Socinian allegation that the New Testament sometimes "accommodated" the Old Testament to its own Christological interests,[51] the Lutherans maintained that the New Testament always interprets the Old Testament correctly. And therefore the theology of the Old Testament

---

50 Abraham Calov, *Socinismus Profligatus, hoc est, Errorum Socinianorum Luculenta Confutatio* (Wittenberg, 1668), p. 76. The Socinians believed that, because of the highly figurative style of Scripture, it was necessary at times to interpret certain pericopes in a way foreign to the intention of the words themselves. See Faustus Socinus, *Disputatio de Jesu Christi*, III, 11, in *Opera Omnia* (Amsterdam, 1656), II, 213.

51 Socinus, I, 292 ff.

must always be seen and understood in the light of the New. *In veteri testamento novum latet, in novo vetus patet.* The analogy of Scripture (*analogia Scripturae*) for classical Lutheran theology was not merely a principle whereby clear passages of Scripture could at times shed light on obscure passages which dealt with the same subject matter. According to this principle, Scripture actually interprets itself, and one *clear* pericope will interpret and open up the implications of another *clear* pericope.[52] And so we see that, considering the old Lutheran posture toward Scripture and hermeneutical presuppositions, the discovery of traces of the Trinity throughout the Old Testament was not so inconsistent after all.

Second, we notice the free use of a very important hermeneutical rule which we have only mentioned earlier, namely that it is proper and necessary in exegesis to draw inferences, or consequences, from Scripture. Such a procedure was categorically rejected by the Socinians, who boasted that their theology was based on Scripture without any consequences.[53] This insistence never to base their doctrine upon inferences drawn from Scripture is really the exegetical root for the Socinian denial of both the deity of Christ and of the Trinity. For there was no one passage, they insisted, which expressly (αὐτολεξεί) and in so many words (ῥητῶς) taught the doctrine of the Trinity. The Lutheran theologians felt quite free to grant this point, but they felt no need for such evidence of express statements in Scripture for the doctrine of the Trinity. Their hermeneutical principle is stated by Calov as follows:[54] "Although we recognize that

---

[52] This principle was sometimes carried to extremes. For instance, Gerhard (*Loci Theologici*, III, 319) makes the following comments on Ps. 105:4 ("Seek the Lord, and His strength: seek His face evermore"): *"Per faciem Dei* intelligitur Dei Filius, ut superius docuimus ex Exod. xxxiii, 14. *per virtutem Dei* Spiritus Sanctus, ut colligitur ex Matth. xii, 28. Luc. xi, 20. invicem collatis."* That similar terms do not in such a case as this imply relationship with other passages does not occur to Gerhard. To apply the *analogia Scripturae,* he feels he must find the relationship between the passages and dig out all the implications for the passage under consideration. At the same time, Gerhard would adamantly insist that he is not departing one hair from the *sensus literalis* of Ps. 105:4, but finding it; for the God of the Old Testament is the triune God, and a vestige of this fact is found in the psalm.

[53] *Catechesis Racoviensis* (Frankfurt and Leipzig, 1739), praefatio. The Lutherans of course insisted that only legitimate consequences or inferences could be drawn from Scirpture, that is, consequences which were inherent in the text itself *(consequentiae Scripturae innatae).* See Quenstedt, *Systema,* P.I, C.4, S.2, Q.5, ekthesis 5 (I, 87).

[54] Calov, *Systema,* I, 804; Baier-Walther, I, 180 ff.

those things which it is necessary to believe for salvation ought to be taught and set forth in Scripture so clearly that all can find them there, still we do not admit that these things are expressed in the sacred writings in just so many words, as though these things which are drawn from the sacred writings by inference, however easy and leading and obvious this inference is, ought not to be considered articles of faith and necessary to believe."

Calov believes he is following the practice of Christ and the apostles at this point, for Christ and His apostles proved many things by inference, notably that Jesus was the Messiah and Savior, and considered these things to be articles of faith. Applied to the doctrine of the Trinity, this hermeneutical rule would also hold true. For Scripture clearly taught that there was one God but three "I"s (ἄλλος καὶ ἄλλος καὶ ἄλλος) whom the church has called Persons. The only conclusion, or inference, from Biblical data such as this is the ecclesiastical doctrine of the Trinity. We notice here how fundamental hermeneutics was at this point. With their radically opposed hermeneutics the Lutherans and the Socinians could not possibly have arrived at the same doctrine. It is significant that the Socinians denied not only that the Old Testament taught the Trinity but the New Testament as well — and this on the basis of the same hermeneutical premise. However, the battle centered primarily in the Old Testament; the Lutherans sensed apparently that if they lost on this ground, they would lose on the New Testament ground as well.

5. GOD THE FATHER

The universal practice in Lutheran theology, after clarifying the Trinitarian terminology and demonstrating the doctrine, was to treat the Three Persons in order. The order of the Persons in the Trinity was not thought to be one of time or of dignity or of nature or of inner composition, but only of mode (τάξις), or, as it was called, an *ordo productionis*.[55] Keeping in mind this order and the *characteres personales* which express this order, Lutheran dogmatics proceeds to discuss each Person.

The Person of the Father came in for very little discussion. Neither His deity nor His personality was in dispute as in the case of the Son and

---

[55] Hutter, *Loci Communes Theologici,* p. 103.

the Holy Spirit. And so no time was spent defending these points of doctrine. Since in the doctrine of the Trinity the term "Father" was a correlative term (in order to be a Father God must have a Son), one might expect the paternity *(paternitas)* and other characteristics *(spiratio activa)* of the First Person in the Godhead to receive a certain amount of attention at this point. This did not happen, however, because it served the purposes of the dogmaticians better to treat such characteristics of the Father within their discussions of the Second Person (His eternal generation, filiation etc.) and the Third Person. And so only a few statements for clarification were made in regard to the First Person of the Godhead, the Father.

The chief point of clarification is that the First Person is Father not in a loose or metaphorical sense, but in the strict and natural sense; namely, He has a Son of His own essence by an actual generation.[56] He is an eternal Father through an eternal generation. This is the hypostatic fatherhood of the First Person, a fatherhood *non* χάριτι *sed* τῇ φύσει. This generation of a consubstantial Son, a generation through which God is Father, is not temporal but antemundane and eternal; for in God there is no time. The "today" of Ps. 2:7 (cf. Acts 13:33; Heb. 1:5; 5:5) is an "eternal today," an always (Ps. 95:7; Heb. 13:8), denoting a generation which is without time and without beginning (ἄχρονον and ἄναρχον cf. Mic. 5:2; Prov. 8:23; Col. 1:17). This eternal begetting of the Son is in accordance with the rule: *interni actus Dei sunt aeterni.*

Of course God may also be called Father because of the many *opera ad extra* which He performs, because He has created and sustains us and all things through His Son and in the Spirit, or because He gives birth to sons by regeneration and adoption (Job. 1:6; 38:7; Gal. 4:6; Matt. 6:9). But in this sense the term may also apply to the entire Godhead (Is. 9:6; Rom. 11:36).[57] There are in fact many passages in Scripture which use the name "Father" not relatively or personally for the First Person, but

[56] Calov, *Apodixis,* p. 115; *Systema,* III, 153; Quenstedt, *Systema,* P.I, C.9, S.1, Thesis 28 ff. (I, 330 ff.). The Lutheran dogmaticians reserve their full discussion of the eternal generation of the Son for their treatment of the Second Person, the Son, and we shall do the same.

[57] Gerhard, *Loci Theologici,* III, 82. Quenstedt maintains that Rom. 11:36 points to all persons of the Trinity, the ἐξ αὐτοῦ to the Father (1 Cor. 8:6), the δι' αὐτοῦ to the Son (John 1:3) and the εἰς αὐτοῦ to the Spirit. *Systema,* P.I, C.9, S.1, Thesis 19 (I, 327). (Cf. I, 424.)

essentially for the Godhead, the entire Trinity. (Mal. 2:10; Matt. 23:9; Eph. 4:6)

The chief Biblical proof for the fatherhood of the Father is found in Jesus' discourse about His heavenly Father. For instance, in John 5:17 Jesus is speaking of the personal fatherhood of God who begets one of the same essence. And the Jews understood Him correctly, for they sought to kill Him. That He is the Son of the Father's essence is clear from the fact that He says He works the same things (ταῦτα) as the Father.[58]

But what about those passages which ascribe to the Father exclusively immortality (1 Tim. 6:15, 16), wisdom (Rom. 16:27), goodness (Luke 18:19) and even deity (John 17:3)? These passages speak of the Father as opposed to creatures and other gods and are not to be taken as excluding the Son and the Holy Spirit from such predications. Christ made this fact clear in His ministry (John 8:16, 28, 29. Cf. Matt. 11:27; 1 Cor. 2:11).[59]

6. GOD THE SON

When the orthodox Lutheran dogmaticians in their treatment of the Trinity speak in turn of the Three Persons, they consider each Person only in reference to the so-called *propositiones personales* and the *opera ad intra*. They do not address themselves to the work of the Father or of the Son or of the Spirit. And when treating the Second Person they do not at this point usually concern themselves with the entire doctrine of Christ. Naturally they are compelled to speak of Christ as the λόγος ἔνσαρκος and mention both natures; they try however to restrict themselves to a discussion of the Second Person in His relation to the other Persons of the Godhead.

Although little was necessary to say concerning the Person of the Father, a great amount of discussion in Lutheran dogmatics centered upon the Second Person of the Trinity. The reason for this was twofold. *First,* most heresies concerning the Trinity centered in some false notion concerning the Second (or Third) Person of the Godhead. This was a particular problem during the later period of Lutheran orthodoxy because Arianism had been revived in the Socinian movement. The true doctrine

[58] Baier-Walther II, 66—68.
[59] Gerhard, *Loci Theologici,* I, 108 ff. (Cotta ed.).

of God and of the Trinity was therefore thought to be best served by upholding the doctrine of the Second Person, His deity, His eternal generation, and the like. *Second,* the Person of Christ lies at the very center of the Gospel and the question of His deity always involves the question of soteriology. This was the emphatic conviction of Lutheran orthodoxy. It is the Son of God who acts on our behalf to redeem us. No mere man could satisfy the justice of God, overcome the devil, destroy hell, and open heaven to us. No mere man could reconcile the world to God.[60] Only Christ the Son of God could by His obedience and sacrificial death offer a ransom of infinite worth to the Father.[61] And so the church, Calov declares,[62] emphasizes Christ's deity in order to urge us to place all our confidence in the finality and certainty of His redemptive work, and then to worship Him for His work of redemption. For here is our only comfort, Calov says, that our salvation is founded on the Rock and that we have eternal life and everything pertaining to it through Him who is eternal life, God over all, infinitely rich in power and wisdom and righteousness and grace. (Cf. Formula of Concord, Epit. VIII, 18.)

The attention given to the Second Person of the Trinity increased as the 17th century wore on. Whereas Chemnitz in the preceding century uses the ancient heresies as a sort of foil for presenting the correct doctrine of the Second Person, Calov, writing three generations later, offers the most thorough, one might say definitive, treatment of all the Biblical and patristic background for the preexistence of the Son, His divine nature, eternal generation, etc. The reason for this lies no doubt in the threat of Socinianism, which had become more aggressive in the 17th century and had gained footholds in Transylvania and especially Poland.

The Socinian doctrine of Christ was basically Arian.[63] The eternity of Christ was categorically denied. The ἐν ἀρχῇ of John 1:1 was taken to mean "in the beginning of the Gospel" in analogy with Mark 1:1. John

---

[60] See Nicolaus Hunnius, *Diaskepsis Theologica* (Wittenberg, 1626), par. 652.

[61] Baier-Walther, III, 71—72.

[62] Calov, *Systema,* III, 534 passim.

[63] John Völkel, *De Vera Religione* (Cracow, 1630), V, 484. This work represents one of the most thorough defenses of the Socinian doctrine on every issue. For a modern study of the Socinian doctrine of the Trinity see E. M. Wilber, *A History of Unitarianism, Vol. I, Socinianism and Its Antecedents* (Cambridge: Harvard University Press, 1946), passim.

8:58 ("Before Abraham was, I am") was said to have nothing to do with eternal generation; in fact, Christ did not exist before Abraham, except proleptically as the Light of the world, the promised Messiah.[64] This was the opinion of "blessed Arius." In similar fashion every passage indicating the eternity of the Son was systematically shown not to apply. For instance, John 17:5 refers not to a glory which Christ possessed before the world, but to a glory which He was predestined to have.

The later Lutherans, beginning with Gerhard, felt constrained to give answer to all these objections and arguments, and this added tremendously in some cases to the length of their section *de Filio Dei.*[65] For the most part three vital issues were taken up: (a) the preexistence of the Son of God, (b) the deity of the Son of God, and (c) the eternal generation of the Son. We shall now try to summarize the orthodox Lutheran teaching on these three points, basing our observations primarily on Calov's definitive study in his *Systema.*

a. *The Preexistence of the Son of God*

There are two ways in which Scripture speaks of the preexistence of the Son, according to Lutheran dogmaticians. Calov says,[66] "The preexistence of the Son of God before His conception in time is described in two ways in Holy Writ. *First* we are told that He existed before He was sent, before He was born, before He took on human flesh; that He went out from the Father, came down from heaven and went into the world before John (the Baptist), already in the time of the prophets and of David and of Moses; that He existed before Abraham, and hence from the beginning of the church, from the very creation of the world. *Second* we are told that He existed before time . . . and before the foundation of the world, from eternity."

What is the evidence from Scripture for all this? That Christ existed

[64] Völkel, p. 486.

[65] By far the most thorough and lengthy treatment *de Filio Dei* is Calov's (*Systema*, III, 235—694) which is even longer than his *locus* on the person of Christ in its usual place under Christology. Many of the dogmaticians (for example, Baier-Walther, II, 74) make only summary mention of Christ's person at this point, although the earlier Lutherans (for example, Selnecker, Heerbrand) presented the entire doctrine of the person of Christ within their *locus* on God. See Heerbrand, *Compendium Theologiae*, 23—38; Selnecker, *Institutiones Christianae Religionis*, I, 93 ff.

[66] *Systema*, III, 261.

in time before His birth and advent is indicated by the following Biblical evidence. (1) He existed before He came into the world and was born of a woman (Gal. 4:4; John 3:17; 1 John 4:9, 10, 14). Actually all the Biblical data which speaks of God sending His Son or of Christ coming from the Father into the world indicates the Son's existence prior to His coming in the flesh (e. g. John 1:15; 3:13, 31; 8:42; 11:27; Heb. 2:14-16). (2) There is much Biblical evidence to show that Christ existed and associated among the Children of Israel throughout the Old Testament. David confesses Him as Lord (Ps. 110:1), and "if David recognized Him as his Lord, surely He had to exist at that very time of David." In the Old Testament, Christ was among God's people as the Angel of Yahweh and was recognized as divine. (For example, Gen. 48:16; Ex. 23:20 ff.; cf. 1 Cor. 10:9) [67]

That Christ existed before the world and *from eternity* is shown by the Lutheran teachers in the following way. Scripture teaches that Christ existed at the beginning of all things (John 1:1). In fact creation is ascribed to Him (John 1:3; Heb. 1:2; Col. 1:16; Eph. 3:9). Therefore He must have existed prior to the creation of all things. In His high-priestly prayer Christ speaks of His glory which He had with the Father "before the world was" (John 17:5). And the apostle Paul expressly says that Christ is "before all things." (Col. 1:17)

Commenting on Paul's statement, Calov says,[68] "Really there is no getting around the fact that the apostle says absolutely that Christ was before all things. And of Him who exists before all things we must say that He is from eternity. Now before all things there is nothing but eternal God — nothing but mere eternity. Furthermore, of Him who is before all things in the sense that all things consist by Him we must likewise say that He is eternal. But all things cannot consist in anyone except in the eternal God who is the basis and support of all things. In just such a way the Son of God is 'before all things' according to the apostle's testimony."

[67] Calov draws heavily from Luther (e. g. *W* 41, 463; 5,553; 3,85) and Gerhard (*Loci Theologici,* III, 329) especially. At this point he is debating not only with the Socinians but with the Lutheran George Calixt, and the Syncretists. That the deity of Christ could be shown from the Old Testament, Calov had already discussed against the Syncretists in the first volume of his *Systema* (I, 754 ff.). In his *Consensus Repetitus Fidei Vere Lutheranae* (Wittenberg, 1666), Calov even tried to make this issue a matter of confession in the Lutheran Church, but the *Consensus Repetitus* was never accepted among any great number of Lutherans.

[68] Calov, *Systema,* III, 270.

Commenting next on Heb. 13:8 (cf. also Ps. 102:27; Heb. 1:10; 7: 3, 13), Calov makes the following interesting observation,[69] "He who is ὁ αὐτός, the same yesterday, and today, and forever, is truly eternal. These words embrace all the differences of duration: past, present, and future, a duration which is not finite but infinite, which is not of time but of eternity. Only this eternity embraces all the differences of duration; and it is an eternity which cannot be grasped by our understanding except under the concept of past, present, and future."

The significance of the data which is assembled in support of the eternity of the Son lies in the fact that eternity is an attribute of God alone. Therefore the Son who inhabits eternity with the Father is truly God. Certain Socinians, when faced with the Biblical evidence, had expressed the opinion that Christ was not "absolutely from eternity" but was a creature who had been made eternal by God, an "eternal creature." Such a suggestion was pure sophistry, according to the orthodox Lutherans. Scriptures know only one eternity, and that is the true and absolute eternity of God. And such an eternity is predicated of the Son. No, the implications of the eternity of the Son cannot be evaded. The Son is to be acknowledged and worshiped as God. He who denies the Son does not have the Father (1 John 2:23). There is no true faith without a knowledge of the Son. Nor can there be saving faith (*fiducia*) in the Son as Redeemer and Savior without believing in His eternal Godhead. No one can know the Father's grace shown us in His Son who does not know the Son.

b. *The Deity of the Son*

Having established the preexistence of the Son before the Incarnation and before creation, Calov next proceeds to speak more explicitly of the divine nature of the Son.[70] The Son's nature is not created, but uncreated and divine; it is not inferior or dependent in any way upon the Father; the independent and supreme Deity is His nature. He is the Son of God not by grace, but by nature. And apart from Him there is no God, for the Father and the Son are only one God in nature (*unus tantum natura Deus*).

Literally hundreds of Scripture passages are evoked in support of the

---

[69] Ibid., III, 271.

[70] This is the common practice among the Lutherans. See Quenstedt, *Systema,* P.I, C.9, 8.1, Thesis 40 ff. (I, 334 ff.). Hollaz, *Examen,* P.I, C.2, Q. 34 ff.

deity of the Son by Gerhard, Calov, and the other dogmaticians. We can only summarize the Biblical evidence according to Calov's grouping of data.

(1) Scripture ascribes names to the Son which can only be predicated of God. The essential name for God, the *nomen* ἀκοινώνητον, is *Yahweh*. And this holy name is ascribed to Christ, the Son (Jer. 23:6; 33:15, 16).[71] In his remarks on Is. 61:1 ff., which is also cited in this connection, Calov asserts,[72] "He whom Yahweh has anointed and upon whom the Spirit of the Lord rests, He who says He has been sent to evangelize the poor, is Himself Yahweh." (Cf. Hos. 1:7; Zech. 2:8 ff.; Ps. 68:17; Is. 6:1; 8:17.) The Son is also called *Adon* or *Adonai* (Mal. 3:1; Ps. 110:1; Heb. 1:6; Ps. 95:6). He is given the divine name *El* (Is. 7:14; Prov. 30:4; Is. 9:6; Ps. 95:7; Is. 35:4, 5).

In the New Testament Christ is called both God and Lord, and this in the absolute sense without any limitations. (For example, *God:* John 1:1; 20:28; Acts 20:28; 1 Tim. 3:15; Heb. 1:8; 1 John 5:20; Titus 2:14; Rom. 9:5; Col. 2:2; Jude 4; *Lord:* 1 Cor. 1:31; Rom. 10:13; 1 Tim. 6:15; Rev. 17:14; 1:8; 1 Cor. 8:6; 2:8; Acts 10:36; and δεσπότης: 2 Peter 2:1; 2 Tim. 2:21; Rev. 6:10)

Calov briefly discusses each passage in this long array. His remarks on John 1:1 directed against the Socinians are typical of his manner.[73] The term "God" is ascribed to the Son, the Logos, he claims, according to His essence and person. The text in no way distinguishes between the essence of the Logos and the essence of God. "And where the text does not make a distinction, it is not our place to make one." The Socinians maintained that the text did not apply because the definite article does not appear before Θεός. "The article makes no difference," Calov replies. Furthermore, the article is used in other passages. (John 20:28; Acts 20:28; Rom. 9:5; 1 John 5:20)

The Socinians also claimed that the Father is called God in the subject, the Son only in the predicate. "But this makes no difference either," answers Calov, "for the person remains God whether the term is found in the subject or the predicate." But as a matter of fact Christ is called God in the subject (1 Tim. 3:16; Acts 20:28). Moreover, He is called accord-

---

[71] Calov, *Systema,* III, 367.

[72] Ibid.

[73] *Apodixis,* p. 118.

ing to His very essence (οὐσιωδῶς) life (1 John 1:2; 5:20), and only the one true God is life in this sense (Jer. 10:10; 1 Thess. 1:9). Christ, the Second Person, is life and light in the dynamic sense (ἐνεργητικῶς) as Giver and Author of life and light (Acts 3:16; John 1:9; 8:12; 1 John 1:5). "He who is true Light and the Author of light is the true God, and this is plain from James 1:17."

(2) Scripture ascribes to the Son divine attributes, the same attributes which are ascribed to the Father: for example, divine majesty and immortality (1 Tim. 6:16), simplicity and immutability (as applied in such abstract titles as light, life, and truth which comport with divine simplicity), holiness and immensity (John 10:30; 14:20), eternity, freedom (John 5:21), power, omnipresence, grace, mercy, righteousness, and omniscience. Lutheran theology laid particular emphasis on those passages which indicated that all the divine attributes are in the Son. (Col. 2:9; Phil. 2:6; John 5:18, 26; 10:30)

(3) The doctrine of the eternal generation of the Son and the doctrine of the procession of the Holy Spirit from the Son were considered strong evidences for the Son's essential deity.

(4) With His divine works the Son proved that He possessed the same power, majesty, omniscience, mercy, and justice as the Father. Scripture portrays the Son as performing works of divine omnipotence such as creation, preservation, and miracles. His divine omniscience is perceptible as He foretells the future or searches the hearts and motives of the people. Divine mercy is seen in His entire work of redemption, for He has paid for our sins, reconciled us to the Father, freed us from the Law, overcome the power of Satan, and brought righteousness and salvation to mankind. His divine mercy is also shown in the way He gathers His church and rules in it. The prophets were inspired, the apostles sent out, the sacraments instituted, the Holy Spirit promised and sent; conversion, regeneration, and remission of sins were brought about; the church was defended and protected — all in the name and by the gracious power of the Son. And at the Last Day divine justice will be seen by all as the Son comes again in the clouds to judge all men. The entire life and saving ministry of Christ were thus seen by Lutheran theology to be one continuous witness to His divinity.[74] In particular His resurrection manifests His divinity

---

[74] Calov, *Systema,* III, 381.

by revealing His divine power over death, a power which applies not only to His own case but also to us, for His rising from the dead gives irrefutable proof of His divine power to raise us up at the Last Day. It is in the power of Christ's deity therefore that a Christian has a real eschatology.[75]

But does the above evidence so eloquently presented by Calov and others really prove the consubstantial deity of the Son with the Father? The Lutheran dogmaticians are all convinced that the divine activities attributed to the Son throughout Scripture are overwhelming evidence of His full deity. They are also convinced that Christ Himself in His ministry insists on just such a conclusion when He says (John 5:19 ff.), "What things soever He (the Father) doeth, these also the Son doeth likewise." Calov remarks,[76] "With these words Christ teaches that absolutely all things which the Father does are also His own works, and He claims for Himself both the identity of the works and an identity in the manner of doing them." Dorsch offers a much fuller discussion of this passage which was thought to be crucial for Christ's own understanding of His person and work in relation to the Father. Basing his remarks specifically on the words, "The Son can do nothing of Himself, but what He *seeth* the Father do," Dorsch makes the following significant observation,[77] "The Son does not see the Father doing something as a disciple sees who learns from his master, but He sees as the Father's only begotten Son without whom the Father does nothing. The Son's knowledge of the Father is not by virtue of having been taught but by virtue of generation. In God knowing and being are the same, and in like manner to receive divine wisdom and to receive the divine essence are the same." Dorsch may have Col. 2:3 in mind at this point.

Continuing in the same vein he says,[78] "The Son sees what the Father does, not after it is done, but because He is the wisdom of the Father through whom the Father acts. Now although certain actions seem to pertain to the Son in a very special way and not to be appropriate to the Father as He acts, we must now understand that the Father not only by willing but also by acting has done whatever the Son has done, and He

[75] Giles Hunnius, *Opera Latina*, I, 115.
[76] *Systema*, III, 383.
[77] *Synopsis Theologiae Zacharianae*, II, 199.
[78] Ibid., II, 201.

has done all these things as the efficient cause, not as the one who actually executes the action. The Son was begotten; the Father has begotten Him. The Son assumed a human nature; the Father gave Him the human nature. The Son died; the Father delivered Him up. The Son rose from the dead; the Father raised Him up. Thus in all these things the same act (*eadem actio*) was done by the Father and the Son, but in the sense that the Son and not the Father was begotten, incarnate, dead, and raised again. For these terms signify not only actions but also the execution of the actions; and this has to do not with the Father, but with the Son who, because of the distinct nature of His person, actually carried them out. Now Christ wants to show that He is by nature joined to the Father, but He wishes to show this in such a way that He might indicate also a distinction. He shows the intimate connection when He says that He can do nothing except what the Father does. He shows the distinction when He says that He sees what the Father does. For it is one thing to be one who sees, another thing to be the one who is seen. Moreover, Christ wants to say that He is equal to the Father in just such a way that He can still rightly be called Son. And it is the part of the Son not to go before but to follow the Father. When Christ says that He can do nothing 'of Himself' He is not referring to His own power and authority, but He is referring to the fact that He does nothing alone without the authority, consent, and will of the Father. . . . Finally, this must be said about Christ seeing what the Father does. It is said that the Son is *shown* all things. This δεῖξις is carried out in such a way that the Father shows all things to the Son as He Himself is actually working through the Son. He does not show things to the Son merely by way of example. And so the Son *sees* — sees as one who is united in wisdom and power with the Father; in this way He sees the Father as the Father does all things."

(5) The deity of the Son is proved, according to Lutheran theology, by the fact that we are called upon to worship and honor Him as the Father (John 5:23). This involves trusting in Him (John 6:29; 14:1), hoping in Him (1 Tim. 1:1), being baptized in Him, swearing by Him (Rom. 9:1), adoring Him, calling on Him, glorifying Him (Rev. 4:11), and serving Him.

(6) Finally, the old Lutheran teachers assembled the many passages in which Christ asserted His deity and consubstantiality with the Father (John 5:17; 10:25 ff.; 14:1 ff.; Matt. 22:44-45). Chief among such pas-

sages was Peter's confession (Matt. 16:16), which Christ Himself approved and which was considered crucial to a correct understanding of Christ's person. We summarize Sebastian Schmidt's comments on this passage which figured prominently in the Lutheran doctrine of the Son, for his comments are typical of the Lutheran understanding of the passage. In contrast, Schmidt points out,[79] to those who believed Jesus to be the Baptist or Elias, a mere man, Peter calls Him "Christ" which designates His work of redemption and "Son of God" which designates His person. He is not a mere human Messiah as the Jews anticipated. He is *the Son* (ὁ υἱός) which can only be understood as the natural and substantial Son of the substance of the Father. Along with the other disciples, Peter sees Jesus in His true humanity. He has heard His voice. He is acquainted with His mother. The remarkable characteristic of his confession is that he calls this man the Son of the living God, and does so, says Schmidt, without any trope. The unity of the person of Christ is clearly confessed here; for "you," like "I" and "he," denotes the whole person. But the predicate "Son of God" denotes clearly the concrete divine nature. This is the only possible meaning of the confession, Schmidt insists. Peter is not employing a trope; he is not speaking of any mutation (as if Jesus *became* the Son of God); he is not speaking of two persons, Jesus and God *(alius et alius)*; if he were doing any of such things, he never would say that the man standing before him was the Son of the living God.[80] And so this historic confession of Peter, approved by his Master, proves conclusively the deity of Christ, the Son.

The discussions on behalf of the deity of the Son in the old Lutheran theology often become intricate, technical, and tedious, and too often marred by polemics. The orthodox Lutherans were aware of this. All theology in those days was done with the same sort of painstaking, relentless thoroughness, and it is doubtful if anyone really questioned the procedure. But the Lutherans would never have apologized for their procedure at this point. To them everything in Christian theology hinges on this article of the divinity of the Son, both the doctrine of God and the doctrine of salvation; and so they feel fully justified in belaboring the

---

[79] Sebastian Schmidt, *Disputatio de Christo ex Matth. XVI. 16* (Strasbourg, 1960), p. 12 ff.

[80] In his zeal Schmidt (pp. 19 ff.) even maintains optimistically that Peter's confession supports by implication all three *genera* of the communication of attributes and implies the three offices of Christ. Cf. Calov, *Systema*, III, 455.

issue as they do. In general the Lutheran dogmaticians overwhelm the reader with the vastness of their evidence (hundreds of Scripture passages are often listed) rather than with the cogency of their evidence. There is usually not sufficient intensive exegesis of the key pericopes and Christological themes which support their doctrine. And what possibly disturbs us the most today is the almost total absence of any defense of the basic Lutheran hermeneutic according to which the Lutheran teachers approached and interpreted the Biblical material which pertained to the subject at hand. For in the old Lutheran arrangement and exegesis of the pertinent texts and themes there is a rationale and consistency which may at first escape the modern reader. These theologians were not merely haphazardly amassing a lot of traditional and questionable evidence for a certain thesis, but were proceeding according to definite hermeneutical rules and presuppositions which they thought were dictated by Scripture itself (see pp. 127—138).[81]

c. *The Eternal Generation of the Son*

Lutheran theology was fully convinced that by appealing to the divine names, attributes, and works of the incarnate Logos sufficient proof had been given for the deity of Christ. However, the Lutheran theologians never neglected to emphasize that there was an *opus ad intra* revealed in Scripture which also proved clearly the deity of the Son. This was the eternal generation of the Son. Most of the Lutherans do not dwell on this mystery at great length, for only a few carefully chosen words can be said of it by way of description. An exception to this rule is Calov, who feels that the doctrine of the eternal generation tells us something more about the sonship of Christ than we learn from His manifestations in the flesh. We must now try to summarize Calov's very long treatment of this subject.

There is nothing original in Calov's approach to the subject. He leans heavily on the theology of the church fathers and the Scholastics. But he

[81] For a discussion of the Biblical hermeneutics of classical Lutheran orthodoxy see Robert Preus, *The Theology of Post-Reformation Lutheranism* [1], pp. 315—39. So far as I know, no study more thorough than this survey has ever been done on the basis of the original sources. For the hermeneutics of individual theologians of this era some excellent studies have appeared. See C. Moldaenke, *Schriftverständnis und Schriftdeutung in Zeitalter der Reformation.* I. Matthias Flacius Illyricus (Stuttgart, 1936); Bengt Hägglund, *Die Heilige Schrift und ihre Deutung in der Theologie Johann Gerhards* (Lund: CWK Gleerups Förlag, 1951).

is very thorough. And his strenuous attempt, typical of Lutheran orthodoxy, to give a detailed Biblical basis for the old ecclesiastical doctrine
affords an excellent example of classical Lutheran dogmatic methodology
as well as a certain amount of insight into the historical doctrine itself.

To Calov the eternal generation is actually the origin of the Logos.
But this origin is from eternity — from before all generations. The Son
of God, who is the same essence as the Father and who is the likeness of
the Father and express image of His hypostasis, comes forth from the substance of the Father, from within the whole *(complexum)* of the Deity.
This generation is to be understood in a passive sense, according to which
the Son was begotten from eternity. No physical connotation can be insin-
uated into the concept. Nor should we confuse this generation with our
spiritual generation or regeneration. The eternal generation of the Son
is unique. Thomas Aquinas described its nature as follows (*Summa Theologica*, P.I, Q.27, a.2): "It signifies the origin of a living being from a con-
joined living principle . . . by way of similitude." [82]

Calov agrees with the church fathers and Scholastics that the generation of the Son should be called mystical and supernatural, and little more
should be said about it. But from the observations above and the Biblical
data which will be forthcoming he believes that a number of attributes
can be ascribed to the eternal generation of the Son, and he lists seven.[83]
(1) It is eternal and unceasing; for it does not begin, but is from eternity
to eternity. And yet it remains apart from any idea of a succession of
moments of time. (2) It is intimate generation, an act *ad intra* involving
the most intimate περιχώρησις. (3) It is necessary. It is not the result
of God's will or decision. It would be wrong to say that God freely gen-
erated the Son when He willed to do so, or that God willed before the act
of generation. Rather the generation is necessary by nature rather than
by will.[84] (4) The generation is a communication to one number of the
essence; the one single and undivided essence is thus communicated to the
Son. (5) It is a communication of the total essence, for the essence is
undivided. (6) The generation does not move or change God in any way.

---

[82] See Calov, *Systema*, III, 536. Cf. John of Damascus, *De Fide Orthodoxa*,
I, Cap. S (*MPG* 94, 814): "Nam generatio quidem est ex substantia generantis:
produci quidem generatur secundum substantiam."

[83] *Systema*, III, 592—600.

[84] Cf. Basil, *Adversus Eunomium*, II, 14 (*MPG* 29, 519 ff.).

(7) The generation makes the Son equal to the Father in every respect, and so the Son is and remains αὐτόθεος.

These seven attributes of the eternal generation of the Son, which may sound abstruse if not paradoxical, are calculated to sum up all that can be said about the eternal generation. They are intended not to explain or open the mystery of the eternal generation, but in many cases rather to safeguard the mystery from false and heretical inferences and interpretations. Calov's statement of the seven attributes comes at the end of his discussion, and the discussion leads to this sevenfold conclusion.

Because of misunderstanding concerning the doctrine, Calov feels that he must make a few points clear before taking up the Biblical evidence for the doctrine. *First,* by virtue of generation the Son is equal to the Father and of the same essence (see attributes 4—7 above). When Scripture calls Him the brightness of the Father's glory and the express image of His person (Heb. 1:3), this likeness is not accidental but substantial. This is the necessary implication of Heb. 1:3 and John 10:30 according to catholic theology.

But as Calov further develops this doctrine he takes his stand on some rather shaky ground. He cites Epiphanius, who, arguing the point from analogy, says,[85] "If the Father begets the Son at all, it can be carried out in no other way than that He be equal to the Father and like the Father. For whatever one begets he begets similar to himself, and not similar only but actually equal and the same (*aequale, ut sit idem* [ἴσου τῇ τουτότητι]). For man begets man, and God begets God." Calov approves of this statement and defends the consubstantiality of the Son of God with the Father in the same manner. It is interesting that such an argument is based on Aristotle who taught that whatever is begotten must be of the same species as that which generates it (*Metaphysica,* VII,7, 103a, 23-24). But such an argument by analogy is extremely precarious. For the analogy breaks down; the generation of the Son is unique, as Calov and the church fathers admitted. In his eagerness to show his agreement with the fathers Calov has taken over as proof what at best can only be used as an imperfect illustration.

The *second* point of clarification which had to be made complements the first point; and it again is intended to safeguard the mystery of the eternal generation from the many historical heresies which have attacked

[85] *Adversus Haereses,* III, I, 86 (*MPG* 42, 525). See Calov, *Systema,* III, 538.

it or sought to explain it. Briefly stated, it is simply that the Son is not begotten from a disjunct principle as in the case of natural generation. According to Calov,[86] "The whole essence of the Father has been communicated to the Son, and the Son is not separate from the Father, but the generation occurs within the very bosom, or whole *(complexum)*, of the Father. Therefore the Son is in the Father and the Father in the Son (John 14:10). And the Son is and remains in the bosom of the Father (John 1:18)." Hence neither the prolation [emission] (προβολή) of Valentinus, nor the separation *(partitio)* of the Manichaeans, who taught that the Son was a part of the substance of the Father, nor the emanation (ἀπόρροια) of the Arians can be admitted. Nor can the doctrine of the eternal generation agree with Sabellius' union according to which the Son is the Father. No, what is taught is a fellowship of the Persons within the essence, not a multiplication, not a division of the essence, not a confusion of the Persons.[87] The issue to Calov at this point is clear: no understanding of the eternal generation may be allowed to threaten the unity of the Godhead.

We must now trace Calov's Biblical basis for the doctrine of the eternal generation. Here he summarizes everything the Lutherans have done before him. And we notice also how closely he remains within the ancient tradition both in his choice of Biblical evidence and his exegesis.

(1) Calov lists the passages which speak specifically of a generation of the Son; Ps. 2:7 and parallel passages.[88] Calov sees the psalm as clearly Messianic and as referring to God's own Son in the strict sense of being born from the substance of the Father. The יֶלֶד when referring to persons designates the offspring from the substance *(substantialis productio)*. The "today" designates the generation as an eternal act not subject to differences of time. God's *actus interni* are also *aeterni*. Nothing temporal can be associated with the divine essence. God remains the same, eternal ac-

---

[86] *Systema,* III, 538—39.

[87] Hilary, *De Trinitate,* VII, 27 (*MPL* 10, 233).

[88] Other passages discussed are Prov. 8:22 and Mic. 5:2. Commenting on the former, Calov says (ibid., III, 544): "The Son of God is called the wisdom of the Father by virtue of the eternal generation, because the Son is in the Father and is born of the Father just as wisdom is in the mind of men and springs from the mind as from a source. Now if this wisdom is a Person, distinct from the Father, a Person who was with the Father from eternity as the Wisdom and Word of the Father, He necessarily had His origin from the Father, just as wisdom springs from the mind."

cording to His essence; there is no past, no future; only present, only today which is an eternal today without any variation or passage of time. The "today" means *semper.* (Ps. 96:6; Heb. 7:17; Ps. 110:4)

(2) All Scripture passages which call Christ the Son of God were taken as inferring the eternal generation. Of special force were those verses which speak of Christ as the Father's own Son (for example, Rom. 8:32; John 5:18). The term ἴδιος can only be used in the case of real and essential generation, the Lutherans held. "Unless the Son is equal and consubstantial with the Father He is not the Father's own Son, but an unworthy offspring." [89]

(3) The terms "only begotten" or "first born" designate the eternal generation in the case of God's Son.

(4) Lutheran theology held that the eternal generation is taught in those passages which speak of Christ as being the image (εἰκών, χαρακτήρ) of God (Phil. 2:6; Heb. 1:3; Col. 1:15). From the analogy of faith it was understood that Christ was an image who is one with the Father even though He has His origin in the Father. The idea was that a perfect image will perfectly reflect that of which it is an image. Only God can generate such a perfect image of Himself. The coessential Son is the invisible God's own image who says, "He that hath seen Me hath seen the Father" (John 14:9). Chemnitz's remarks on Heb. 1:3 express the unanimous Lutheran understanding at this point,[90] "The Son of God is not an image which passes away, as the appearance of a figure in a mirror is an image and passes away; but He is a distinct and abiding image, just as a coin is the express image of its mold. But because the coin is the image of the form of the mold only, it is not the image of its substance. Therefore the text adds χαρακτὴρ τῆς ὑποστάσεως, that is, an image not just of qualities in God, but the substantial and entire image by the communication of God's very essence."

Chemnitz later explains what he means by a communicated essence,[91] "The Son is the substantial image of the Father, because the essence of the Father has been communicated to Him. I say communicated essence, be-

---

[89] *Systema,* III, 550—51. Calov's dependence on the fathers here is brought out by citations from Basil, Bernard, Ambrose, Gregory of Nyssa, Theophylact, Chrysostom, and especially Cyril of Alexandria, Hilary, and Augustine.

[90] *Loci Theologici,* I, 51.

[91] Ibid.

cause the Father in begetting the Son did not give up His essence to the Son in such a way that He divested Himself of it; but He gave it up with the result that one and the same essence would be in the Father and in the Son and common to both. Nor did the Father hold back anything so that the Son did not have all. Nor did He give all things to the Son so that He Himself no longer has all; but as Christ says (John 16:15), 'All things that the Father hath are Mine.' And (John 5:26), 'For as the Father hath life in Himself so hath He given to the Son to have life in Himself.' "

(5) The Lutheran teachers believed that the Biblical practice of calling the Son the Logos and the wisdom of God inferred the eternal generation of the Son (for example, John 1:1 ff. and Proverbs 12; but also Heb. 4:12 and 11:3). The reasoning at this point was based largely on the analogy between the generation of the eternal Logos and the birth of words in our minds. For instance, just as our mind is never without a word and no word without a mind, so it is with God and the eternal Logos. The conclusion is: "The generation of the Son is eternal just as the mind of the Father is eternal. The Father is never without the Son just as the Son is never without the Father (John 8:29; 10:30)." [92] Using the same analogy, Calov also shows that there is no possibility [capability of feeling or suffering] in the Father in begetting the Son, just as there is no change in the mind when a word goes forth from it (Basil, Athanasius). Immanence too is suggested by the analogy: the thought of the mind is given birth in the mind and yet remains in the mind; in like manner the Son is from the Father, and yet He remains in the Father (*a Patre est, & nunquam non in Patre permanet*).[93]

(6) Finally the whole of Lutheranism sees the eternal generation of the Son reflected in all the passages of Scripture which speak of Christ's glory (John 12:40-41; Is. 6:1 ff.; 2 Cor. 3:7 ff.), and also in those passages which call Him light (John 1:9; 8:12; 12:35; cf. James 1:17; 1 Tim.

[92] Calov, *Systema,* III, 570.

[93] Ibid. 571. Following the fathers who called the preexistent Logos a *repraesentatio* (ἀπεικόνισμα) *Patris,* just as a word is a *repraesentatio mentis,* Calov comments, "Ut noster λόγος, ita est in mente, ut mentis etiam nomine significetur: veluti cum dicimus, *haec est mea mens, etc.,* ita Filius Dei est in Deo, ut sit ipse Deus. Interim uti mens ipsa & conceptus mentis differunt realiter: sic Pater & Filius distinguuntur realiter, non quidem *ut subjectum & accidens,* sed ut *personae distinctae,* quia λόγος hic substantialis & ὑποστάτικος est." Calov follows John of Damascus, *De Fide Orthodoxa,* I, 6 (*MPG* 94, 803).

6:16). "For what else," asks Calov,[94] "is that procession and origin of light from light but a certain kind of generation?" From these figures Calov along with the ancient church before him used the analogy of light and its rays in speaking of the eternal generation. But further conclusions may be drawn from such imagery, according to Calov. We can conclude that the eternal generation was necessary "just as the rays of the sun do not go forth freely but of necessity and naturally." It is eternal: the rays of the sun coexist with it and so long as it remains they cast their beauty; "in like manner the Son was begotten from eternity, He existed in eternity with the Father, and He goes forth from the Father." From the figure of light Calov also concludes that the eternal generation is pure and direct and inseparable.

What shall we say by way of comment to these reflections of Calov's on the eternal generation? There is no doubt that Calov would insist throughout that he is not finding any mystical sense in the passages which he interprets, but is adhering to the *sensus literalis* as found in the light of the analogy of Scripture. And yet Calov is clearly indulging in a type of speculative exegesis from analogy here which we ordinarily do not find in his exegetical works. And without the virtually universal precedent of the church fathers and the Lutherans before him one wonders if Calov would have gone quite so far.

It can be pointed out, of course, that Calov is merely using the various analogies suggested in Scripture as illustrations and not as proof. For instance, in a somewhat guarded fashion he says, "The generation of the Son of God is implied *(insinuatur)* when the Son of God is called the Word or wisdom of God." [95] He later [96] points to the many places where the analogy fails. He says, "Our words have their beginning in time; the Word of God has no beginning. Our words come later in time than the mind; such is not the case with the Word of God and God the Father. Our words are measurable and finite; that Word is unmeasured and infinite. Our words are many; that Word is one."

In the light of such remarks we are tempted to ask why Calov and the orthodox Lutherans employ the various analogies for the eternal generation so often, when the analogies break down at so many points. And

[94] Calov, *Systema,* III, 565.
[95] Ibid., III, 567.
[96] Ibid., III, 572.

why not use the Biblical material which speaks of Christ's glory and which calls Him life simply to prove His deity, and not try to apply it to the doctrine of the eternal generation? The explanation for the Lutherans' exegesis at this point can be found in their deep reverence and respect toward the ancient church fathers, a reverence which expressed itself not only here, but in every *locus* where the fathers had spoken.[97]

7. THE HOLY SPIRIT

If one were to read only what Lutheran theology says about the Holy Spirit in its *locus* on God, one could only conclude that Lutheranism teaches a quite truncated pneumatology. For in this particular section of Lutheran dogmatics the personality and deity of the Holy Spirit is proved — but little more. This procedure is quite in harmony with the dogmatic purpose of the Lutheran teachers which was at this early stage to speak of the persons of the Trinity only in reference to their *characteres personales* and *opera ad intra*. The work of the Spirit, like the work of Christ, is therefore not treated at any length at this point. We may well complain here too that to discuss the Spirit of God apart from His *opera ad extra* is a highly questionable procedure. But again there were overriding reasons which convinced the dogmaticians that their procedure was appropriate. First, their innate Lutheran fear of all enthusiasm makes them feel more comfortable speaking of the work of the Spirit in the context

[97] With all their insistence upon the *sola Scriptura*, the Lutherans after the Reformation were fully convinced that their theology was within the stream of catholic tradition, and this in contrast to the theology of Rome. And in their insistence that they were following in the catholic tradition they were fully in accord with the Lutheran Confessions and the Lutheran Reformers themselves. See Peter Fraenkel, *Testimonium Patrum, the Function of the Patristic Argument in the Theology of Philip Melanchthon* (Geneva: Librairie M. Droz, 1961). Fraenkel discusses also the confessional writings of Melanchthon as they bear on this matter. This conviction, that they were in the catholic tradition, expressed itself not only in polemics like Gerhard's massive *Confessio Catholica* or Chemnitz's huge and erudite *Examen Concilii Tridentini*, which support the Lutheran against the Roman doctrine with thousands of citations from the fathers, but it is demonstrated also in the Lutheran Confessions themselves (for example, "The Catalog of Testimonies" for the Lutheran Christology following the Formula of Concord), and in works of positive theology by Chemnitz, Gerhard, and Calov in particular. Lutheran theology was always deeply engaged in patristic studies — we recall that Gerhard wrote the first book in patrology and coined the term — and was most reluctant to reject any real consensus of the fathers except when the Gospel was clearly threatened. And so it is natural that in the doctrine of the eternal generation they would repair to the fathers for help and insight.

of the means of grace through which the Spirit always works, or in their sections on soteriology and ecclesiology. Second, as with *theology*, Christology and pneumatology are discussed throughout dogmatics. In this sense, all theology is *theology*, Christology, and pneumatology. As a matter of fact, the work of the Spirit is discussed rather deeply at several points in Lutheran dogmatics: in the section *de Scriptura* (inspiration), in the *locus* on the means of grace, in the section on soteriology (regeneration, conversion, *unio mystica*, the gift of faith, sanctification, the Christian life) and also, perhaps unexpectedly, in the section on man (freedom of the will).

Much of the Biblical proof for the personality and deity of the Holy Spirit had been raised in the previous discussions concerning the Trinity. However, because of the Socinian aberration, many of the Lutherans of the 17th century felt constrained to give detailed attention to the deity and personal characteristics of the Spirit in a specific discussion on the issues. The Socinians denied both the personality and the deity of the Holy Spirit. They denied that the Scriptures ever expressly attributed divinity to the Spirit. He may be called God only in the sense that the things in God are called God, but never as a distinct divine Person.[98] The Racovian Catechism says bluntly, "The Holy Spirit is nowhere in the Scriptures called expressly God, and though in some places the things of God are attributed to Him, still it does not follow that He is either God or a Person of the Deity." [99] The fact that divine operations are attributed to Him in no way implies that He is a divine Person; God merely works through the Spirit as He does through Christ.[100] Although He is not a divine Person, nevertheless the Spirit is eternal, like the vision of God or the righteousness of God.[101] What then is the Spirit? The answer to this question is not quite clear in Socinian theology. At times it seems He is an influence, at times a manifestation. But one thing is clear: The Spirit does not play the part in soteriology that He does in Christian theology. He is not a personal cause of the Virgin Birth of Christ or of man's conversion, but is only an impersonal means used by God.[102]

[98] Smaltz, *Refutatio Disputationis de Spiritu Sancto,* p. 5.
[99] *Catechesis Racoviensis, seu Liber Socinianorum Primarius* (Frankfurt and Leipzig, 1739), Cap. I, 35, p. 89.
[100] Ibid., Cap. I, 38, p. 89.
[101] Völkel, *De Vero Religione,* V, 493.
[102] Smaltz, p. 22.

The issue between Socinianism and evangelical theology at this point was therefore quite clear. And the Lutheran theologians set about to prove, once again on the basis of Scripture — for the Socinians would accept arguments only from the *nuda Scriptura* — the personality and deity of the Spirit.

But the first order of business is to state just what is meant by the specific personal characteristic of the Holy Spirit. It is the specific personal characteristic of the Holy Spirit to be spirit. In other words, that He is the Spirit means more than that He is one Person in the Godhead which is spirit (John 4:24); it is His personal characteristic to be breathed from the hidden majesty of the Deity.[103] This characteristic which distinguishes the Spirit from the Son and the Father is usually called procession, or spiration. It is called a *spiratio passiva* because it is never said in the Scriptures that the Spirit breathes, but always that He is breathed.[104] This procession is an eternal procession from the Father (John 15:26), an eternal going forth *(emanatio processio)*, not merely a temporal sending *(missio)* by the Father.[105]

Dorsch puts it as follows:[106] "The Holy Spirit is said to proceed from the Father through an eternal procession of being breathed. This eternal procession is His eternal characteristic whereby He is distinguished from the Father and the Son while being in the absolute unity of the divine essence." It is true of course that Christ sends (πέμψω, future tense) the Spirit (John 15:26) in time, but this is something far different from the procession of the Spirit (ἐκπορεύεται, present tense) which points not to His mission but to His substance (cf. Rev. 22:1).[107] The passive nature of the Spirit's procession does not imply that the Spirit is somehow imperfect or lacks something.[108] Just as the Father is the source of the Son's generation and can be said to produce by generation the Son and communicate His essence to Him in an eternal act, so the Father and the Son may be said to have produced the Holy Spirit by spiration in an absolutely

103 Giles Hunnius, *Opera Latina*, I, 119.

104 Giles Hunnius, *Opera Latina*, I,119. Quenstedt, *Systema*, P.I, C.9, S.1, Thesis 54 ff. (I, 339 ff.).

105 Calov, *Apodixis*, p. 125.

106 *Synopsis Theologiae Zacharianae*, II, 217.

107 Calov, *Apodixis*, p. 115.

108 Dorsch, *Synopsis Theologiae Zacharianae*, II, 211.

simple and eternal act.[109] That this procession is a *personal* characteristic is seen from the many personal *opera ad extra* attributed to the same Spirit of God: witnessing, comforting, convincing, speaking the truth, glorifying Christ, and the like.

There is no need to do more than summarize the kind of Biblical evidence and procedure the Lutheran theologians employ in their argument for the personality and divinity of the Spirit. It was their conviction that the personality and deity of the Spirit were concepts so closely linked that in most cases the same Biblical basis was thought to support both.

First, it was pointed out that the Holy Spirit is spoken of in a very special manner throughout Scripture.[110] He is represented as one who is pure spirit and who possesses His essence *(spiritualitas)* in Himself. He is represented as having no beginning and as being unbound by time and circumstances like the human spirit.

Second, the Lutheran teachers appeal to the many personal terms which Scripture invariably employs when speaking of the Spirit.[111] He is said to be shed abroad in personal terms (Joel 2:28; Titus 3:5-6; Rom. 5:5); in every case it is an ἄλλος who is shed abroad (John 14:16) by either the Father or the Son, a He, a distinct center of consciousness. If He were no different from the Father, or if He were a mere influence or afflatus of the deity or a mere power residing in God, then He would not be consistently represented as an ἄλλος and as being sent personally by Christ or proceeding personally from the Son and the Father.[112] In John 14:16 we have a clear case of one person, Christ, sending another person (ἄλλος παράκλητος), of two persons distinguished from each other as ἄλλος καὶ ἄλλος. In John 16:8 the Spirit is explicitly called ἐκεῖνος which denotes a person.

Third, the Lutheran teachers try to show the personality and deity of the Holy Spirit by the many personal works and activities ascribed to Him in Scripture. This is particularly apparent in the history of Jesus as presented in the gospels: His birth, His temptation, His baptism, etc.

---

[109] Ibid., ". . . Sic et Pater ac Filius spiratione producit Spiritum Sanctum, in simplicissima aeternitate."

[110] Ibid., II, 185.

[111] Ibid.

[112] Calov, *Apodixis,* p. 125 *passim.*

In every case the Spirit of God is present actively as a person.[113] In fact it is more through His activities than through specific statements concerning His person that we learn of the Spirit's personality and deity: He searches the deep things of God; He speaks through the prophets; He certifies the doctrine of Christ; He convicts us of sin; He converts us, sheds love abroad in our hearts, teaches us the truth of the Gospel, comforts us, strengthens us in our struggle against the flesh; He creates a New Testament ministry and gives gifts to His church (Pentecost; 1 Cor. 12).[114] These are activities of a person, a free, intelligent, independent person.[115]

In pressing for both the deity and personality of the Holy Spirit, John Dorsch makes much of the fact that the Spirit is represented as the author of God's covenant with men (Zech. 9:10 ff.; Titus 3:5).[116] "In the covenant of Baptism the Spirit acts as a Person along with the Father and the Son in carrying out the covenant." To be baptized in the name of the Holy Spirit is to be baptized on His personal authority and into the name of His divine Person. For in the formula of Christ His name is joined with the Father and the Son. The term "Spirit" in this formula cannot be taken as an *idioma* of God or a creature or a mere something coming from God (*aliquid Dei*). Acts such as baptism are carried out in the name of a person. It would be absurd, for instance, to baptize in the name of love or freedom. Christ here must be referring to three personal divine names, not to two names and a virtue (Socinianism). Dorsch sums up his position as follows,[117] "Baptism is a covenant type of action, and it is as such that a man enters a covenant. Something which is not a person cannot receive anyone into a covenant relationship. He in whose name men are baptized is the one who receives men into a covenant. Now men are baptized into the name of the Holy Spirit. And so we conclude that the Holy Spirit is not merely something, but is a Person."[118]

---

[113] Jacob Martini, *Synopsis Totius Religionis Photinianorum Novorum* (Wittenberg, 1633), pp. 217, 227, 232.

[114] Selnecker, *Institutiones Christianae Religionis,* I, 244 passim.

[115] Cornelius Martini, *Theologiae Compendium,* p. 93. See Dorsch, *Synopsis Theologiae Zacharianae,* II, 190, 195.

[116] Dorsch, II, 191.

[117] Ibid., II, 192.

[118] Dorsch (II, 190, 193) is most insistent that certain verbs (like βαπτίζειν) are ascribed to the Spirit, which are always according to the New Testament activities of a person, for example, making intercession (ἐντηγχάνειν), helping

The tripartite formulae of the New Testament, particularly the Pauline benediction of 2 Cor. 13:14, are further indication of the distinct divine personality of the Holy Spirit.[119] In Paul's prayer, or benediction, the κοινωνία of the Holy Spirit is treated as something communicated to us, and according to Dorsch it included the love of God and the grace of Christ. Paul prays that the entire Trinity be graciously present with the Corinthians, and it is the Person of the Spirit who effects this. Just as love and grace are personal divine activities, so also is the κοινωνία of the Spirit.

Finally, the references to the sin against the Holy Spirit were thought to show clearly His divine personality.[120] It is the specific work of the Spirit of God to witness (Heb. 10:15), and He witnesses as a divine personal Lord. Therefore he who insults or blasphemes the Spirit (Heb. 10:29; Matt. 12:31) does so to God, not in the general sense as if "Spirit" referred in such instances to the entire Godhead; for Christ distinguishes between the sin against the Spirit and the sin against Himself. "The term Spirit in this case must be understood hypostatically in such a way that this specific sin by reason of its particular character can be called 'the sin against the Holy Spirit' in contrast to sins against the Son." [121]

We mentioned that the Lutheran doctrine of the Trinity represents no new dogmatic development. As we have seen, the Lutheran teachers make every effort to remain within the catholic tradition both in their use of the old established terminology and in their exegesis. But in the point we have just discussed they have progressed beyond the church fathers. While following the pious exegesis of the ancients, they go farther. Never before had such a broad Biblical basis been given the doctrine of the Trinity — at least never concentrated as it was within one *locus.* For the most part the speculative development of the doctrine with its homiletical overtones is absent. This is particularly true as they organize and carry out their arguments for the personality and deity of the Holy Spirit. But in all their struggle for Biblical proof, the old Lutheran dogmaticians did not lose

(συναντιλαμβάνειν), being insulted (ἐνιβρίζειν), and the like. This is one of his chief arguments.

119 Dorsch, II, 193.

120 Ibid., II, 194.

121 Ibid., "At si vox Spiritus, quando peccatum in Spiritum Sanctum describitur, simpliciter sumeretur communiter seu essentialiter pro ipsa οὐσία et essentia divina, aut virtute Dei substantiali absoluta, tum non esset peccatum non in Filium, non in Patrem, sed aequaliter in hunc et illum.

sight of two very important aspects of the Trinitarian doctrine. First, the doctrine is viewed and applied in the economy of God's salvation. Second, the doctrine actually supports the unity of God: not only are all the *opera ad extra indivisa,* but the *opera ad intra,* although distinguishing the Persons, reveal an inter-Trinitarian procession which is eternal and unchanging and of God Himself.

PART TWO

The Doctrine of Creation

Creatio Prima
Its Significance and Its Use

CHAPTER FIVE

One of the most impressive contributions of post-Reformation Lutheran theology is the article on creation. As the theologians from the period of orthodoxy teach this doctrine and attempt to relate it to all Christian theology and apply it to life, they manifest not only a good deal of deep Biblical insight but also a definite orientation in the Gospel which is not nearly so apparent in their *locus* concerning God. Their doctrine of creation is quite unencumbered with scholastic distinctions or with any cosmological or metaphysical speculation but is drawn directly from the Scriptures and for the most part is presented in a very practical way which pertains to the concrete Christian life. Rarely is a point made (for example, the *creatio ex nihilo,* or the *creatio per verbum*) which does not have a definite practical relevance and application.

The first thing we notice in the orthodox Lutheran creation theology is the very slight attention paid to the *creatio prima.* Quenstedt, the most thorough of all the great dogmaticians, devotes only five pages to the subject, not even touching upon the hexaemeron, and really indicating rather little interest in the *creatio prima* as such.[1] And this is generally the case among the dogmaticians.[2] In Melanchthon's *Loci Communes*

---

[1] *Systema,* P.I, C.10, S.1, Thesis 9 ff. (I, 415—19).

[2] See John Deutschmann, *Antiquissima Theologia Positiva* (Wittenberg, 1694), p. 205 passim. Calov, *Systema,* III, 885 ff. Hollaz, *Examen,* P.I, C.3, Q.5 ff. (362 ff. [351 in 1750 edit.]). Selnecker (*Institutiones Christianae Religionis,* I, 257) presents practically nothing on the subject except a very strong polemic

the doctrine of creation was presented as having its terminus in the providence of God, and was treated as one article. This practice was followed by Chemnitz.[3] Beginning with Hutter[4] the Lutheran dogmaticians chose to follow the Scholastics of the Middle Ages and separate the two articles in order, Hutter says, to give proper emphasis to each. But as in the case of Chemnitz, the emphasis was soon placed almost wholly on the *creatio continua* (divine providence).

So little attention is directed to the *creatio prima* as such that it is not always easy to find a full and adequate definition of it.[5] And we must often follow a discussion rather closely to determine just all that is involved in the initial creation of all things and the theological significance of it all. In general[6] the Lutheran teachers began by noting that creation means either to make something from nothing or to produce something from any unwrought or unorganized thing. In Christian theology the doctrine of creation excludes any idea of preexistent matter or time. But even the second meaning implies in a sense a creation from nothing, inasmuch as it involves a production from something which has no disposition or tendency for order.[7] This initial creation of all things must be distinguished from God's continuous creation in the generation of species and in His providential care over all things *(creatio continua)*. Creation

against Aristotle. An exception to the rule is Heerbrand (*Compendium Theologiae*, p. 53) who, although treating the subject in a rather systematic and unimaginative way, still gives more attention to the *creatio prima* than to divine providence.

[3] *Loci Theologici*, I, 101 ff.

[4] *Loci Communes Theologici*, p. 197.

[5] We might cite the brief definition of Brochmand as typical: "Creatio est actio externa totius Trinitatis: qua Deus, immensa bonitate commotus, res omnes creatas, visibiles et invisibiles, sex dierum intervallo, sapientissime et ordine concinno condidit, ut manifestam faceret suam bonitatem, sapientiam atque potentiam, ad utilitatem hominum." See Jesper Rasmus Brochmand, *Definitiones Articulorum Fidei* (Copenhagen, 1662), p. A2. This definition, which contained some fine points (for example, that creation is the result of God's goodness and was performed according to order and plan), is still quite incomplete. No mention is made of the creation from nothing or of creation through the Word or of the use of the doctrine. Quenstedt's definition (P.I, C.10, S.1, Thesis 9 [I, 415]) is almost identical, and so is that of Sebastian Schmidt (*Compendium Theologiae* [Strasbourg, 1697], p. 73). Perhaps the shortest definition is Calov's (*Systema,* III, 885): "Creatio est actio, qua Deus Pater per verbum in Spiritu S. virtute infinita, in tempora omnia, quae sunt e nihilo produxit ad laudem gloriae suae."

[6] Bechmann, *Annotationes*, p. 201; Calov, *Systema*, III, 903.

[7] Quenstedt, *Systema*, P.I, C.10, S.2, Q.5, Ekthesis 5 (I, 429).

was never regarded as a process whereby God set things in motion. Deism and notions of "theistic evolution" in an ancient or modern sense were quite foreign and repugnant to the creation theology of historic Lutheranism. Rather the creation of all things and of our first parents was considered to be a deliberate, definite, and specific action of God.[8] Creation occurred by the absolutely free will of God and not by any natural necessity. This freedom extended not only to the acts of creating but to the kind and manner of creation which God exercised. The free act of creation was willed and decreed by God in eternity and carried out in time. This means that God created time and in His freedom took time to create.[9]

The Christian doctrine of creation as a free act of a powerful, wise, and good God has been threatened, according to Cort Aslakssøn,[10] by four major errors which have recurred throughout history. (1) The Aristotelian doctrine that the world is eternal. (2) The theory of ancient and modern philosophers (Democritus, Leucippus, and Epicurus) that the world came into being by accident *(ex fortuito atomorum concursu coaluisse).* (3) The view that the world came into being by someone other than the triune God (Gnosticism). (4) All forms of dualism (for example, Manichaeism) which recognize two principles (one good and one evil) of creation. Against these errors the Christian doctrine of special creation affirms a threefold mode of creation, Aslakssøn says. First, by producing all things God showed His power. Second, by separating all things and thus giving them individuality, suitability, harmony, and classification God showed His wisdom. Third, by adorning these things with functions, beauty, and charm, God showed His goodness.

This last point was very important in Lutheran theology. The God of creation is not only omnipotent and wise, but good. It was by His good will that all things were made, for "He wills to communicate His own goodness to all creation."[11] It is the good and loving God who creates. Aslakssøn[12] goes to great lengths to show that God's goodness and wisdom have made for us the best possible world, not according to any Leibnizian

[8] Bechmann, *Annotationes,* p. 202.

[9] Cort Aslakssøn, *De Creatione Disputatio Prima* (Copenhagen, 1609), p. A3v.

[10] Ibid.

[11] Bechmann, *Annotationes,* p. 204.

[12] *De Creatione Disputatio Prima,* p. BR2.

or philosophical argumentation, but in the simple, ingenuous fashion of a believing Christian. To him Scripture has informed us what the goal of creation is. It is the glory of God. His power and goodness and wisdom are engraved in His creation, and therefore we should glorify Him for His goodness. And the goal of creation is man's glory also, man's happiness and well-being, man's health and honest delight in life, man's institutions, but best of all man's fellowship with God.

A number of basic concerns occupy the attention of the Lutheran theologians as they struggle to set forth a balanced and distinctly Christian doctrine of creation.

1. "CREATIO PER VERBUM"

Lutheran theology stressed a creation *per verbum*. This meant that God created by speaking, by commanding. No idle speculation was expended concerning the nature of the speaking of God which was an obvious anthropomorphism. What was important was that it was a real word, there was an actual speaking of some kind, a real action which resulted in the creation of all things.[13] Creation *per verbum* for most of the Lutheran dogmaticians meant that God actually "spoke" a word: creation occurred *per verbum* προφορικόν. For Heb. 11:3 tells us that creation took place ῥήματι θεοῦ, not τῷ λογῷ θεοῦ. But this view in no sense left the Logos, the Second Person of the Trinity, out of the picture. Creation is often attributed specifically to Him in Scripture (John 1:3; Col. 1:16; Eph. 3:9; 1 Cor. 8:6). It is also through this personal Word, the λόγος ὑποστατικός, that God made the world.[14] And this personal Word

13 John Conrad Dannhauer, *Hodosophia Christiana* (Leipzig, 1695), p. 279: "Solo verbo, scilicet reali, Deus enim res loquitur, Dictio Dei est jussio et productio ipsa. Nec alio verbo mundus creatus est, quam quo conservatur, quod est ῥῆμα reale."

14 Sebastian Schmidt, *In Epistolam ad Hebraeos Commentarius*, p. 1274. See also p. 1190. Cf. also Dannhauer, op. cit., p. 270; Hollaz, *Examen*, P.I, C.3, Q.10, Prob. b (p. 367 [356]). The precise relation between the verbum προφορικόν and the λόγος ὑποστατικός presented a problem which the Lutheran dogmaticians struggled with at length. They saw great significance in the fact that both Scripture, or the Gospel, and Christ were called the Word. The reason for this, they believed, lay in the fact that God revealed Himself both through a written and spoken Word and through His Son. The Lutheran dogmaticians concluded that although the prophetic Word and the hypostatic Word are not to be confused, still there is an intimate relation between the two. Christ, the hypostatic Word, is the nucleus and content of the spoken and written Word; but at the same time

has created and upholds all things through His Word.[15] Commenting on the "God said" of Gen. 1:3, Calov says what seems to be the general Lutheran position,[16] "The 'God said' denotes not merely a word of command; but inasmuch as God does not command anything or do anything except through His hypostatic Word 'through whom all things were made' (John 1:3), the term 'God said' must here, where the creation of all things is spoken of, be taken, on the one hand, as the Word by whom God the Father spoke, the hypostatic Word [17] through whom the Father speaks and

God deals with people and makes Himself known by means of oral and written proclamation. See Calov, *Systema*, I, 457. This was about as far as any of the dogmaticians went in the matter. Cf. Robert Preus, *The Theology of Post-Reformation Lutheranism*, pp. 269—73.

[15] This is the correct interpretation of Heb. 1:3, according to Brochmand (*Commentarius in Epistolam ad Hebraeos*, pp. 25—26). The passage teaches that the Son of God "upholds and preserves all things without any labor or difficulty." Brochmand then comments, "He easily preserves all the things He has made τῷ ῥήματι δυνάμεως. Now the words of the Logos or Son of God are not empty and fleeting words but are filled with mighty power. Indeed whatever exists anywhere is the work of divine words. For God made everything by speaking (Ps. 33:9), and man does not live by bread only but by every word that proceeds from the mouth of God (Matt. 4:4). All things must necessarily adjust themselves to the pleasure and will and purpose of God; and so mighty are the decrees of the Divinity that even those things which are not, appear at the summoning of God (Rom. 4:17)." This statement shows once more the close relation between creation and providence in Lutheran theology.

[16] *Biblia Testamenti Veteris Illustrata* (Dresden and Leipzig, 1719), I, 223. See also *Systema*, I, 702; *Commentarius in Genesis* (Wittenberg, 1671), p. 148. In another place (*Biblia Testamenti Veteris Illustrata*, I, 992) Calov puts it as follows: "Illud אָמַר explicandum est ita, quod Pater in Filio loquens & operans lucem fecerit." Cf. also Sebastian Schmidt, *Super Mosis Librum Primum, Genesis Dictum, Annotationes* (Strasbourg, 1697), p. 4. Gerhard's comments are much the same. See John Gerhard, *Commentarius super Epistolam ad Ebraeos* (Jena, 1666), p. 379: "ῥήματι θεοῦ verbo jussionis ac mandati, in quo inerat Verbum hypostaticum, Dei Filius, Gen. 1:3, Ps. 33:6."

[17] A few of the old Lutheran theologians took the creation *per verbum* to refer exclusively to the activity of the personal Logos. A rather interesting, if unconvincing, argument for this opinion is presented by Jacob Martini. He says (*De Tribus Elohim*, II, 503), "Since God is immutable, He did not begin to speak for the first time on the first, second, and following days of creation, when the things that were made came into being. But He spoke from eternity, and as a consequence also on those specific days when days began to coexist with eternity He spoke on the first day, Let there be heaven, earth, and light; He spoke on the second day, Let there be an expanse in the midst of the waters, and let it divide the waters from the waters; and He spoke in similar fashion on the other days. Actually, we are told in the first chapter of Genesis that God created all things by speaking, and Psalm 33 tells us that the heavens were established by the word of the Lord, and John 1 says that all things were made by the Word. Now, it is not said that this divine speaking had its beginning at that time when all things

works and without whom He neither speaks nor works, and, on the other hand, as the word which God spoke or uttered, the prophetic word, the word of command, as a divine impulse." Calov feels that such a statement summarizes the relationship between the hypostatic Word and the spoken word as they pertain to the creation of all things.

The reason for the emphasis on the creation *per verbum* is to bring into sharp relief and stress a fiat creation and thus to ward off both Aristotelianism and its doctrine of an inactive god and also all pantheistic cosmologies. God's creation *per verbum* distinguishes God as the living and personal God who acts by speaking and whose speaking is always action. The doctrine of creation *per verbum* tells us not only something about how God made the world and all things, but it tells us something about God Himself. For God is still the active, living Creator God, creating a church through His Word, and creating a new heaven and earth for His elect when temporal things have passed away. And all is done through His hypostatic and spoken (and written) Word.

were made. And since the creation account is silent on this point, it is obvious from this account and other texts that the speaking here can in no sense be understood as the word or speaking which are subject to change or which pass away. Since God is immutable He does not make anything by means of any function or quality which is distinct from Himself, but He produces all things by His own essential might. And so we might present our position as follows.

"That speaking through which all things were made is either a creature or an uncreated Word.

"It is not a creature because it was through it that creatures were made.

"Therefore if it is anything at all, it will have to be an uncreated Word.

"Now it certainly is something, according to the teaching and testimony of Moses in Genesis and of Psalm 33 and of John 1, and therefore it must be the uncreated Word.

"Furthermore, this uncreated Word is either God or is not God.

"We cannot say that it is not God, for whatever is outside God is something created, a creature.

"Thus the uncreated Word is God Himself. And so it is manifest that this speaking of God at creation does not refer to a word or quality which passes away, but to the hypostatic Word which in the fulness of the time became man, namely the Son of God Himself."

The strained logic employed by Martini here is due to his fear that the doctrine of fiat creation threatens God's transcendence and immutability. But this is the problem connected with any *opus ad extra* of God, and it is strange that Martini should have been bothered so much at this point. As a rule Lutherans simply assert that creation involves no change in God, and let it go at that. Certain Lutherans agreed with Martini, but on purely exegetical grounds, that creation *per verbum* referred only to the hypostatic Word. (See Giles Hunnius, *Opera Latina*, II, 642; Martin Geier, *Opera Omnia*, I, 488.) Most agreed with Calov's position. Some, like Gerhard (*Loci Theologici*, IV, 4-7), do not show enough interest to commit themselves.

2. "Creatio ex Nihilo"

The term "create" was recognized by the Lutheran teachers to be a very flexible term in Scripture, often used metaphorically for "make" or "recreate" or "change" (Ps. 51:10; 102:18; Is. 57:19), at other times used interchangeably with "make" (Ps. 124:8; Rom. 1:20) in the more general sense.[18] For the sake of clarity, however, Lutheran dogmatics was compelled to distinguish between "create" and "make." Strictly speaking, creation refers to the fact that God in the beginning called the heavens and the earth into existence from nothing *(ex nihilo)*. The whole context and tenor of the creation story in Genesis 1 indicated that the בָּרָא in this instance means to create from nothing, and does not simply mean to establish or make in the sense of the Greek κτίζω.[19] To Lutheran theology therefore, much of what God did in the six creation days was not creation, strictly speaking, that is, creation from nothing. In fact the consensus was that the entire immediate creation *ex nihilo* took place on the first day of creation,[20] when God made heaven and earth and the abyss (Gen. 1: 1, 2). The general belief was that these three, which alone were created *ex nihilo*, were first a rude, confused, and shapeless state (Gen. 1:2; cf. Jer. 4:7), and only on the subsequent days of creation did God separate and divide and work things out more fully and in an orderly way.[21] What was created *ex nihilo*, usually called *rudis moles*, actually had existence, although it could be called a sort of "chaos." But the Lutheran dogmaticians were quick to point out that this Biblical picture was in no sense to be associated with the Aristotelian idea of prime matter *(prima materia)*.

---

[18] Quenstedt, *Systema*, P.I, C.10, S.1, Thesis 9, nota 2 (I, 415); Chemnitz, *Loci Theologici*, I, 105.

[19] Salomon Deyling, *Observationum Sacrarum in qua Multa Scripturae Veteris ac Novi Testamenti Dubia Vexata Solvuntur* (Leipzig, 1735), I, 18—20. Cf. Quenstedt, *Systema*, P.I, C.10, S.1, Thesis 13 (I, 417). It was also thought that Ps. 33:9 implied a creation from nothing. Chemnitz says (*Loci Theologici*, I, 102): "The following statement teaches that things were made from nothing: 'He spoke, and it was done; He commanded, and it stood fast' (Ps. 33:9), that is, things came forth by God as He spoke and gave commands." The closest Scripture came to declaring the creation *ex nihilo* explicitly was Heb. 11:3, and for this reason a great deal of exegesis was expended on this passage to show its bearing on the doctrine. See Sebastian Schmidt, *In Epistolam ad Hebraeos Commentarius*, p. 1,274.

[20] Cort Aslakssøn, *De Creatione Disputatio Prima*, p. A3v.

[21] Chemnitz, *Loci Theologici*, II, 111; Hutter, *Loci Communes Theologici*, p. 199.

Moses had no desire in Genesis to teach such philosophical theories. Heaven and earth and the abyss did not lack all form and structure in the Aristotelian sense; such a notion would be utterly opposed to the intent of Genesis 1.[22]

What was the significance of the *creatio ex nihilo?* Why did Lutheran dogmatics stress this doctrine so consistently? There were several reasons for this. First, the *creatio ex nihilo* very clearly showed that God was the one *causa efficiens* of creation and precluded any other cause whatsoever, even an instrumental cause.[23] There was no *materia ex qua* of creation; and the world cannot be its own cause. All that exists came into being at God's Word and command (Rom. 4:17; Heb. 11:3). Thus, the *creatio ex nihilo* proclaims that God is both living and transcendent. This being the case, we can see that the doctrine constituted a strong repudiation both of Aristotelianism with its doctrine of an inactive god and a necessarily eternal world and of pantheism which failed to distinguish between God and His creation and denied the transcendence of God.[24] Again we see that the right doctrine of creation tells us something most important and comforting to know about God.

Second, the *creatio ex nihilo,* properly understood and applied, wards off every notion of deistic Stoicism with its denial of God's total involvement in His creation. As they develop this important point the dogmaticians relax their distinction between the notions of "create" and "make" and include both together as belonging to the *creatio prima.* Chemnitz states the Lutheran position,[25] "God did not create matter in order that it might just remain a void and shapeless mass, but He did so in order that through His Word He might produce of that matter the classes and divisions *(genera)* of all creation, as described in Genesis 1, and arrange each of them according to a fine and lovely order. This is what it means 'to make.' For עָשָׂה means to prepare or adapt."

[22] Hutter, ibid.; Quenstedt, *Systema,* P.I, C.10, S.2, Q.7, obs.3 (I, 433).

[23] Baier-Walther, II, 96; Quenstedt, *Systema,* P.I, C.10, S.1, Thesis 11 (I, 417); Hutter, p. 199.

[24] Chemnitz, *Loci Theologici,* I, 105: "Creare vero significat ex nihilo aliquid fabricare, diversum a substantia creantis." We might bear in mind that in the later period of orthodoxy pantheism was not dead. Deyling (I, 22) directs the burden of his remarks at this point against Spinoza who taught, according to his presuppositions regarding substance, that creation from nothing was both absurd and contradictory.

[25] Chemnitz, *Loci Theologici,* I, 105.

Chemnitz's theological concern here is to avoid any notion which would separate God from the creation and from the upholding of all things. Nothing has come into being without God; nothing has come into being by itself or by chance or in any sense remote to His total control. God is a living and active God intimately concerned with every step and aspect of His creation. (Ps. 136:5; Psalm 33)

This view, that the mighty and all-wise God was totally, one might say meticulously, interested and involved as He created all things and as He now upholds all things, is brought out, according to Chemnitz, by a vast amount of Biblical imagery: e. g. "form" (Gen. 2:7; Is. 43:7), "prepare carefully" or "establish" (Ps. 74:16), "command to be" (Ps. 33:9; 148:6; Wis. 1:14), "make beautiful" or "adorn" (Job 26:13), "found" (Ps. 89:11; 104:8), "stretch" (Ps. 136:6; Is. 42:5), "build" (Heb. 3:4; cf. 1 Peter 3:20; Heb. 11:7), "frame" or "construct" (Heb. 11:3). It is very obviously Chemnitz's conviction that the בָּרָא and עָשָׂה, the *creare ex nihilo* and the *facere* of Gen. 1:31 both belong to the doctrine of creation and to deny either would be disastrous to our notion of God and His intimate relationship to His creation — and in particular to man.

3. CREATION AND THE GOSPEL

The doctrine of creation is never viewed as a mere cosmology in Lutheran theology, as a mere aetiological reply to certain persistent questions which man poses about the origin of things. The Biblical doctrine of creation, according to historic Lutheranism, is something which should be put to use. Without question, this concern to use the doctrine of creation evangelically is one of the most persistent themes to run through the creation theology of classical Lutheranism.

The doctrine of creation is used first of all in Lutheran theology to show man his importance to God. For he for whom the world was created is man, and there is nothing in all creation which does not have the purpose of serving man and adorning his life with blessedness.[26] "God made all things for man," says Quenstedt,[27] "and He made man for Him-

[26] Deyling, I, 299: "Homo, cui nihil non servit vitam vitaeque commoda instrumenta & ornamenta."

[27] Quenstedt, *Systema*, P.I, C.10, S.1, Thesis 17 (I, 418). See Chemnitz, *Loci Theologici*, I, 116; Baier-Walther, II, 76.96.102.

self. Ps. 115:16: 'The heaven, even the heavens are the Lord's; but the earth hath He given to the children of men.' That is to say, God resides in heaven, but the earth, rich and abundant with the greatest variety of good things, He has given to man to possess." This is no mere idle thesis of Quenstedt's, but a bit of profound counsel on the approach one should take toward God's world. There can be no hostility toward nature or God's creation, but only friendship and enjoyment of what God has made for man and given to man.

The orthodox Lutheran creation theology is optimistic. For everything in the humdrum, daily life of man, every event of history, every movement and occurrence in nature, even the most insignificant and infinitesimal, has been brought about and directed for the benefit of man. Nothing, great or small, is outside God's creation and sovereign will. And God's will is not only sovereign, but good and loving, that is, directed always toward our good. This does not mean that creation somehow becomes redemption in Lutheran theology. Such an idea would represent a hopeless confusion to the old Lutheran theologians. There is nothing of the modern notion of creation grace in the old Lutheran doctrine. But it is a very strong emphasis in Lutheran theology that the creator God is a God of grace,[28] that God's creation was an act of love and has a benevolent and loving goal in mind.

And it is a very strong emphasis too that we are to *use* the doctrine of creation in such a way that the man in Christ sees all God's activity in creation as the activity of a loving and beneficent God who is personally and intimately concerned with all His children right now. The Lutheran creation doctrine is as antideistic as it can be, and yet, all in all, remarkably free of all notions of magic and superstition, as we shall see. It is a doctrine which makes constant dependence on the God of love and constant communion with Him the key to meaningful and happy life on earth.

Second, the doctrine of creation is to be used doxologically. The great creation pericopes in Scripture (Job 38; Ps. 104; Is. 40) are seen by the old Lutherans primarily not as cosmologies, but as great hymns of praise to God, the "magnificent Creator." [29] Seeing God's magnificent creation

[28] Mentzer, *Opera Latina,* I, 29.

[29] This is Geier's understanding of Psalm 104 (*Opera Omnia,* I, 1571). It is also Sebastian Schmidt's understanding of Job 38. See *In Librum Ijobi Com-*

causes us to adore Him for His goodness and power and wisdom and to give ourselves to Him in doxology.[30] In his remarks on Heb. 1:2 Sebastian Schmidt says,[31] "Earth and the heavens are the most noble and wonderful of works. Why? Because they are the works of God's hands. The Son of God has founded the earth with His hands and the heavens are the works of His hands. And what God has formed with His hands is perfect and noble and wonderful. Indeed the apostle wants to say with the psalmist that the foundation of the earth and the creation of the heavens are a work which bring wonder and admiration to all men's reason."

Not just anyone can apply the doctrine of creation in the two ways just mentioned. Lutheran theology maintained that only a Christian could do this, only one who approaches the doctrine of creation from the point of view of the Gospel. All the Lutheran teachers held and made much of the fact that creation from nothing was an article of faith, a pure article of faith *(articulus purus)*, which could not be known from the light of nature or from philosophical principles.[32] Without faith no one could know that creation was an act of God's goodness and love and transcendent freedom, for no human could anticipate how God would exercise His freedom and love.

Commenting on Heb. 11:3 and its reference to the creation of all things, Sebastian Schmidt says,[33] "When he [the author of Hebrews] says that we know by faith, he shows that we will not know without faith."

mentarius (Strasbourg, 1705), pp. 1415 ff. Schmidt sees the section as a divine challenge to Job or any man who would question God's justice and wisdom. God's impenetrable marvelous creation silences man at this point and can evoke only wonder. Schmidt takes the whole piece as a highly figurative poem glorifying God's wisdom and majesty which is not to be used for cosmological interests. Calov (*Biblia Veteris Testamenti Illustrata*, I, 919), while agreeing with Schmidt's understanding, attempts at a few places to tie the chapter in with the Genesis account of creation, which was thought to be more historical. But he too says that the burden of God's speech in the chapter is to show Job the inscrutable wisdom of God and the divine majesty and goodness which are apparent in creation, but often only to faith, and God's wonderful governance of all things. Calov sees Is. 40:12 in much the same way as a glorifying of the immense power and wisdom of God (ibid., II, 176).

[30] Geier, I, 427 f. Geier is commenting on Ps. 33:6.

[31] *In Epistolam ad Hebraeos Commentarius*, p. 149.

[32] Quenstedt, *Systema*, P.I, C.10, S.2, Q.1 (I, 419). See also Hollaz, *Examen*, P.I, C.3, Q.10; Calov, *Systema*, III, 911 ff.

[33] *In Epistolam ad Hebraeos Commentarius*, p. 1272.

It is very important to understand what Schmidt means in this statement, what he means by "know" and what he means by "faith," or more precisely, what he thinks the writer of Hebrews means by these two verbs.

First he explains what is meant by "know" in the verse.[34] "The word 'to know' in sacred Scripture is not always taken in its very strict sense as meaning 'to comprehend fully a thing,' but it also designates any kind of knowing. Hence in this passage we have a reference not to a knowledge according to which we completely comprehend the creation of the world and how something can be made from nothing, but we have a reference to our incipient knowledge and understanding which will be made perfect in the life to come. But although incipient, this knowledge is nevertheless far superior to any natural or philosophical knowledge." Why is it superior, according to Schmidt? Not only because it is correct as far as it goes, but because it is theological and practical, a knowledge which can put the doctrine of creation to use. Reason and philosophy are powerless *(languidus)* to cope with the doctrine of creation — committed as they are to such axioms as: nothing can come from nothing — powerless to make any sense out of it and powerless to apply it theologically. No, says Schmidt, faith must be added before creation means anything to us — not a theoretical but a practical faith which directs what it knows to definite goals and purposes.

Schmidt then proceeds to tell us what he means by faith in the short statement cited above. He means justifying faith,[35] faith in the Gospel, faith which views and applies the doctrine of creation soteriologically. "And what else is the purpose and range *(scopus)* of faith," he asks, "than the justification and salvation of man? Therefore to know in this context (Heb. 11:3) will indicate at the same time the direction of the knowing toward a definite goal. For justifying faith has its very own special activity; after it has accepted the justification itself which is offered in the Word, it then accepts everything else which can strengthen it in its acceptance of justification. Among other things which strengthen faith is very deservedly the article of creation; from this article faith understands that He who was able to create all things and in particular man himself is

---

[34] Ibid., p. 1189.

[35] Ibid., p. 1188. Schmidt is convinced that the entire long pericope in Hebrews 10 and 11 is speaking of justifying faith (cf. Heb. 10:38) as it works its way out in the life of a Christian.

able also to justify a poor sinner and to save him forever. If we keep this fact in mind, it will not be difficult to see that the faith spoken of in this verse is justifying faith."

This is a highly significant statement of Schmidt's. For it shows the setting into which Schmidt wishes to place the doctrine of creation. To him creation is a doctrine to be employed for our spiritual edification, to be used evangelically. This is Schmidt's constant emphasis. Again he says,[36] "The enlightenment and knowledge of faith exceed and surpass that of nature also in respect to the creation of the world, especially in this, that faith can use those things which are known soteriologically to confirm and establish itself in the article of justification and eternal life. The apostle offers an example of this in the patriarch Abraham (Rom. 4:17). Here he shows us well how the holy patriarch put to use that which he knew by faith concerning the creation of the world. The apostle tells how Abraham believed in God who raises the dead and calls into being things that are not. And so now when the apostle says, πίστει νοοῦμεν, by faith we know, he means to say that we know soteriologically."

We must quote Schmidt once more on this important point, as he seeks to orient the doctrine of creation to the Gospel and make it serve the Gospel in the concrete situations of practical faith-life. Still commenting on Heb. 11:3, he says,[37] "It is by faith that we understand the work of creation. And we understand it in such a way that we are convinced that God who has created all things is the one who also can re-create us in Christ and make us over anew for His glory. We are convinced that God who once made all things good, including man, did not make man a sinner, but is able by His grace to free the man in Christ from sin. We are convinced that God, who did not make things which are seen from things which appear, is able to accomplish for our salvation those things which we are unable to see or understand."

The lack of emphasis upon the original creation of all things, the stress (which we shall note in the next chapter) on the *creatio continua* and divine providence, and the insistence that creation is an article of faith to be viewed and applied evangelically — these three facts illustrate the

[36] Ibid., p. 1272. Cf. also p. 1188.
[37] Ibid., p. 1274.

marked similarity between the creation theology of Lutheran orthodoxy and that of Luther and the Lutheran Confessions.[38]

4. THE HEXAEMERON

Although the Lutheran teachers in their exegetical works on Genesis always traced the progress of God's activity during the six days of creation, usually following Luther quite closely, their works in dogmatics pay rather little attention to the hexaemeron. Quenstedt offers no discussion of the six creation days at all, and the other dogmaticians (Chemnitz, Gerhard, Calov, et al.) present only very cursory discussions. The reason for this relative lack of interest in the hexaemeron was probably that nothing was thought to be at stake or of theological significance in the account of the six days, except that it showed divine order and wisdom and goodness.

The Lutheran dogmaticians reject the interpretation of St. Augustine, Athanasius, and others who believed that all creation was accomplished in a moment and the account of the six days was merely Moses' way of indicating that God made the world according to order with certain things following and depending on others.[39] They preferred to interpret the account as teaching that creation occurred at successive intervals.[40] No

[38] For a brief discussion of the doctrine of creation in Lutheran confessional theology see Robert Preus, "Biblical Hermeneutics and the Lutheran Church Today" in *Crisis in Lutheran Theology*, Vol. II, ed. by John Warwick Montgomery (Grand Rapids: Baker Book Company, 1967), pp. 87—88 passim. In the light of the above observations it is odd to note Werner Elert (*The Structure of Lutheranism*, p. 450) faulting the Lutherans of the post-Reformation era for not presenting creation in the light of the joy of faith. He accuses them of assigning a "false position . . . to the doctrine of creation," but never explains what he means by this. He then says that when they speak of creation, the dogmaticians have not yet given the reader "any knowledge whatever of what faith is." He offers no evidence of this, and his remarks seem bizarre in the light of Schmidt's statements cited above. It is true that the dogmaticians for the most part offer only a brief resume of justifying faith prior to their *locus* on creation (see, e. g., Hollaz, *Examen*, Prol. II, Q. 19), but this does not imply that they do not view the doctrine of creation in the light of faith. In fact as they develop their doctrine of *creatio continua* and providence, they usually give the reader a very good idea of what faith is, as we shall see. It is interesting that Gerhard, perhaps because he shares somewhat the same concerns as Elert, takes up the person and work of Christ in his *Loci Theologici* immediately after the *locus* on God and before his discussions of creation, man, and sin. But such a procedure did not win approval by the other dogmaticians, probably because they thought it best to discuss sin before discussing the Gospel and faith.

[39] See Augustine, *De Civitate Dei*, II, 7 (*MPL* 41, 322).

[40] See, for instance, Quenstedt, *Systema*, P.I, C.10, S.2, Q.6 (I, 431 ff.).

great issue was made of this matter, and Augustine was never hereticized; for the ancient theory did guard against the false doctrine of spontaneous creation or evolution from the essence of God (pantheism). But it was felt that the theory of instantaneous creation did not do justice to the Genesis account and tended to undermine the intent of that account which was to underscore the wisdom and order of God's creation. There was simply no good reason, theological or hermeneutical, for departing from the *prima facie* meaning of the pericope. The detail with which the account rehearses the work of the six days was thought to indicate the clear theological purpose of the account.

Gerhard expresses his disapproval of the view of instantaneous creation with the following comment:[41] "We must not depart from the record. God could have produced all things at once in one moment, but in His great goodness He desired to extend the work of creation to six days." Why? Gerhard offers no answer. "It is enough," he says, "for us to know that it was God's will even though we cannot fully explain the reasons for His decision." Bechmann speaks in much the same manner,[42] "The historical narrative of Moses was set forth to the common people in so direct and clear a genre that the words can correctly be interpreted in no other way. For who of the ordinary people would ever have understood Moses to mean one split instant when he speaks of six days?" And Bechmann adds that the days ought to be taken as normal solar days, according to their prima facie usage, although יום may designate a period of many days in some cases (Deut. 4:37 [38,39]; Gen. 2:5 [4,5]). This is the more natural interpretation, he feels. It is clear from such arguments that it was on hermeneutical and not theological grounds that Augustine's doctrine (as well as Philo's allegorical approach to the text) was rejected and a literal hexaemeron accepted.

Like the rest of the Book of Genesis, the account of creation was taken as history by the Lutheran teachers. It was called the *historica narratio Moses* or the *historia Mosaica* or the *historia creationis*.[43] This is perfectly

41 *Loci Theologici*, IV, 16.

42 *Annotationes*, p. 212. Cf. Quenstedt, *Systema*, P.I, C.10, S.2, Q.6 Bebaiosis 2 (I, 432).

43 Baier-Walther, II, 78; Bechmann, *Theologia Polemica*, p. 179. This was also Luther's view (*WA* 42, 15). Bechmann (*Annotationes*, p. 212) maintains that only a historical interpretation of the text adequately explains the origin of

compatible with the goodly amount of anthropomorphism and highly figurative imagery which one finds in the story. And because the account was taken as history the things and actions mentioned cannot be allegorized away. For instance, God's speaking was a real event, although we cannot know the nature of it; the light created on the first day was real light, although again we cannot know its nature or whether it had an orbit.[44] That the creation account was taken as history was considered to be perfectly compatible with the definite theological purpose of the narrative. The theological intention and purpose of the story was to glorify God and to proclaim His wisdom and power and goodness; and this purpose is achieved by telling us a history, by giving an actual glimpse of what happened at the first creation, a glimpse of the order of God's creation. For the creation history was believed to offer a revealed account of the order of creation. What was the nature of this order? In this account Quenstedt says,[45] "Moses does not follow any order of nature or of importance or of thought, but an order of time." Such was the only viable interpretation of the pericope, Quenstedt thought, if the account is to be taken as history and not as allegory.

We must now follow the Lutheran teachers as they attempt to trace God's day-by-day creative activity during the hexaemeron. For their discussion of the hexaemeron reveals some significant aspects of their creation doctrine. For the most part we notice a brief and ingenuous Luther-like account of the order of creation with no apologetic overtones whatever and no attempt to structure or imply any world picture or cosmology. Their exegesis represents a very simple, one might say naive, attempt to get at the probable intention of the pericope which was recognized as being very difficult because of the subject it treated. The overarching concern was to let the text speak for itself, even though it leaves hosts of questions unanswered and seems to conflict at times with our observation of nature.

Sabbath observance (Ex. 20:9-10). Cf. Quenstedt, *Systema*, P.I, C.10, S.2, Q.6, Bebaiosis 1 (I, 431). Cf. also fons sol. 1 (I, 432). Cf. also Calov, *Systema*, III, 1023. Sebastian Schmidt (*Super Mosis Librum Primum, Genesis Dictum, Annotationes* [Strasbourg, 1697], p. 1) calls all of Genesis *historia sacra & divina.* There was no such notion as prehistory in those days.

44 Bechmann, ibid. Calov, *Systema*, III, 938.

45 Quenstedt, *Systema*, P.I, C.10, S.2, Q.6, Bebaiosis 3 (I, 432).

a. *The First Day of Creation*

It was generally held among the Lutherans that Gen. 1:1 was a general introductory statement that God created everything without exception. The verse therefore was not to be taken necessarily as step one in an order of creation.[46] Heaven and earth in this verse were understood as the rude material from which all subsequent things were made. This meant that the immediate creation *ex nihilo* took place only on the first day, a view not incompatible with certain modern gap theories of creation. This rude material, it would appear, was part watery and part earthen. It was absolutely vast like a mass without dimensions. Its nature was raw, unformed, confused, utterly obscure and devoid of vegetation and life.[47] The abyss, according to Hutter,[48] was an immense force of waters under which the raw material lay. Later it was gathered together and was called seas. It was called an abyss because its depth lacked any foundation. Baier[49] favors the idea of Chemnitz that the abyss was a chaotic mass *(globus)* of unformed matter which later became sky and water and earth.

In any case this view meant that, strictly speaking, heaven and earth as we know them today were not made directly *ex nihilo* on the first creation day. Such a theory granted that God in the first act of creation made something confused and unfinished. But the Lutherans, convinced that this is the meaning of the Biblical account, are not disturbed by this, and feel that it does not necessarily militate against an order in God's creation. Quenstedt says,[50] "We must not say that God's creation is confused, but only that the work of creation at this point was rough, unformed, and imperfect. And because the act of creation is perfectly planned for definite ends *(ordinatissima)*, therefore a progression took place in creation from the more rudimentary to the more complete. All this does not pertain

---

[46] Chemnitz, *Loci Theologici,* I, 111; Aslakssøn, *De Creatio Disputatio Prima,* p. A3v. This was also Luther's position (*WA* 24, 26). Sebastian Schmidt says (*Super Mosis Librum Primum, Genesis Dictum, Annotationes,* p. 3): "Generalis itaque in hoc versu est propositio vel titulus operis creationis; quod deinde specialiter juxta sex ejus dies et certa opera distinguitur."

[47] Chemnitz, ibid.

[48] *Loci Communes Theologici,* p. 210.

[49] Baier-Walther, II, 81.

[50] Quenstedt, *Systema,* P.I, C.10, S.2, Q.7, obj. dial. 6 (I, 435).

to God's power, to what He as the omnipotent One could have done, but to His will and wisdom, to what and how He in His wisdom was pleased to act." There are two things to note in this approach: first, the conscious attempt to get the sense of the Biblical account and stay with it at all costs, and second the lack of any concern to harmonize the account with any correct world picture.

This common view held by Quenstedt and Gerhard and Chemnitz was not shared by all the Lutherans. Bechmann[51] maintains that the heaven mentioned on the first day of creation was actually the airy heavens which we know and see. He gently differs with Luther,[52] averring that the latter followed the Vulgate too closely at this point. So there was no real uniformity on this point. And this was often the case on details of interpretation.

On the first day God also created light. What was this light? It was not a reference to the creation of angels, as Augustine and some of the church fathers believed. Chemnitz is of the opinion that the light in this case has reference to the universe and to the fact that God now removed the darkness and obscurity from the created matter. Gerhard is more inclined toward Luther's opinion that light in this case was actually something corporeal, but immersed within the raw material and therefore somewhat obscured. Bechmann goes even further in developing this theory and suggests that this light actually had an orbit which accounted for the days of creation.[53] He suggests also that the light could have been the sun in a somewhat undeveloped state, but does not favor this conjecture.

b. *The Second Day of Creation*

On the second day of creation God created the firmament which was above the waters, and He divided the waters. By certain rabbis the firmament was taken to mean the air. But Gerhard[54] prefers the view that firmament was the whole system of the universe, all the heavenly bodies

[51] *Theologia Polemica* (Jena, 1719), p. 276. Bechmann feels that the emphatic ה before שָׁמַיִם makes his point. Baier (Baier-Walther, II, 81) lists the various views among the Lutherans on this issue.

[52] *WA* 24, 26; 42,6.

[53] *Theologia Polemica*, pp. 285 ff.

[54] *Loci Theologici*, IV, 16. Cf. Luther, *WA* 42, 18—19.

and their orbits, if they had them. It is called רָקִיעַ because it gives the appearance of a tent or a carpet or curtain or shell (Ps. 104:2; Is. 40:22; 42:5).

Gerhard adds, "It is called firmament (στερέωμα) not because it was formed from some very hard material or because it occupies a stationary position, but because of its definiteness; for at this point was fixed the terminus of the human search for knowledge." We notice the lack of interest in cosmological speculation and the clear theological explanation for the difficult term. Chemnitz takes the same position. He assumes that the root meaning of רָקִיעַ denotes expansion, and he says that God in the second day created extension *(res extensissima)* and from this extension which He made from nothing He then formed the heavens.[55]

What about the waters above the firmament? Some like Philo thought the idea of waters above the firmament was impossible and allegorized at this point. Those Lutherans who struggle with the problem of identifying these waters (Chemnitz does not) believe that a literal interpretation is called for, however difficult and incredible the thought. But what possible purpose have such waters? Gerhard submits no answer to the question, but their existence he will not doubt. "Think," he says,[56] "of the power of God, think of the waters of the Red Sea and the Jordan erect like walls, think of clouds rushing along in the sky, and you will be able to take more easily your reason captive in obedience to faith." That is all he says. His total Biblical orientation to theology makes it impossible for him to find any difficulties in what he believes Scripture is saying.

A generation later, however, this matter took on new importance as a controversy developed between the Lutherans and the Calvinists. The Calvinists for the most part (Calvin, Alsted, Zanchi, Piscator, Junius, et al.) interpreted the waters in the verse to refer simply to clouds and thought the whole idea of supercelestial waters to be contrary to common sense, *"incredible,"* Calvin said.[57] The Lutherans for the most part held that, although there was no indication of such waters from nature, Scripture was sufficiently clear in affirming that such waters existed.[58] True,

[55] *Loci Theologici,* I, 112. See also Hutter, *Loci Communes Theologici,* p. 210; Calov, *Systema,* III, 941 ff.

[56] *Loci Theologici,* IV, 17. Gerhard's approach here is very like Luther's (*WA* 24, 33).

[57] *CR* 23, 18.

[58] In particular Quenstedt, *Systema,* P.I, C.10, S.2, Q.8 (I, 435 ff.); Calov, *Systema,* III, 1034 ff.

Scripture never tells us the purpose of such supercelestial waters (τὸ πῶς καὶ διότι) except in the general sense that all created things are made to serve and glorify God (Ps. 148:4), but to affirm the existence of real waters above the heavens seems to be the intention of the pericope. And with this observation they leave the matter. Quenstedt, whose discussion of the subject is the longest, says merely,[59] "We must distinguish between the book of Scripture and the book of nature. We do not perceive these supercelestial waters with our senses nor do we know of them by our reason; only from Scripture do we understand that they exist and what they are."

Karl Barth [60] sees in this rather lengthy apologetic of Quenstedt's a highly instructive commentary on both the strength and weakness of the later orthodox doctrine of creation. Its strength rests in its insistence upon employing the *sola Scriptura* principle here in arriving at a position which presented difficult problems and refusing to allow any extra-Biblical considerations to influence their exegesis. Barth sees its weakness in the narrow interest shown by Quenstedt: Quenstedt makes more of the existence of the supercelestial waters than of the purpose of the creation account, hinted at in Ps. 148:4, which is doxological. Barth is correct in his criticism of Quenstedt. But his remarks hardly hold against the Lutheran creation doctrine of the entire period. The theologians preceding Quenstedt say little or nothing of the supercelestial waters. Some of the Lutherans of Quenstedt's day agree with the Calvinists that the water referred to is simply clouds or something similar.[61] And Bechmann's last words on the subject are, "But since this question does not touch upon the foundation of faith, anyone should be permitted free judgment in the matter." Even those contemporaries who agree with Quenstedt make rather little of the issue.[62] Furthermore, as we have shown above, the Lutheran creation theology as a whole emphasized strongly the doxological purpose of creation. We can only conclude, therefore, that Quenstedt is unique in his making a great issue of the supercelestial waters.

[59] Quenstedt, ibid., Ekthesis 1 (I, 435).

[60] Karl Barth, *Church Dogmatics,* III, I, 137 ff.

[61] For instance, Martin Geier, *Opera Omnia,* I, 1578; Baier-Walther, II, 84—85; Bechmann, *Theologia Polemica,* pp. 288—91.

[62] See, for example, Calov, *Systema,* III, 947. Calov argues the case at more length in his exegetical works. See *Biblia Veteris Testamenti Illustrata,* I, 226 ff.

c. *The Third Day of Creation*

At the end of the second creation day the earth was like an open abyss, like a garment, with the waters of the abyss higher than the submerged land. Now on the third day at the rebuke of God the waters recede, and dry land and mountains and valleys appear.[63] Often the Lutheran teachers interpret Ps. 104:6 ff. as a sort of homiletical commentary on the third day and see God's creative activity of the third day in the light of the psalm.[64] This is a great wonder (Ps. 33:7) that water is now distributed around the globe in seas and rivers and there is a place for man to live (Job 38:11-12). On the first day earth was created rude and confused; now on the third day it is made habitable for men. The vegetation provided for man in this day is also not a creation from nothing, but is produced "suddenly" from the earth itself, even though no seeds were planted, no watering or cultivating was made, and the sun had not been made. The first vegetation therefore did not come about through any natural process. Those who speculate that the earth was created in the fall because vegetation was flourishing therefore miss the point of the text which is that God's creation and every aspect of it was absolutely supernatural and not to be judged according to our present knowledge of things.

d. *The Fourth Day of Creation*

The Lutheran teachers will not speculate whether God made the heavenly bodies on the fourth day from the light which He created on the first day or in some other way.[65] What is important is that God formed the sun and heavenly bodies to serve man in seasons and days and nights. Apart from this, nothing is said by the Lutheran dogmaticians in regard to the work of the fourth day. Gerhard[66] takes the occasion to express strong warnings against astrology. There is nothing in the creation account to suggest such superstition, he maintains. He believed that certain weather conditions could be predicted by the position of heavenly bodies (he believes the pericope allows for this), although one must exercise

[63] Chemnitz, *Loci Theologici*, I, 112.
[64] Calov, *Systema*, III, 948.
[65] Chemnitz, *Loci Theologici*, I, 113; Baier-Walther, II, 87.
[66] *Loci Theologici*, IV, 18.

extreme caution, since there is much which is not known in such matters. But to suppose that one can predict human affairs by the stars ignores God's providence and the power of our prayers which may change the course of history and human affairs. It is better to fear God and to pray, Gerhard says, than to speculate in astrology. The idea that thievery and other crimes of men were destined in the stars is a denial of God's power and of man's responsibility. Astrology cannot anticipate God's or man's will.[67]

e. *The Fifth Day of Creation*

On the fifth day God made fishes and birds not from nothing but from earth itself. And "what a stupendous wonder this is," says Chemnitz,[68] "that among the aquatic creatures and the birds there is such a great difference — for the fish dies in the air and the bird suffocates in the water — and yet when God speaks they are both produced from the same material." We see again that the Lutheran dogmaticians see in the work of the fifth day, as in the fourth, no grist for speculation in cosmology or natural science, but only ground for wonder and praise.

f. *The Sixth Day of Creation*

In the sixth day God made animals and man in the same manner as He worked on the fifth day: He makes life from an inanimate element. And as the earth produced animals and men at God's command this is no less a wonder than God's first creation from nothing. But as God makes man He does not say, "Let there be," but rather "Let us make." God shows deliberation as He creates human nature. He prepares the material from which He makes the human body (Gen. 2:7). He does not say, "Let the earth bring forth," but He forms, fashions, molds (יָצַר), cf. Job 10:8. He makes animals living souls; but into man He breathes the spirit of life which does not pass away when man dies (Eccl. 12:7; Matt. 10:28).

---

[67] These comments of Gerhard's show how far he is from the magic world picture which dominated much of the thought even after Luther. Both Melanchthon and Chemnitz regularly read horoscopes. But actually Gerhard is leaning heavily on Luther here for his comments. For in his comments on this same verse Luther rejects the proposition "Astrologiam inter scientias numerandum esse," and with even more detail than Gerhard (*WA* 42:33). Cf. Elert, *The Structure of Lutheranism*, p. 417.

[68] Chemnitz, ibid.

Unlike the animals, man was created for eternal fellowship with God (although this immortality was lost through the Fall). By divine inbreathing therefore God makes man something very special: He thereby gives to man wisdom, light, and righteousness; He makes man in His own image, an image lost by the Fall, but restored again by Christ through another inbreathing of the Spirit (John 20:22). Like light and the abyss and the angels, man's soul was created from nothing.[69]

The details of anthropology which concerned post-Reformation Lutheran dogmatics were not discussed within their *locus* on creation, since most of these matters had to do with man after the Fall, and we cannot therefore discuss these matters in our present study.[70] The one fact of anthropology that was brought out in the discussion of creation and in particular the sixth day of creation was that man was the culmination of God's creation. The entire creation leads to what God did finally on the sixth day when He made man in His image. We have already mentioned this when we noted that creation was to be taught, according to the old Lutherans, in such a way that man learns to know how important he is to God. On the sixth day this importance of man to God was highlighted, for on that day God gave all the world, the world which He had created good, to man.[71]

What may we say in comment on the Lutheran treatment of the hexaemeron? We must bear in mind of course that in affirming their simple interpretation of the hexaemeron the early Lutherans were faced with no severe challenges to their exegesis of the narrative. They saw no prominent scientific world picture as seriously challenging their interpreta-

[69] Chemnitz, *Loci Theologici,* I, 113; Bechmann, *Annotationes,* p. 212. It was only the soul of the first man which was created *ex nihilo,* however. The Lutherans were all convinced traducianists in their doctrine of the origin of man's soul, in contrast to the Roman Catholic doctrine of creationism. See Quenstedt, *Systema,* P. I, C.12, S.2, Q.3 for a very complete presentation of the Lutheran position.

[70] The subjects discussed under anthropology were the following: (1) the image of God, (2) the freedom of the will, (3) the constitution of man (dichotomy as opposed to trichotomy), (4) the origin of the soul (traducianism as opposed to creationism), (5) the immortality of the soul (that man does not perish like an animal but has an existence after death. This was not to be confused with Aristotelian or Platonic ideas), (6) the state of the soul after death (blissful fellowship with God rather than soul sleep, purgatory, etc.). These were the usual subjects, although not all were discussed by all the dogmaticians. The subject of sin was reserved for a special *locus.*

[71] Gerhard, *Loci Theologici,* IV, 18,239. Cf. Quenstedt, *Systema,* P.I, C.12, 5.1, Thesis 1 (1715 ed. I, 730).

tion, and there was no evidence then from extra-Biblical sources which might point to a different understanding of the text. And it is quite doubtful if any such considerations would have prompted them to change their interpretation.

They are satisfied with Luther's ingenuous historical approach to the narrative and they follow him very closely, trying to picture what might have taken place in those creation days, but satisfied that they were given in Scripture only the most fragmentary glimpse of the how of creation. Like Luther, they indulge in a good deal of homiletical application throughout their commentary, and we find them often praising the goodness and wisdom and power of God manifested in the account of creation.

Like Luther, they took for granted that the Biblical account of creation could actually tell us something about how God created the world and perhaps also something about our physical universe (after all, there can be no conflict between the book of nature and the book of Scripture). But only rarely do they become specific on this matter, and not so often as Luther did.[72] All in all, their discussions of the hexaemeron are not very original, not very spirited, and only bear out what they say when they speak in general of creation and its significance and use.

---

[72] We shall have occasion to return to this subject in our final chapter on the Lutheran world picture.

Divine Providence

CHAPTER SIX

In the final paragraph of his *locus* on creation Martin Chemnitz makes the following significant statement concerning the proper understanding of the doctrine.[1] "Creation must not be understood," he says, "in such a way that God left His handiwork, like a laborer who leaves a house when it has been finished or a ship when it has been constructed. In the article of creation we must always include God's continuous upholding and preserving of the things He has created. The church must understand that God is working every day in the world and that He embraces in a very special way and with fatherly kindness those to whom He has given His Word, defends them, upholds them, nourishes them, frees them from all dangers and troubles, and sees to it that they who seek the Lord shall not be in need of any good thing (Ps. 34:10)." At this point Chemnitz abruptly breaks off his discussion, realizing that he is no longer speaking of creation in the strict sense but of divine providence. And so it must be.

A Christian cannot speak of creation without speaking of providence. The Christian doctrine of creation in contrast to the doctrine of the philosophers includes the fact that God is active in the world now (Matt. 6:31; Acts 17:24-26). This is apparent in every Lutheran discussion of the subject. The doctrine of creation must be presented, says Chemnitz in the very beginning of his discussion of creation,[2] in such a way that it

---

[1] *Loci Theologici,* I, 108.
[2] Ibid., I, 102.

shows that God is present in His creation now, "acting with absolute freedom, sustaining His creation, and directing all things according to His great mercy and giving good things to us, helping us, and preventing secondary causes from harming us." This, says Chemnitz, is precisely how the Scriptures apply the doctrine of creation (Acts 17:22-28; Heb. 1:2-3; Col. 1:16, 17; 1 Tim. 6:17; 4:10), reminding us always that God is a living God who provides us daily with good things to enjoy (Psalms 100; 103; 125; 144). In the Fourth Petition we indicate our recognition of the fact that we do not live by fate but by the living God who scrupulously cares for us. Because it is difficult for the human mind to accept this fact, particularly in times of trouble, God challenges us to try Him, as it were, to commit our ways to Him (Ps. 37:5) and call on Him in every trouble. (Ps. 50:15)

It is in just such a context that the doctrine of providence is always seen and approached in Lutheran theology. Providence is viewed as God's ongoing creative activity, as God's *creatio continua*.[3] The Lutherans stress this point at great length; providence is never to be thought of as mere knowledge, precise and perfect knowledge, and awareness of all things, but it is an ἐνέργεια which extends to everything which is not God.[4] Just as there is no Christian doctrine of creation which does not lead directly to the providence of God — John Deutschmann says that a Christian "hastens" from the doctrine of creation to the article on God's providence[5] — so there can be no Christian doctrine of divine providence which is not seen as creative, as God's work, and His creative work exclusively.

---

[3] Dannhauer, *Hodosophia Christiana*, p. 307: "Nihil est aliud conservatio quam continua creatio." Also in the Biblical thought pattern, creation and providence belong inseparably together, according to Lutheran theology. In his comments on Is. 40:12 Schmidt says, "Fecit autem in creatione, cum omnia fecit in ordine, pondere & mensura, facitque hodie in conservatione, in qua omnia, ut creavit sustentat & portat." Sebastian Schmidt, *Commentarius super Illustres Prophetias Jesaiae* (Hamburg and Frankfurt, 1693), p. 349.

[4] Stephan Gerlach, *Theses de Providentia Dei* (Tübingen, 1591), p. A2r.

[5] John Deutschmann, *Disputatio Theologiae Biblicae de Providentia Divina ex Rom. XI.36* (Wittenberg, 1688), p. A1r. Very clearly Gerlach subsumes the doctrine of creation under providence and not vice versa. See *Theses de Providentia Dei*, p. A2v.

1. THE MEANING OF DIVINE PROVIDENCE

A typical definition of divine providence goes as follows:[6] "God's providence is His activity of knowing and seeing all things. In this way He cares for the entire world and every single creature in the world, both great and small; and He attends their movements, actions, and passions, that He might effectively and mercifully advance all things which are good, strictly contain and severely punish all evil, and bring all things to His glory and the salvation of pious men." There are a number of concerns voiced in this definition (such as the definite eschatological and soteriological purpose of divine providence) which we will trace later in this chapter. But the strongest emphasis is unquestionably the all-embracing nature of God's providence and the personal nature of His providence.

God's providence is an all-embracing activity. It applies to both nature and history (Heb. 11:3; Jer. 10:23; Acts 17:25).[7] Nothing is outside God's providence. He is intimately involved with everything that is and happens. This is precisely Paul's point in Rom. 11:36:[8] all things (τὰ ταύτα) are the object of God's providence. But providence is not only universal in the general sense that it extends to all things and all classes of things (Col. 1:17; Heb. 1:3). Providence is also very specific: it embraces everything individually, even the lowliest and despised of the creatures of God (Ps. 147:9),[9] the most trifling things as well as the noblest things. "For just as God continues to produce things of little value, He also takes care of them, since His care is nothing else than a continuous creation."[10]

God's providence is a personal activity of His.[11] It is not a force

---

[6] Brochmand, *Definitiones Articulorum Fidei*, p. A4.

[7] Bechmann, *Annotationes*, p. 295.

[8] Deutschmann, *Disputatio Theologiae Biblicae de Providentia Divina*, p. A3r.

[9] Hutter, *Loci Communes Theologici*, p. 218.

[10] Bechmann, *Annotationes*, p. 296.

[11] It was common for the Lutherans to cite Rom. 11:36 again at this point to show that providence like creation was a personal work of the Trinity. See Deutschmann, pp. A4r-B3r. The ἐξ αὐτοῦ, καὶ δι' αὐτοῦ, καὶ εἰς αὐτόν was taken as referring to the Three Persons of the Trinity, although the singular pronoun designates the one undivided essence. Thus the one God personally (ὑποστατικῶς) carries out His work of providence, as He did creation. The conclusion was that the ἐξ αὐτοῦ denotes the Father as the source of all things and the source of the care of all things. The διὰ αὐτοῦ denotes the Son who is often represented in

which has been set in motion and then operates according to predetermined laws. The God of providence is not a remote first cause, a *Deus ex machina*. Nor does providence mean only that God preserves what He has created and that He sustains those things which He has put in motion, such as the reproduction of life, the seasons, and the like (Matt. 4:4; Ps. 74:16). No. God actually enters personally and intimately into the affairs of nature and of men.[12] He enters the world directly, setting bounds to things and putting things in order — all things and things in particular, controlling events or limiting their effectiveness, encouraging and approving and actually effecting good actions among men, and prohibiting or directing or setting bounds to men's evil actions. God is directly and personally active in everyone's life (Job 10:8; Ps. 139:5) so that nothing in anyone's life happens by accident. (Job 14:5)

From this brief summary of the Lutheran understanding of providence we can perceive the great practical importance of the doctrine. The Lutheran teachers knew that they were not involved in any academic discussion at this point but were dealing with a matter of life and death for Christianity. The rule and lordship of the Creator God is at stake. Moreover, a good many principles and beliefs basic to Christianity and an ordered life and society are undermined if the providence of God is denied. Without divine providence we cannot depend on the orderly performance of nature. In fact there is no sense in nature at all, if God is not controlling all things, no purpose in nature or life, and therefore no possibility of indicating future events or of understanding and controlling nature. Furthermore, there can be no natural knowledge of God and no rationale for human behavior — for social and political action and ecclesiastical organization. Therefore, says Hutter,[13] he who denies divine providence can only become an Epicurean or a virtual atheist.

The fact is that by nature all men tend to be either Stoics or Epi-

---

Scripture as the means through whom all things were made and are now supported (John 1:3; 1 Cor. 8:6). The εἰς αὐτόν refers to the Spirit in whom all things have their termination. The idea was that in the first creation the Father "spoke" the creation of all things, the Son made all things spoken by the Father, and all this that the Spirit might behold the creation.

[12] Bechmann, *Annotationes*, p. 297. Hutter, *Loci Communes Theologici*, p. 218.

[13] Hutter, ibid.

cureans.[14] They see how often the wicked prosper and the pious suffer, and they despair of finding any sense in the world or in life. And so the doctrine of divine providence is a very difficult doctrine to hold. It is in every case an article of faith, Gerhard says; it cannot be observed or proved empirically. And so the Christian must simply trust that God's providence is absolutely righteous; and this is often learned only through suffering. (Job 21:7 ff.; Ps. 73:2)

The doctrine of providence is something like the doctrine of justification in Lutheran theology; it is easy to formulate but difficult to hold on to and apply. For this reason a great deal of discussion centered on the doctrine of providence. First, the Lutheran dogmaticians struggled with the problem of how best to present the doctrine. And there were a great number of rather original approaches. Second, they attempted to give answer to a large number of difficulties which the idea of providence introduced.

2. The Various Approaches to the Doctrine of Providence

The doctrine of providence was approached and presented in a variety of ways. There was a constant attempt on the part of the Lutheran dogmaticians to improve the presentation of their predecessors. It is doubtful, however, if any real improvement took place after Chemnitz.

a. *The Approach of John Gerhard*

The most elaborate and complicated — and the most unsatisfactory — treatment of providence is that of John Gerhard. He sees God's providence in terms of three distinct acts: (1) God's foreknowledge, (2) God's decrees, and (3) God's regulating and governing all things according to His power and wisdom and goodness.[15] Concerning God's *foreknowledge* Gerhard does not say a great deal that he had not already dealt with in his *locus* on God. The *decrees* of God (πρόθεσις, προορισμός) Gerhard understands as being carried out in Christ, e. g., His decree to send Christ, to save all who believe in Christ, the decree of election (Rom. 8:28; 9:11;

---

[14] Gerhard, *Loci Theologici,* IV, 132.
[15] *Loci Theologici,* IV, 55 ff.

Eph. 1:9, 11).[16] But by analogy he includes also God's *creatio continua* and preservation of all things as a decree, since "whatever God did in time He decreed to do in eternity."[17] Strictly speaking, since God's decrees are acts of goodness in Christ, they cannot embrace anything evil. God did not will or decree the fall of man. He foresaw evil, but He foresaw and decreed good, that is, everything which comports with His goodness.[18] Often Gerhard just speaks of two decrees in this context: creation (and

[16] The earlier Lutherans do not bring the decrees of God into their discussion of divine providence. It is interesting that Gerhard links providence especially with the decree of election. He discusses election immediately after his *locus* on providence, and subsumes election under the broader concept of providence. This seems a strange procedure for a Lutheran. Ordinarily election was treated much later in dogmatics, in the *locus* on soteriology (Quenstedt, Baier), after the stage had been set, as it were, for such a discussion. But Gerhard had set the stage for such a discussion to a certain extent. He had already discussed the person and work of Christ, and he introduces his treatment of predestination and election with a brief discussion of God's universal mercy, the soteriological purpose of God's creation of all men in Adam, and the universality of Christ's work of redemption. But he has not yet discussed man and sin. This somewhat illogical procedure is no doubt due to Gerhard's viewing predestination primarily in a formal sense as an act in eternity, a decree of God, to be reckoned with and established theologically before taking up the actual redemptive deeds of God in history. The older Lutherans, on the other hand, seldom call predestination a decree (The Formula of Concord, XI, calls predestination a decree only once) and view the doctrine functionally as a Gospel preachment.

[17] *Loci Theologici*, IV, 81.

[18] Gerhard is making a very delicate point at this juncture, and it is doubtful if he is very successful. The principle he is enunciating is obviously not meant to conflict with what he later says when he makes both election and reprobation decrees, and parallel decrees at that (*Loci Theologici*, IV, 215 ff.). God decrees to damn unbelievers, Gerhard says, but He does not will (according to His *voluntas antecedens*) that anyone perish. In making election and reprobation parallel decrees Gerhard is closer in a formal sense to Calvinism than to the Lutheranism of the Formula of Concord. The Calvinists thought that predestination embraced both election and reprobation (see Bartholomew Keckermann, *Systema Theologicum* [Geneva, 1602], C.1, p. 196). This was rejected by the Lutherans (see Calov, *Apodixis*, p. 326), yet they too make the two decrees parallel: the decree of election was κατὰ πρόγνωσιν *fidei, quod illos ab aeterno praevidit finaliter in Christum credituros* (ibid., p. 328) and the decree of damnation was *ex praevisa finali incredulitate* (ibid., p. 333). See also Hollaz, *Examen*, P.III, S.1, C.2, Q.6 (p. 655 [645]) where the parallelism is even more obvious: "The regenerate are elect κατὰ πρόγνωσιν, according to the foreknowledge of persevering faith in Christ. . . . Similarly the unregenerate are reprobate according to the foreknowledge of final unbelief by which the atonement of Christ is stubbornly rejected." Such a parallelism made election and reprobation like two species of one genus and would have been impossible for the earlier Lutherans who consistently made election Gospel and damnation Law and never brought the two concepts together in such a fashion. See Formula of Concord, SD, XI, 81.82.

providence) and restoration (redemption). The third distinct act of God's providence, according to Gerhard, is God's *sustenance* and loving care over all things — providence in the narrow sense. And here Gerhard discusses providence in the same way his forerunners (Chemnitz, Selnecker, Hutter) had done. It is clear throughout that Gerhard, as he attempts to put providence in its proper setting, differs from Chemnitz. Whereas the latter views providence as proceeding naturally from the doctrine of creation, Gerhard sees providence as belonging also within the context of God's foreknowledge and decrees (particularly predestination).

b. *The Approach of Nicolaus Selnecker*

Selnecker's approach to the doctrine of providence resembles Gerhard's in some respects but is much simpler. He begins with a definition of three degrees or grades or providences.[19] *First* is God's general or universal providence whereby He sustains and upholds all things, such as the orderly movements of heavenly bodies, regular rainfall, growth on the earth, etc. (Matt. 10:29; Acts 17:28; Col. 1:17; Psalms 24; 33). This is the very sense of *creatio continua;* for if God should withdraw His presence from His creation it would instantly perish.[20] *Second,* Selnecker speaks of God's *providentia specialis.* God not only sees and hears and sustains all things, but He guides and moderates all things so that they serve His purposes either to punish (Law) or to save (Gospel). All, even the most insignificant things, are thus regulated by Him; all things must comply with His will and execute His commands. *Third,* Selnecker speaks of God's *providentia peculiaris* which pertains to the elect who believe in Him. This pertains to God's work in the church. All things, all of nature, all events in history, every occurrence great and small, serve God's elect (Psalm 1; Matt. 10:30; Rom. 8:28-39; Ps. 36:5). This brings Selnecker to the subject of God's presence which, he feels, must be discussed in just

---

[19] *Institutiones Christianae Religionis,* II, 304 ff. Hutter follows the same line (*Loci Communes Theologici,* 218 ff.). Most of the later Lutherans follow Selnecker in speaking of these three grades of providence.

[20] Brochmand puts it well (*Commentarius in Epistolam ad Hebraeos,* p. 25): "All things would sink into nothing unless sustained by the Son of God. For just as they were founded by the Son they continue so long as they are kept from crumbling and perishing by the Son."

this context, and also the subject of election. He speaks of four modes of presence, as we have already seen; [21] but there are two modes which particularly pertain to God's providence. First is God's universal and repletive mode of presence whereby He is present to all things (Is. 66:1 ff.; Jer. 23:24; Psalm 139), above, beneath, outside, inside all things. Second is God's presence in His church through Word and promise — present in the hearts of His people; present with His power and Spirit; moving, protecting, forgiving, and saving His elect. Selnecker then breaks into a brief discussion of election as it is viewed in the light of the Gospel; and he touches a theme at this point which becomes very important in the Lutheran theology of providence, namely, that providence always has an evangelical and soteriological aim. It is not merely that God keeps things in order and guides all things according to His absolute wisdom, but He does all for our sake who are His children through faith in Christ — to strengthen and keep us in faith and confirm us in our love toward Him. (Rom. 8:28 ff.)

c. *The Approach of Stephan Gerlach*

Even more simple is the approach of Stephan Gerlach to the doctrine of divine providence. Gerlach presents God's providence under three aspects: creation, sustenance, and governance.[22] The *creatio prima* is viewed as an aspect of providence, that is, it is used to bolster and confirm the doctrine of providence. *Sustenance,* according to Gerlach, means that God preserves the beautiful order within His creation, for example, the orbits of the heavenly bodies, the seasons and fertility of the earth, the essential properties of things and in general His laws of nature. Sustenance means that God cares for us as He does for all things, and this involves individual and personal care and concern (Matt. 10:29-31). In a very special way this pertains to the church. *Governance,* according to Gerlach, is God's wise rule over all things. God as Lord controls and sets bounds for all things of past, present, and future sometimes directly Himself, sometimes by means of nature and secondary causes. In no sense is He bound by anything within the created order as He works providentially. In absolute freedom He controls and guides *(administrat)* all things *vel*

---

[21] See Selnecker, II, 314 ff. Cf. above, Chapter III, footnote 84, and Selnecker, III, 244.

[22] *Theses de Providentia Dei,* A2v.

secundum, vel contra vel super naturam.[23] For He has made asses speak and closed the mouths of lions and kept fire from burning. And even natural occurrences God puts to new uses — like eclipses and natural calamities. One sees in Gerlach's approach a very practical presentation of the doctrine of providence, geared again to the needs and comforts of God's people. What is important to him is that believers recognize God's absolute power and control over all nature and history and in need draw strength and comfort from this fact.[24]

d. *The Approach of Martin Chemnitz*

The most impressive treatment of divine providence is that of Martin Chemnitz.[25] Chemnitz approaches the notion of providence with the same very simple and practical purpose in mind as Gerlach, namely, to offer comfort to Christians in every exigency of life. He presents the doctrine of providence under several points, and his procedure is not very logical; but in an admirable way he achieves his main purpose which is to offer a broad Biblical picture of the doctrine and to make it as practical and comforting as possible.

Chemnitz begins with the observation that the providence of God receives special consideration in the church because of the false opinions of philosophers and agnostics who either reject it or distort the doctrine. He also notes that Christians in time of trouble or temptation sometimes doubt God's providence. But the doctrine holds great comfort for the believer, he says. What is so unique and comforting about the Christian doctrine of providence? And now, having posed this question, Chemnitz lists the many points which explain all that is involved in the doctrine.

(1) All things and events are directly present to God. He sees and knows and understands them all *now* (Ps. 33:13, 15; Ps. 34:15, 18; Ps. 73:11 passim; Ps. 94:11 ff.). This is not just some sort of detached observation on His part, but an attentive providence which includes God's intimate and loving care and lordship (Ps. 33:13, 15).[26] He helps those who pursue good and hinders the ways of the evil.

[23] Ibid., A4r.

[24] Ibid., A4v.

[25] *Loci Theologici,* I, 115 ff.

[26] This is often expressed by the Lutheran teachers. God never observes His creation or the affairs of men as a mere spectator, says Sebastian Schmidt *(Super*

(2) God upholds all things in their natural order and preserves His creation, and He does so as one present and active. (Ps. 119:91)

(3) It is a characteristic of God's providence to have individual concern with His creatures and with the individual needs of all. This should be the constant comfort of the Christian as he lives according to his calling in life.

(4) More precisely, God actually continually preserves and *assists* the order of things which has been established by Him. He not only allows the sun to rise, but He brings forth *His* sun (τὸν ἥλιον αὐτοῦ) each day, *He makes* it rise (ἀνατέλλει), Matt. 5:45 (cf. Is. 40:26). He does not just ordain that rain gather in clouds and come down on occasion, but He determines, He *sends,* the rain (Ps. 135:7; Jer. 10:13). To be sure, God instituted and set in motion the laws of nature, but not in such a way that He is some sort of spectator to what occurs, a remote cause far from it all. For instance, God has established the order of procreation; from the union of male and female men are born. Yet we still confess with Job 10:8: "Thine hands have made me and fashioned me together round about" (cf. Ps. 139:5, 13; Ps. 119:13). And so these laws, which are empirically discovered, dare not be used against what is known by faith, namely God's direct and causative activity in the disposition of all things. To be sure, God works through secondary causes, through an ordered creation; but *He is working,* preserving, upholding, and effecting all things. This means that many of the phenomena of life can be explained naturally and also according to God's direct providential activity.[27]

(5) Although providence extends to all created things, there are degrees, as it were, of providence; it pertains especially to human beings (1 Cor. 9:9). "God's providence in respect to all other creatures has its goal in man (Matt. 10:31; Rom. 8:20). It is because of the sin of man that nature has been subjected to vanity."[28] And in an even more special

Mosis Librum Primum, Genesis Dictum, Annotationes, p. 4), but God's seeing is always a preserving. "Et vidit Deus, quod bonum esset q.d. ideo conservavit, sicut creatum erat."

[27] Cf. Sebastian Schmidt, *In Librum Ijobi Commentarius* (Strasbourg, 1705), p. 1381. One considers an eclipse of the sun, Schmidt observes, and one can predict it and trace natural causes for it. But at the same time one sees it as a "wonderful work of God," that is, a direct providential activity.

[28] Chemnitz, *Loci Theologici,* I, 118.

sense providence pertains to the church of God. (Ps. 33:13, 18, 19; 1 Tim. 4:10)[29]

(6) God's providence is adjusted to different objects. For instance, in a mountain where no man goes, God cares for the animals by providing grass (Ps. 147:8, 9). But in a different way He cares for man, who is expected to be wise as he lives in God's creation (Matt. 10:16) and to live by the sweat of his brow. However, Scripture teaches that secondary causes avail nothing unless God adds His aid and blessing (Ps. 127:1; 1 Tim. 6:17). Therefore we should never put our trust in secondary causes, but only in the living God who gives us all things to enjoy.

(7) The irrational objects of providence possess a sort of propensity to fit into the providential activity of God (Ps. 104:27; 145:15). And it may be said that in their irrationality they understand the providence of God (Ps. 104:21) better than man who is beset by the darkness of sin. (Matt. 6:30)

(8) God is not enmeshed within the created order or bound by the laws of nature. Chemnitz says,[30] "God is not bound by secondary causes, as though He could do nothing more than appeal to these secondary causes. Apart from the order of usual secondary causes and contrary to the ordinary course of nature God is willing and able to help His church and punish the wicked, and all this in such a way that He either hinders, alters, mitigates, or overcomes secondary causes." He is not the god of the philosophers, says Chemnitz, who have taught a closed universe in which God does not or cannot move and act freely. But Scripture teaches all over that God is free to operate providentially within the created order. All this means three things to Chemnitz. First, whatever God does through secondary causes, He is able to do alone without them. Second, God is able to produce through secondary causes other effects than those which would ordinarily occur through secondary causes. Third, God is able to impede, alter, or soften the results of secondary causes even after they have been put into action. (Job 10:5-7; Rom. 4:19)

In Chemnitz's delineation of divine providence we find a very practical approach to the subject: Chemnitz is trying to inform the reader how the doctrine of providence can be used; He is showing the child of God how

[29] This is the emphasis of all the dogmaticians. See, for instance, Jacob Martini, *Synopsis Totius Religionis Photinianorum* (Wittenberg, 1633), p. 44.

[30] *Loci Theologici*, I, 118.

to draw comfort from the doctrine. His presentation, we notice, contains all the major points which the later Lutherans stressed. But his very last point underlines something which was not made quite so clear and emphatic by the others, namely, the importance of linking providence with God's absolute freedom and omnipotence. The article of divine omnipotence, according to Chemnitz, like the articles of divine omnipresence and divine wisdom, have as their main function to comfort the believer that he can rest secure in God's providence and that he can depend upon God in every way and under every circumstance. If necessary God will perform a miracle and break the laws of nature to answer the prayers of His people and help them in their need. God is unhampered and free, free to act wisely and lovingly; no matter how much the believer feels caught within the inexorable nexus of secondary causes, God is free and able to help him and is in fact doing so. To confirm the Christian in this conviction is the main purpose of teaching the doctrine of providence.

3. THE PROVIDENCE OF GOD AND THE PRESENCE OF GOD

Chemnitz's discussion of divine providence showed us that providence is a manifestation of God's power, according to Lutheran theology. From the presentation of Selnecker we observed previously that God's providence is a manifestation of His presence. And we noticed how Selnecker spoke of both God's repletive and gracious presence in connection with God's providence. We might recall also that a good deal of the concern of the Lutheran dogmaticians, as they treat God's presence so extensively in its usual place in dogmatics, was to safeguard His present and active governance over all things and especially His gracious protection of His church.

As Jörg Baur has remarked,[31] Lutheran theology never chooses to speak of God's presence according to empirical or philosophical categories, but, as Baur puts it, "in the Biblical sense as an operative personal presence." For instance, Quenstedt rejects the notion of divine presence according to the "philosophical sense," which on his definition denotes a "mere substantial nearness, an inactive continuity, that is, a closeness, a being there, or existence of an uncreated being in relation to a created

---

[31] *Die Vernunft zwischen Ontologie und Evangelium*, p. 106.

being." [32] No, in the Biblical sense divine omnipresence is "personal" and "operative," either in a general or a specific way, either in power or grace or glory (Gen. 1:2; Jer. 23:23; Col. 1:17; Acts 17:28, 29). God's presence to Quenstedt is an activity.

From such a dynamic idea of God's presence (which is nevertheless always substantial) we can see that Quenstedt has virtually identified God's presence with His providence *(concursus)* in this context. And in fact Quenstedt calls God's omnipresence here an *actus providentiae.* Later Quenstedt calls God's omnipresence an "activity" of divine providence, or "personal presence" to all of God's creatures, a presence illocal, undivided, or uncircumscribed in nature or mode (Gen. 1:2; Ps. 139:7 ff.; Acts 17:27, 28).[33] And this presence, he says, corresponds exactly *(coincidit)* with that element of divine providence called "divine concurrence," whereby God actively invades *(influit)* His creation, as it were.

This means the following, according to Quenstedt: [34] "God not only empowers secondary causes (sets in motion the laws of nature) and upholds them, but He directly enters into the action and operation of a creature in such a way that the effect is accomplished not by God alone or by the creature alone or by God in part and by the creature in part, but it is accomplished by God and the creature in one complete working power with God as the universal and first cause and man as the participating and secondary cause."

God is always the efficient cause of any concurrence of causes, and this in the sense that all activity has its origin in and is sustained by the *present and acting God.* True, in a certain sense the heavenly bodies may be called the universal causes of the actions of the sublunaries, but in respect to God they are subordinate causes.

All this discussion of God's active presence means in simple language that God, who is present everywhere and unfettered by space or place or any created secondary cause, is also actively engaged in upholding all things. He has His hand in everything. And so the practical application of God's presence is found in the proclamation of divine providence.

[32] *Systema,* P.I, C.13, S.1, Thesis 10, nota (I, 532).
[33] *Systema,* P.I, C.13, S.1, Thesis 16 and nota (I, 532).
[34] Ibid., P.I, C.13, S.1, Thesis 15, nota (I, 531).

4. PROVIDENCE AND CHRIST'S KINGDOM

Although there are certain manifestations in nature and history which point to God's providence, only the Christian can make use of God's providence effectively. For the Christian, Chemnitz reminds us,[35] depending upon God's testimonies to the church, sees God graciously ruling and intervening in His creation in order to forgive men their sins for Christ's sake. To Chemnitz the doctrines of creation and providence are meaningful only when viewed from the perspective of the Gospel. This important emphasis is not so apparent in the later dogmaticians until we read further into their works. But they too make it clear that divine providence, to be fully understood and appreciated, must be seen in the light of Christ's work which culminated in His exaltation, His glorious ascension to the right hand of power (1 Peter 3:22).[36] For His exaltation is complete; He is exalted above all creatures (Eph. 1:20-22). It is the incarnate and exalted Christ, Christ the Savior of all men, who rules over all things.

And so the Lutheran notion of providence is very closely related to the doctrine of Christ's kingdom of power. Like an Atlas, Christ upholds all things by the Word of His power.[37] He is the great אֵל גִּבּוֹר (Is. 9:5), מוֹשֵׁל (Micah 5:1), παντοκράτωρ (Rev. 16:14), the Lord of all (Acts 10:36). His dominion is absolutely unlimited, and exercised over all creatures without exception (Ps. 8:7-9; 1 Cor. 15:27-28). So closely is Christ's reign of power associated with providence that the two are at times practically equated by Quenstedt. He says,[38] "Christ's reign of power consists in this, that He rules and upholds as one who is present and absolutely powerful both in heaven and earth, that He subjects all creatures to Himself and rules according to both natures in the midst of His enemies." Although it is the incarnate and exalted Christ who now rules, still from the beginning He has ruled all things as the Son of God. (John 17:5)

---

[35] *Loci Theologici*, I, 104.

[36] Quenstedt, *Systema*, P.III, C.3, Memb. 2, S.1, Thesis 69 ff. (III, 264 ff.).

[37] Ibid. See also Brochmand, *Commentarius in Epistolam ad Hebraeos*, p. 25.

[38] Quenstedt, ibid., Thesis 72 (III, 264). Cf. Baier's statement (Baier-Walther, III, 128): "Regnum *potentiae* est, quo Christus huic universo potenter dominatur, idque conservat et providentissime gubernat. Ideoque subditi in hoc regno sunt omnes creaturae."

For Quenstedt it is most important to recognize that it is Christ our substitute and brother, Christ the Savior, who now rules all things. And He rules for our sake, for the sake of His church.[39] The kingdom of grace and the kingdom of power belong together at this point; the *creatio continua* and the ongoing saving activity of Christ are *una numero potestas.* The kingdom of power and of grace and of glory is one kingdom *(regnum)* embracing as its *objectum* "absolutely all creatures." Christ is Lord of all things in heaven and in earth and under the earth (Phil. 2:9-10), and all things are put under His feet that He might be Head of the church (Eph. 1:22). This is no cosmic redemption in the modern sense, no incipient universalism, which Quenstedt advocates here. He is simply linking redemption with creation and insisting that the latter is made to serve the former by the exalted Christ. This is seen by the fact that Quenstedt, when referring to Christ's rule in general, refers to His activity of grace:[40] His rule is in the world, but it transcends the world, being infinite and eternal; it is not a mundane rule, but spiritual and heavenly, and therefore not always perceived. But Christ's rule — and at this point Quenstedt is primarily thinking of Christ's kingdom in the New Testament sense as His gracious rule [41] — is a divine rule in the strictest sense; it is universal, omnipotent, carried out with absolute wisdom; and it is not a rule *in absentia,* but Christ the God-man "is present personally, near and actively at hand . . . among all creatures and every creature both in heaven and on earth." [42]

We see at this point how very closely Christ's (or God's) presence, His rule over all, and His redemptive activity are linked in Lutheran theology. God's presence and His providence cannot be viewed *nude* as something inactive, but always dynamically and in the light of their goal which is eschatological and soteriological, namely God's glory and our glory.[43] *Regnum potentiae ad regnum gratiae ordinatum.*[44] All creation is seen as being in the service of the Gospel and of those who believe it.

[39] Quenstedt, ibid.

[40] Ibid., Thesis 63, obs. 1 (III, 262).

[41] Quenstedt identified the kingdom here with the Gospel. See ibid., Thesis 78, obs. 1 (III, 265): "The Gospel is the Gospel of the kingdom."

[42] Ibid., Thesis 63, obs. 3 (III, 262).

[43] Ibid., Thesis 73 (III, 265).

[44] Ibid., Thesis 77 (III, 267).

For it is within the created order [45] and through the social orders (church, state, and home) [46] which are also instituted and sustained in the world by God that the Gospel, the kingdom of grace, comes to man. "It is," says Quenstedt, [47] "the Messiah who exercises dominion over the whole circle of the earth, but He rules especially those with whom He has made covenant, who have been washed clean in His blood and freed from the rule of Satan." And so we see that in Lutheran theology the doctrine of creation and providence is viewed from the perspective of the Gospel and applied evangelically.

5. The Problems with Divine Providence

The doctrine of divine providence has always opened up a long series of vexing questions. Why is there evil, if God's providence extends to all things? Why does a good and omnipotently providential God allow sin at all? Since evil exists, does God concur with it? What becomes of man's freedom in the light of divine providence? Can man resist God, if divine providence is always totally in control? Is divine punishment justified, if God upholds and supports all things? And what about the problem of God's hardening some men?

Many of the Lutheran dogmaticians make no attempt to answer all of these questions. They rather emphasize their belief in God's providence in spite of these difficulties, for, after all, divine providence is an article of faith. It is certain that the problems encountered by their adherence to the doctrine do not provoke the Lutherans to modify their doctrine in the slightest. The problems did however in some cases call forth a good deal of discussion and a more precise, if not always more satisfactory, statement of the Christian position. As we might expect, the earlier Lutherans like Chemnitz and Gerlach offer rather simple answers to the problems and remain closely within a Biblical framework. The later Lutheran dogmaticians go more deeply into some of the difficulties and give serious attention to the problems and to the answers given. Why? Be-

---

[45] Ibid., Thesis 84 (III, 270): "Locus regni gratiae est mundus."

[46] Baier-Walther, III, 724 ff.

[47] Quenstedt, loc. cit., Thesis 77 (III, 267).

cause of the inherent importance of the matter. To deny providence is to deny that God is a living God; it is to deny the Christian faith.

a. *The Cause of Sin*

The doctrine of divine providence raises the question of the cause of sin. The Augsburg Confession had dealt with this problem in a very naive manner by saying simply (Article XIX): "Our churches teach that although God creates and preserves nature, the cause of sin is the will of the wicked, that is, of the devil and ungodly men. If not aided by God, the will of the wicked turns away from God, as Christ says in John 8:44, 'When the devil lies, he speaks according to his own nature.'" This is the only thing the Lutheran Confessions mention in connection with God's providence and the problem of sin and its cause.

Chemnitz seeks to follow this very simple approach by voicing a plain categorical denial that God is the cause of sin. He refuses to consider the various logical and philosophical aspects of the problem, but on the basis of such Scriptures as 1 John 2:16 and Genesis 1 he insists that the origin of evil lies not in God but in the devil and the evil will of evil men. He says,[48] "With both hands, indeed with all our hearts, we must hold to this true and pious opinion, that God is not the author of sin. He does not will sin, He does not coerce those who will to sin, nor does He approve of sin. No, rather He is indeed terribly angry with sin, as He declares so often in His Word, by the continuous punishments and miseries He sends upon the world and by His threats of eternal wrath. This wrath against sin has been demonstrated by the Son of God in a particular way when He came to become a sacrifice for sin and to show that the devil was the author of sin and to appease by His death the overwhelming wrath of the Father."

This is a very instructive statement: the wrath of God against sin, poured out against the Son, is God's supreme act of love and at the same time the strongest testimony against the suggestion that God could in any sense be the cause of sin. Again the suggestion is that the problems connected with providence are solved in the cross of Christ, in the Gospel.

But Chemnitz goes on. To be sure, he says, God upholds all things, even the fallen world, and He knows all things, all the sins of men.

[48] *Loci Theologici,* I, 127 ff. See also Gerhard, *Loci Theologici,* IV, 87—132.

But He does not will evil or sin and is in no sense the cause of it. "God foresees the transgression of Saul," he says,[49] "but He does not will it to happen nor does He move Saul's will. Rather He permits the will of Saul to function in such a way that unhindered it does the opposite of what He wills. Yet all the time God marks off the point where Saul will be held in check. Meanwhile this foreknowledge *(praevisio)* does not bring about necessity nor does it change the will of man as man acts in a certain way."

Stephan Gerlach makes the same kind of observation. He says,[50] "God does not will evil actions, nor does He approve them, but He does permit them, set bounds to them, and restrain them." God's foreknowledge of evil does not make Him the cause of evil, Gerlach insists. True, God hardens men,[51] blinds them, punishes sin with sin, but always for a righ-

---

[49] Chemnitz, ibid.

[50] *Theses de Providentia Dei,* p. 9.

[51] The Lutheran theologians never tone down the Biblical theme of God's hardening, a theme which seemed to make God the cause of sin. However, in their opinion, such hardening is not imposed by God arbitrarily but as a result of man's sin and hardening. This is seen in the example of Herod, who first hardened himself, and then God hardened him (Bechmann, *Annotationes,* p. 307). At the suggestion of Satan a man willingly hardens and blinds himself, and God allows such a man to do so and abandons him to his own blindness. Bechmann says: "Atque ita Diabolus suggerit: Homo consentit: Deus deserit." Calov states the paradox which seems apparent in the issue even more baldly. God hardens the sinner and does not always give repentance, Calov says (*Systema,* II, 554), but the cause of any lack of repentance is always the man himself, who out of indifference or neglect or malice puts off repentance. God meanwhile is always active in His grace, calling sinners, and inviting them to repentance. According to Calov, the fact that God permits sin in no sense implies that He condones it or is the cause of sin. At this point he chides Peter Martyr, who said that when God removes His grace in certain instances from sinners, he was in a certain sense *(aliquo modo)* the cause of sin. It is doubtful whether Martyr, a Calvinist, really differs with Calov on this point, however. Martyr offers a tremendously long discussion to show that God is not the cause of sin. See Peter Martyr, *Loci Communes* (Zürich, 1580), p. 53 ff. If God were the author of sin, he asks, why would He forbid it and punish it? It is in the context of God's permitting sin that Martyr says things which are objectionable to Calov. "God rules and governs sin," Martyr says (ibid. p. 57), but in the sense that sins "cannot escape the providence of God." Thus God ruled the obdurate Herod. Herod was the cause of his own rebellion. God is said to have hardened him — but in the sense that He overruled his sin and used it for His own glory. In no sense does Martyr imply that God is the cause of sin — he even shuns the idea that God is the cause of the cause of sin — but follows the same traditional line as Calov. It seems that Calov has been unfair at this point. Calov believed that the Calvinistic doctrine of predestination made God the author of sin, and he thought that this would be apparent also in the Calvinistic doctrine of providence. At times the whole discussion of the cause of sin was turned into a polemic against Calvinism. For instance, Andrew Schaafman

teous cause. And in the end *all* things, bad and good, serve His purpose (Acts 2:23; Gen. 39:17-23; 45:5). This is an immensely comforting doctrine, Gerlach believes. All things are blessings to those who hold to God. For His good and gracious will always wins out. God's providence is seen not only as an act of omnipotence but as an act also of utter goodness. "God wishes," says Gerlach, "to be known and recognized as one who is omnipotent and absolutely glorious in all His acts of providence, and also as one who is good and well disposed toward men." And Gerlach, like Chemnitz, leaves it at that — in a paradox with no real attempt to harmonize God's goodness and omnipotence, except to say that they are united in God's providence. This is the same ingenuous practice also of Calov [52] who appeals simply to the Biblical evidence that God tempts no one (James 1:13-14), that He is essentially good and holy (1 John 1:5), and that all His works are good and right (Deut. 32:4; James 1:17). And God's benevolent providence infers that God cannot be called the cause of sin, not even *per accidens*.

b. *Providence and Contingency*

Does providence destroy contingency in the universe and in the affairs of men? Again the dogmaticians with one voice answer no. And again Chemnitz offers the most simple and unsophisticated answer to the problem. He says,[53] "That God upholds nature does not oppose contingency and human freedom. Eve's will was the cause of her action. For freedom of choice was a gift bestowed at creation upon the human race, and divine sustentation did not violate that gift. Also today our freedom, however great, is not hindered by divine sustentation; but God upholds Saul as he is, and the will of Saul is itself the cause of his evil action." [54] The sig-

---

said that all the problems related to divine providence can be solved by upholding three basic Biblical principles: (1) that God earnestly wishes to save all who have fallen into sin and death, (2) that Christ the Redeemer was sent for all and died for all, and (3) that the Gospel promises are for all. Many of the Lutherans, however, never bring the Calvinists into the discussion. See Andrew Schaafman, *Libri II Controversiarum de Peccatorum Causis* (Frankfurt, 1597), p. H4r.

[52] *Systema,* II, 354.

[53] *Loci Theologici,* I, 129. Cf. I, 145.

[54] When Chemnitz speaks of freedom here he refers only to that limited freedom which the unregenerate man has in his fallen state, "a sort of freedom in that to some extent he can maintain outward discipline." See Martin Chemnitz, *Examen Concilii Tridentini,* ed. Edward Preuss (Berlin, 1861), pp. 129—44;

nificant thing about this brief statement is that Chemnitz makes no effort to harmonize providence and contingency, but only to state the paradox rather starkly.

Hutter [55] goes more deeply into the problem. He insists that he is speaking of contingency and necessity from a Biblical and not a strictly logical point of view. Hutter lists three grades of necessity which appear to have some Scriptural warrant. (1) There is the necessity for certain things which have been divinely predicted. (2) There is a necessity for certain things which arise from immutable causes. (3) There is a necessity for those things which are true, although contingent. It is this last category wherein a contradiction seems hidden. Here God's providence and contingency seem to be at odds. For example, Jesus says that there must be offenses, and Paul says that there must be heresies. Here are examples of things taking place immutably, and yet not by absolute necessity, but only *ex accidente*, conditioned by divine foreknowledge. With all this intricate and involved terminology Hutter is really only trying to affirm two Biblical themes: (1) the reality of divine providence, and (2) man's responsibility and guilt for his own sinful actions. His discussion becomes somewhat more edifying as he addresses himself next to a single disturbing case from Scripture, namely, Judas' betrayal of Christ.

According to divine providence this betrayal must be regarded as necessary (according to a *necessitas consequentiae*,[56] that is, a conditional necessity), for God saw from eternity that Judas by his persistent ill will and by a definite plan would betray Christ. But from the point of view of contingency Judas was able to resist the desires of his depraved will and not betray Christ. However, if Judas had resisted this temptation, then God would have seen this from eternity and thus again the providence of God would not and could not have failed. This discussion does not really solve anything, for it begs the question. But at least Hutter, like Chemnitz, has focused our attention on the paradoxical nature of the Biblical evidence

Loci Theologici, I, 183 ff. Lutheranism held that the unregenerated man has no freedom to approach God or please Him, but his will was bound to sin.

55 Hutter, *Loci Communes Theologici,* p. 228.

56 Hutter is using the same distinction as Anselm here between a *necessitas praecedens, quae causa est, ut sit res* and a *necessitas sequens, quam res facit.* See Anselm de Cantorbery, *Pourquoi Dieu S'est Fait Homme,* trad. ed. René Reques (Paris: Les Editions du Cerf, 1963), II, 17 (p. 434).

relative to the problem and on the importance of maintaining both God's providence which is infallible and man's freedom.

That there is contingency in the universe does not mean that things happen by chance. Chance implies that there is no meaning or purpose in the universe. But this is never the case. If a man is a hunchback or deaf and dumb, this is not something that happened by chance without any reason. "No," says Gerlach,[57] "it is not by chance that a man stands, sits, gets up, walks (Ps. 139:3), that a single hair falls from the head (Luke 21:18), that a sparrow flies up or down. Even when lots are deposited in a jar the reading of them is regulated by God." Such a rejection of chance, Gerlach maintains, does not support any theory of fate or determinism, as if there were no contingency, as if Christian prayers were useless and all God's threats and promises pointless. The doctrine of determinism and any derivative of it is blasphemy against God and His providence.

A *via media* must be maintained between absolute determinism and the doctrine that things happen by sheer chance. This *via media* is found in the Christian understanding of contingency. Contingency exists in all things outside God.[58] But necessity exists in all things as they pertain to God and His providence — not a simple or coercive necessity (*necessitas coactionis*) but a hypothetical necessity which is dependent upon God's providence. For God sees all things according to their goal. Again this fact does not violate our freedom of movement. For God's knowing all things does not predetermine them. God does not force us to act. But even the sins of men are controlled by God in such a way that even the worst designs are changed to the advantage and welfare of the godly.[59] This is what the Lutheran teachers mean when they say that contingency in human affairs does not oppose divine providence but is subject to it and subordinate to it.

c. *Providence and the Circumstances of a Man's Death*

In accordance with His providence God has determined the length of every man's life, and He established the time and circumstances of

---

[57] *Theses de Providentia Dei*, p. 22.

[58] Ibid., p. 23.

[59] Hutter, *Loci Communes Theologici*, pp. 229—30.

every man's death. This fact is perfectly consistent with contingency and with man's freedom, according to the Lutheran teachers. But how are the ideas of providence and contingency reconciled in this particular case? Bechmann [60] deals at some length with this particular problem; and because his remarks bring into sharp relief certain aspects of the doctrine of providence, we shall trace his discussion. He begins by resorting to a distinction. He differentiates between God working through *ordinary, general providence,* according to general laws and the course of nature, and God working through *special, extraordinary providence,* apart from secondary causes and the course of nature. And this distinction lies behind his entire discussion.

According to the first kind of providence God sets the limits to a man's life according to the contingent circumstances of the natural realm, including the man's own temperament and secondary causes. From eternity God foresees every man's hereditary characteristics and how each man will be permitted by environment to conduct his life. And so God determines events to occur in accordance with this foreknowledge. For instance, as God foresaw in His omniscience that a certain man would have a good disposition and good health and could reach 60 years of age, He determined *(decrevit)* to allow that particular man's characteristics and the natural course of secondary causes to concur so that the man reach just such an age. However, if God foresaw a man who could live to be 60 but was totally intemperate and careless, God would not prevent such a person from sinning and exposing Himself to danger and thus losing his life before 60 years of age. In all this God is working through *ordinary providence.*

But God at the same time determines the circumstances and time of a man's death according to His special and *extraordinary providence.* For He who is the First Cause is not bound by secondary causes, nor is He compelled to make use of them; but He works freely apart from secondary causes and the usual course of nature, shortening or lengthening life according to His grace or judgment *(ex gratia vel ex ira).* In His grace God lengthens the lives of His people or sometimes shortens them to spare them the dangers and miseries to which they would be subject (Is. 57:1-2). In His wrath He often enters into history and shortens the lives of tyrants or evil doers (Ps. 55:23). The termination of man's life, how-

[60] *Theologia Polemica,* p. 331 ff.

ever, does not happen by absolute necessity, but by what Bechmann calls hypothetical necessity. It was a necessity dependent upon God's fore-knowledge and decision.

It appears that Bechmann has not really solved anything by the expediency of his distinction. He has, however, through the distinction which seems paradoxical underlined two very important points in Lutheran creation theology. First, he has noted that God as creator has established an order of creation which is consistent and reliable, which man can search and understand and over which man can gain dominion. Second, he has stressed the equally important fact that God is not bound by the order of creation. And it is Bechmann's point that this freedom of God over all creation is not merely a freedom in principle but a freedom which God actually exercises. God actually enters into history with acts of judgment and mercy — acts which control or suspend or violate secondary causes. The *first* point Bechmann stresses in order to preserve man's responsibility to exert dominion over nature, for example, to discover and use medicine to prolong and save life. The *second* point he maintains to preserve a very realistic doctrine of God's active personal presence in His creation, a providential activity whereby God hears and is responsive to the needs and prayers of His people even to the point of prolonging their days by turning the course of history or nature. (1 Kings 19:5; Jonah 4:6; Is. 38:2-5)

d. *Divine Concurrence with Sin*

Probably the most persistent and troublesome problem connected with the doctrine of divine providence centered in the relation of providence to the ongoing daily sins of men — in the question how divine providence concurred with the evil actions of men. This was a tricky question. It could not be answered in any way which would imply that God willed sin, for then God would be made to contradict Himself and His goodness. On the other hand, the question could not be answered in any Manichaean manner which would make sin independent of God and place it beyond His control. Concerning this second matter the Lutherans were all very emphatic in their insistence that God works all things in all, that even the devil and the wicked exist in Him and cannot act without Him.[61]

---

[61] The Lutheran dogmaticians, especially the earlier ones (see Chemnitz, *Loci Theologici*, I, 145), are most anxious to show that the unlimited sovereignty

The problem was to reconcile this fact with God's concurrence with sin. Sensing the danger, Bechmann once more falls back upon the expediency of a distinction as he attempts to grapple with the problem.[62] He distinguishes between sin viewed *materially* as an objective positive act (this would include also sins of omission, since such sins were always involved with an act) and sin viewed *formally* as wickedness *(deformitas)*, as an immoral act. Nothing can happen without God's concurrence, Bechmann insists. Therefore it must be said that He concurs with sinful actions viewed materially as mere actions. However, because God in His goodness never takes pleasure in iniquity (Ps. 5:4) and in His righteousness loves righteousness (Ps. 11:7) and is so offended by sin that He sends His Son as a payment for it, He must not be said to be the cause of sin. But He concurs with sin only in the sense of allowing it.[63] And even as He permits it, He sets limits for sin, and in His providence uses it as a blessing or as a judgment. The classic example of such divine concurrence with sin is the crucifixion of Christ; here is an example of the most horrible hatred and rejection of God and at the same time of God's merciful guidance.

Gerhard's discussion of the problem of concurrence is far more thorough than Bechmann's or any of the other Lutherans' and for this reason is more satisfactory.[64] His approach is not to solve the problem by resorting to distinctions but to list what he thinks are several basic Biblical principles, or data, relative to the problem. With such an approach he does not solve the problem, strictly speaking, but he does offer a more *Biblical* answer to the problem, so far as Scripture gives any answer at all. He finds seven motifs which seem to relate to the problem of God's concurrence with the evil actions of men.

of God is opposed to any form of Manichaeism. The doctrine that God controlled wisely all things, even the forces of darkness, was considered to be a source of great comfort and reassurance in times of trouble and suffering. To stress this comfort was precisely Paul's point in Col. 1:16, as he says that all things were created and exist by Christ and for Him. The κυριότητες, ἀρχαί, and ἐξουσίαι, according to Gerhard, include also the demons and show the absolute sway of Christ's rule and control over all things. See John Gerhard, *Annotationes Posthumae in Epistolam ad Colossenses* (Jena, 1660), p. 34 ff.

[62] Bechmann, *Theologia Polemica,* p. 349 ff.

[63] Chemnitz, (*Loci Theologici,* I, 145) employs the picture from Is. 54:16 at this point: God creates the smith, but when he forges weapons against God, he does so without God.

[64] *Loci Theologici,* IV, 87—99.

(1) God sees and knows all that transpires, and no evil escapes Him. (Ecclus. 23:18-19)

(2) God upholds all creation (Acts 17:28) in His goodness, and this even when man falls into sin. Meanwhile men always have the opportunity to return to God in repentance.[65]

(3) Divine providence concurs with evil actions in the sense that it permits them. What exactly is meant by this *permissio,* a notion which we have run across throughout our survey of the Lutheran doctrine of providence? Gerhard answers,[66] "God as a matter of fact does not will sin, but He also does not prevent it; this in effect is His permission. Now God does not against His will allow sin, but allows sin willingly. However, His permission and His will pertain to two different objects. Permission pertains to sin itself. God's will refers to the final outcome of the action toward which God in His wisdom will guide the action." This point Gerhard believes becomes clear when one traces the analogy of Scripture as it treats God's dealing with sinful men. God's hardening recorded in Rom. 1:24 will be seen in the light of His *permissio* in Acts 14:16 (cf. Deut. 28:28 with Hos. 4:16). Examples of this divine concurrence with sin, according to this overall picture whereby God permits sin but controls it and turns it to His good purpose, are common in Scripture according to Gerhard. (Ps. 81:12-14 and 1 Cor. 10:13)

But does not the notion of divine *permissio* conflict with the sovereignty of God's providence? Does the notion not suggest that there are things with which God does not concur? [67] Gerhard's comments thus far have been calculated to show that such a charge is unfounded. *Permissio* must always be viewed in the light of final causes which occur according to God's sovereign providence. But lest there be misunderstanding he faces the problem head on. He says,[68] "That God permits sin must never be

[65] An implicit distinction lies behind this second point, namely the distinction between an action and a sinful action. See ibid., IV, 96: "The action as action is not sin. Otherwise all actions would be sin. But the wickedness and defect in the action is sin. Furthermore, the wickedness and defect do not arise from a universal cause, but from the proximate cause, namely the will of man."

[66] Gerhard, ibid., IV, 96. Cf. IV, 100.

[67] Gerhard charges Theodore Beza with just such objections to the notion of *permissio.* See Theodore Beza, *Ad Acta Colloquii Montischelgardensis Tubingae Edita Theodori Bezae Responsionis Altera* (Geneva, 1588), II, 182 passim. I have been unable to find Beza making such objections.

[68] *Loci Theologici,* IV, 100.

understood as though Divine Providence is weakened even in the slightest degree. This is not the permission of one who is unaware of what is happening — for God knows of men's sins and for wise reasons of His own does not prevent them from happening. Neither is this the permission of one who is unwilling, if by unwilling you mean that God is forced into something — for just as God forces no one to sin, so no one by his sins can force God into anything. No, God disapproves and detests sins and in this sense is correctly said not to will sins; and it is proper to believe this. Neither is this the permission of one who does not care — for God sets limits to evil actions and brings good forth from them." The providence by which God permits evil actions and concurs with them is, according to this statement, totally omniscient (God is completely aware of what is happening) and good (God brings forth a good result from what is happening). Gerhard feels that on such a basis the providence of God has been completely safeguarded, as one teaches the doctrine of *permissio.*

(4) God concurs with evil actions by deserting the evildoer. Such abandonment of the sinner can only be called concurrence in a very broad sense. For we usually think of abandonment as a reaction against sin rather than a concurrence with it. Gerhard understands this, and feels that the theme of God's abandonment of the sinner must be brought into the broad discussion of His concurrence with sin. He insists that such abandonment is not in any sense the cause of sin, although when God abandons the sinner, he often persists in his sin. For instance, the fall of Adam was not the result of God's abandoning him but was itself the cause of God's abandoning him. And so it always is. Today too "when man resists the Holy Spirit and plunges into sin, God in His grace abandons the man and takes from him what He gave." (Cf. 1 Sam. 15:26 with 1 Sam. 16:14. Also Is. 5:4-6) [69]

It is significant what Gerhard has said at this point: the two examples he cites from Scripture are simple cases of divine judgment against those who have turned against God; and yet Gerhard says that God "in His grace" abandons those who rebel against Him. This is no contradiction to Gerhard, for he views all of God's acts of judgment in this sense of abandonment as having a gracious purpose. In this sense Gerhard can speak in the same way of God abandoning Job and Paul and the Jews,

[69] Gerhard, IV, 97.

though Job and Paul were believers, according to Gerhard, and the Jews not. Gerhard considers God's abandoning of any man always to be corrective in purpose, a sort of gracious medicine which is divinely applied in order that sinners might be brought to repentance. God in His providence summons nature and history to aid Him in His ongoing redemptive purpose toward fallen men.

(5) God concurs with evil actions when He delivers a sinner over to Satan. In this case God acts as a just judge, but only after man has brought destruction upon himself. And as the sinner's sins increase, God punishes sin with sin (cf. Ezek. 14:9 with Jer. 14:14). Whereas God's abandoning of the sinner (in point 4) was marked as an act of grace, there can be no mention of grace as God delivers the sinner to Satan and punishes sins with sins. Here God is concurring with the sins of a man whose period of grace is over, even while he lives.

(6) Divine providence concurs with evil actions by restricting and setting limits to such actions. An example of this is the case of Job. According to His redemptive purpose God fixes limits to men's sins and to the evil which can befall man.

(7) God concurs with evil actions in order to bring forth good from these evil actions according to His gracious purpose (Is. 10:5-12). His omnipotence and wisdom is a gracious omnipotence and wisdom at work always to bless men (for example, God's guiding the life of Joseph).

By mentioning the seven Biblical motifs (which overlap each other a bit) as they relate to the subject of God's concurrence with sin, Gerhard has not settled the logical difficulties connected with the problem. To say that God concurs with sin not by willing sin as such but by permitting it immediately raises the question, why does God permit men to sin at all? Gerhard considers this question too, but again he replies in such a way that he does not face the logical difficulties of the question. He merely says that God, as He allows men to sin, reveals Himself to men as wise and mighty and good and merciful and righteous. As He permits sin He is instructing the sinner to trust in Him and nothing else, to solicit His help in all trouble, to praise Him for His wisdom and goodness, and through suffering to see beauty in life and all creation.[70] This is a Biblical answer as far as it goes, but does not, strictly speaking, answer the question,

---

[70] Gerhard, *Loci Theologici,* IV, 99.

why does God permit sin? No doubt Gerhard did not want to go further into the problem than to mention what Scripture says relative to it. He realizes that he could not go further into it; for ultimately the problem remains, as it did for Job, unsolvable; one must simply believe that the God who permits sin is both gracious and sovereignly provident. Luther would have answered the question in his bald, paradoxical, almost impatient fashion. But this was not the way of the dogmaticians and especially the later ones. Why these theologians were so much more bothered by the problems connected with providence than were the Lutheran Confessions is hard to say. There were no overt controversies which opened up such questions. The answer may lie simply in the increasing tendency to systematize and answer questions.

It might have been kinder to the Lutheran dogmaticians of the post-Reformation era to have omitted their discourses on the problems related to divine providence. Their answers were closely oriented to Scripture, it is true, as they struggle with these problems, but they provide us with little more insight into the nature of God's providence than we already gained from studying their simple Biblical presentation of the doctrine. Furthermore, the preoccupation with these problems (which is really a chapter in apologetics) may tend to make providence itself a problem rather than a mighty manifestation of the living God's *creatio continua* and an activity carried out in the service of God's soteriological purposes. This is said not so much in criticism of their doctrine, which we have tried to show was in many ways impressive as well as Biblical, as of their method of dealing with the doctrine which either bores the reader or distracts him from the main theme.

The Lutheran World Picture

CHAPTER SEVEN

The doctrine of creation and providence immediately raises the question of a world picture. For everyone who believes in creation and providence will have some sort of world picture. It will be a theological world picture, to be sure, based upon God's revelation in the book of Scripture, and not a scientific world picture based upon experience from the book of nature. But since the book of Scripture and the book of nature are both from God and agree with each other, it follows that the Christian doctrine of creation will answer some cosmological questions of tremendous moment, for instance: the genesis and purpose of the universe, the relation of God to the universe, the relation of man to the universe, and the relation of man as a part of the universe to God. These are theological answers, to be sure, but they pertain to the real world, the world also of science, and alone can be the solid basis for a correct and Christian outlook toward life and the world. For this reason a Christian creation theology cannot be indifferent to the recurring cosmologies and world pictures developed by the scientists and philosophers through the course of history.

The Lutherans of the 16th and 17th centuries had to face up to the theological implications of the world picture of Descartes or Spinoza or Kepler or Newton. This does not imply that a theology of creation and providence will become a substitute for scientific investigation or theory. No Lutheran theologian ever entertained such a thought. Rather, a theology of creation should support the independent investigations of science. But theology has also the right and duty to condemn any world picture (such as pantheism, determinism, tychism) which undermines Christian doctrine in such articles as creation or providence or redemption. And it has the right and duty to approve — or at least not to condemn — those cosmological views which seem to support Christian doctrine.

What has just been said would represent the conviction of all the Lutheran theologians of the post-Reformation era and of all the Lutheran scientists as well. Such a position was the natural result of their creation theology. But we have voiced really nothing more than a few formal principles. We have stated merely the formal posture toward scientific cosmologies which one would expect to result from a Lutheran creation theology.

In the present chapter we propose to answer two important concrete questions relative to the creation theology of Lutheranism. *First,* what was the actual response and attitude toward the emerging scientific world picture of the day introduced by the astronomical hypotheses and observations of Copernicus, Brahe, and Kepler? Was the Lutheran creation theology capable of accepting this new cosmology and working with it? *Second,* what was the relation, if any, between the Lutheran theological world picture and the new scientific world picture of the day?

1. LUTHERAN THEOLOGY AND THE NEW SCIENTIFIC WORLD PICTURE

The reactions of Lutheran theologians to the astronomical discoveries and speculations of the 16th and early 17th centuries and to the new world picture which gradually developed were varied, to say the least, ranging from virtual indifference to active participation in the scientific investigations of the day. Some reacted against the new world picture, supposing it to contradict the Biblical cosmology. Others, like Cort Aslakssøn, who was solidly grounded in astronomy, saw no contradiction but agreement, and attempted a synthesis of the observational data with the Biblical statements concerning the world and the universe. But for the most part Lutheran theologians took little interest in what was taking place and in its bearing on theology. So there was no unanimity among the Lutherans in their response to the new world picture of their day.

This is quite understandable. The so-called Copernican revolution was certainly not much of a revolution in its own day. The idea of an earth which moved was not new. Long before the Reformation in the 14th century Nicole Oresme and Jean Buridan had taught the possibility that the earth was not stationary but moved on its axis.[1] Furthermore, Copernicus's *De Revolutionibus Orbium Coelestium* caused so little stir that its first edition of 1,000 copies never sold out. The book described an incredibly complicated and unworkable system which, based on the Pythagorean idea of a heliocentric universe, had the planets run to as many as 48 epicycles. The system was extremely difficult to follow and even more difficult to accept, for it violated the law of parsimony.

The real father of the Copernican revolution — if it is proper to use the word "revolution" in this context — was Kepler. It was not until the publication of his *Astronomia Nova* in 1609 that serious thought was given by theologians to the subject of the new cosmology, and then only by a few and usually in an amateurish and unenthusiastic way. It must be remembered also that Kepler himself was a curious mixture of mystic and empiricist, and for this reason even many of the scientists (for example, Galileo) failed to take him as seriously as they should have. And so it was not until well into the middle of the 17th century that Lutheran theologians began to relate the new cosmology to the theological world picture of Scripture.

We must bear in mind that as children of their time the old Lutheran theologians looked at the world and the universe in a way far different from our manner today. As we have seen, they had a very realistic, childlike belief in God's presence and mighty providence in nature and in the affairs of men. In a thousand cases where we would explain events by natural causes they found God at work, directly at work — or demons at work. To a greater or lesser degree they were still possessed with magical or superstitious ideas of the workings within the universe. It was impossible that they should think otherwise, and we can hardly fault them for this. We can only marvel that their *sola Scriptura* approach to all theological issues emancipated them from as much of the medieval superstition of their day as it did. For they were often relatively untouched by the astrological and magic thinking of their day — as untouched as some of the very scientists who were making the advances and emancipating them

[1] See A. C. Crombie, *Histoire de la Science de Saint Augustin à Galilée (400 to 1650)* (Paris: Presses Universitaires de France, 1959), I, 279 ff. See also R. Hooykaas, *Natural Law and Divine Miracle* (Leiden: E. J. Brill, 1959), pp. 209 ff.

from that older world picture. Concerning the scientists of this era, Arthur
Koestler had made the following provocative statement,[2] "As we watch
the working of the mind of Kepler (or Paracelsus, Gilbert, Descartes)
we are made to realize the fallacy of the belief that in some point between
the Renaissance and the Enlightenment man shook off the 'superstitions
of medieval religion' like a puppy getting out of water, and started on the
bright new road of science. Inside these minds we find no abrupt break
with the past, but a gradual transformation of the symbols of their cosmic
experience — from *anima matrix* into *vis matrix,* moving spirit into
moving force, mythological imagery into mathematical hieroglyphics —
a transformation which never was and, one hopes, never will be entirely
completed." In fact one will find far less mystical speculation and metaphysical *idées fixes* in the theological treatises of the 17th century Lutherans than in the scientific treatises of Kepler. And this is understandable. They were not consumed with the desire to discover the mystery
of the orbits of the heavenly bodies but concerned only to present systematically the teaching of Scripture.

Werner Elert[3] has shown with much detailed evidence that Luther
emancipated evangelical theology from the Aristotelian world picture
which was dominant in his day. Because of this, Elert claims, there was
little hostility and no intolerance among Lutheran theologians, including
Melanchthon, toward the views of Copernicus and the new world picture
which was developing. Lutheranism's transcendence of the medieval world
picture made it possible, according to Elert, for the views of Copernicus
to find acceptance first of all in the Lutheran universities such as Wittenberg and Tübingen. Assuming that Elert's thesis is essentially correct,[4]

---

[2] Arthur Koestler, *The Watershed, a Biography of Johannes Kepler* (New
York: Doubleday & Company, 1960), p. 57. If Koestler is right in this thesis,
then the "Copernican Revolution" was a very gradual thing and all but imper-
ceptible in its time. He greatly expands this thesis in *The Sleepwalkers* (New
York: Macmillan, 1959).

[3] *The Structure of Lutheranism,* pp. 415 ff.

[4] Two points in Elert's thesis seem to be pretty well proved by the facts.
First, Luther's doctrine of Christ's exaltation, ascension, session at the right hand
of power, and the various modes of God's presence certainly transcends the world
picture of Aristotle. Second, there was a great interest on the part of many Lutherans (Erasmus Reinhold, Michael Maestlin, Joachim Rhaeticus, Tycho Brahe,
Johann Fabricius, Samuel Dörffel) in astronomy and acceptance of the new world
picture. But that the latter point is the result to any degree of the former and
that Luther's theology created a climate of openness among Lutherans to indepen-

we must now examine the theology of the post-Reformation Lutheran teachers to see precisely what their reaction to the new world picture was. We have intimated that it was a mixed reaction. We must now trace the three types of response to the new world picture which we notice among the Lutheran theologians of the late 16th and 17th centuries.

a. *Antipathy to the New World Picture*

It is not until the middle of the 17th century that we find an overt rejection on theological grounds of the new world picture among Lutherans. This is understandable, for it was only then that the new world picture had established itself as being generally acceptable to any except a few savant astronomers. By far the strongest negative criticism is offered by Calov in his comments on the hexaemeron.[5] Taking a good deal of imagery and popular expressions from Scripture in an extremely literal way (for example, Ps. 119:90; Eccl. 1:4, 5; Ps. 19:6; 74:16-17; Gen. 1:16; Jer. 31:35-36; Ps. 104:19; Joshua 10:12; 2 Kings 20:11), he argues that the sun moves and the earth is in a stationary position in space, depending for its position only on God's power.[6] This would mean that there was no natural explanation for the position of the earth. The Biblical phrase "foundations of the earth" (Ps. 102:25; 104:5) Calov understood as an expression for God's power. In every case Calov failed to see that the statements of Scripture which assigned a stationary position to the earth were not statements concerning astronomy or a world picture, but statements expressing God's benevolence or wisdom or providence.

dent research in the sciences is a very tenuous hypothesis. Elert's main basis for his thesis is a letter from Hafenreffer to Kepler warning Kepler againt trying publicly to reconcile his astronomical hypotheses with the Scriptures. On the basis of this Elert says, "Here Hafenreffer unreservedly acknowledges the autonomy of research in the field of natural sciences." Klaus Scholder has called Elert's whole argument "onesided" and this last statement "somewhat absurd." See Klaus Scholder, *Ursprünge und Probleme der Bibelkritik in 17. Jahrhundert* (München: Chr. Kaiser Verlag, 1966), pp. 65, 69. And perhaps he is not too harsh. Elert has dug deep and come up with slender evidence for such a thesis. It is hard to believe that Hafenreffer was so little a child of his time and so far ahead of the pack as Elert implies.

  [5] Calov, *Systema*, III, 952 ff. Calov even includes a special question on the fixity of the earth in his polemical section (*Systema*, III, 1036—49). Hollaz is the only other major Lutheran theologian to follow Calov, and he speaks just about as strongly on the matter.

  [6] *Systema*, III, 952: "Locata autem terra est non quae moveretur sive in gyrum, seu alia ratione, nedum quae moto suo tempora definiret, quod luminaribus datum est officium, sed quae stabilis & immota consisteret."

Calov believed that he could find answers in Scripture concerning the nature of the universe — although in fact he finds rather few.[7] For instance, the moon, he says, cannot in itself be dark, getting its light from the sun; for Moses calls it a light. He is willing to admit, however, that the moon is not so large as the stars even though it is called a great light in contrast to the stars. In this case he sees the Scriptures speaking according to appearances, phenomenally. Calov also discusses the distances of the stars from the earth, their measurements, the mountains and valleys on the moon, the question of life on other planets, and the dangers of astrology. Throughout his discussions he brings in the opinions of Kepler, Aristotle, Brahe, Ptolemy, and others concerning the points under discussion; and, subjecting them all to Scripture, he freely voices his criticism.

But Calov does not lose sight of the main purpose of the creation account and the use to which the doctrine of creation ought to be put. He goes into much detail showing homiletically how the account of each day of creation is to help us to know God better in His power and wisdom and goodness. Calov's doctrine of creation, except for this one point, does not differ from that of the other dogmaticians who do not deal with the new astronomy and the question of the earth's fixity.

Why does Calov take the strong stand he does against the astronomy of his day? There are no apparent theological reasons for his opinion on the fixity of the earth. He has no objection to movement as such. The notion of a Copernican revolution, according to which man somehow lost his importance because the earth was no longer thought to be at the center of the universe, does not occur to him, or to any other Lutheran who shares his point of view. As a matter of fact, the Lutheran doctrine of God's immensity and transcendence over time and space would tend to make them quite unconcerned with this aspect of Copernicanism. No, Calov's reasons for his position are completely exegetical. He believes that the Scriptures assert certain things about the fixity of the earth and the movement of the sun, and he will attack any opinion which tends to conflict with what Scripture says.[8] The only principle at stake for Calov as he

[7] *Systema,* III, 954 ff. In this respect Calov does not differ in this discussion from Luther. See *WA,* 42, 1 ff.

[8] Some of the Calvinists took the same position as Calov. See Gisbert Voet, *Selectarum Disputationum Theologicarum Pars Prima* (Utrecht, 1648), p. 638; Matthias Martini, *Quaestiones Theologicae & Philologicae in Librum Josuae* (Bremen, 1624), p. 20. Voet, who takes as strong a stand against the new astron-

states his case is the Scripture principle: to him no extra-Biblical position or opinion or even observation could set aside what Scripture asserts to be the case. But in this matter all the Lutherans, even those who did not enter into the present discussion, were at one with him.[9]

b. *Agreement with the New World Picture and Attempts to Reconcile it with Scripture*

Before the middle of the 17th century the new world picture developed by Copernicus, Brahe, and Kepler was almost never discussed in Lutheran dogmatics. The Lutheran theologians were either unaware of what was taking place, or they considered these new hypotheses as having no direct bearing on theology. The latter may be the case with Matthias Hafenreffer, who was a personal friend to Kepler, and who had firsthand knowledge of the latter's views. Hafenreffer felt that Kepler's views should remain hypotheses, good and workable hypotheses. And he was weary of any attempt of Kepler to reconcile these hypotheses with Scripture.[10]

However, there were a few individual theologians at the turn of the 17th century who felt that there was no real conflict but rather harmony

omy as any of the Calvinists, argues from Scripture in the same way as Calov, listing arguments from Scripture where it is said that the earth is stationary (Eccl. 1:4; Job 26:7) and where the sun moves (Ps. 19:5-6; Eccl. 1:5.6; Joshua 10:12-14). — But Voet's approach differs from Calov's in that Voet essayed to oppose the Copernican system not only from Scripture but also from other authorities, mathematicians, and astronomers. He mentions Ptolemy, Aristotle, David Christian (professor of mathematics at Marburg), Brahe, and many other authorities. Voet also supports the action of the Roman Church against Galileo — an illustration of the tragedy of dependence upon authorities, for Voet had plenty of them! All in all, however, Voet's strictures were very mildly put. Cf. ibid., p. 700.

[9] Calov, *Systema*, I, 608. See Mentzer, *Opera Latina*, I, 776; Gerhard, *Loci Theologici*, II, 36; Dannhauer, *Hodosophia Christiana*, p. 39; Dorsch, *Synopsis Theologiae Zacharianae*, I, II, 11: "Auctoritas ejus est tanta, quanta Dei, qui in ea & per eam dominium suum gratiosum exhibet." It was Calov's opinion that Scripture's authority extended also to those places where Scripture happened to mention the things of nature, and this was the position of his contemporaries. Calov, *Systema*, I, 552. Cf. *Socinismus Profligatus*, p. 62; Quenstedt, *Systema*, P.I, C.4, S.2, Q.5, fons sol. (I, 116).

[10] Werner Elert, *The Structure of Lutheranism*, p. 429 passim. This was also the attitude of Hutter (See *Loci Communes Theologici*, p. 213). Hutter feels that the question of whether there were many heavens, introduced by the church fathers, could well be left for the astronomers to decide. So also the nature of the stars. To him the Scriptures taught merely that there was the atmosphere, there was the vast heavens of the stars for the astronomers to study, and there was the heaven of eternal life which existed in God. This is all the farther he would go.

between the new world picture and what Scripture says about the world and the universe. And they considered it quite in order to demonstrate this harmony between the book of Scripture and the book of nature as well as they were able. The Norwegian theologian Cort Aslakssøn, who was professor at Copenhagen from 1600—1624 (the year of his death), and who accepted the Formula of Concord, had studied as an assistant under Tycho Brahe for some time and was fully conversant with the latter's astronomical findings and hypotheses. Convinced that the prevailing views of astronomy as understood by Brahe were completely compatible with the theological world picture of the Bible, Aslakssøn wrote several books, showing how a synthesis was possible.[11] However, it must be borne in mind that Brahe still kept the earth as the center of his system, with the sun and moon revolving around it and the five planets as satellites of the sun.

Another Lutheran theologian at the turn of the century, who was concerned to show the agreement between the new world view and Scripture, was Melchior Nicolai, professor at Tübingen during the first quarter of the 17th century. His approach, however, was to show that Scripture as it speaks of the universe and the things of nature had no intention of speaking astronomically or scientifically. In speaking of the sun and the stars and the fixity of the earth, Scripture used poetic licence, according to Melchior Nicolai,[12] or simply spoke phenomenally as things appear to the senses. From our vantage point the earth does not move. Nicolai maintained that Scripture should not be used to influence or judge the findings of the astronomers, for it was not the intention of Scripture to present a final system of cosmology. In speaking of the things of nature Scripture also often uses the popular expressions of the day, according to Nicolai. He even thought that Scripture, if anything, intimated the movement of the earth.

By the turn of the 18th century those Lutherans who believed, like Nicolai, that Scripture had no intention of teaching a specific cosmological

---

[11] *De Natura Coeli Triplicis* (Sigena of Nassau, 1597); *De Mundo* (Copenhagen, 1605—7). In his *Physica et Ethica Mosaica* (Copenhagen, 1613) he tried to show that Brahe's new cosmology agreed in essence with that of the first chapters of Genesis. For an excellent account of his activities see Oskar Garstein, *Cort Aslakssøn* (Oslo: Lutherstiftelsen, 1953).

[12] I am dependent upon Calov for my information on Nicolai. See *Systema,* III, 1037 ff. Nicolai is one of the few Lutherans Calov opposes as he tries to prove the fixity of the earth from Scripture.

world picture had a completely different problem on their hands. Their quarrel was no longer with orthodox Lutherans like Calov, who read the phenomenal language of Scripture literalistically and insisted that the new world picture was wrong, but was with skeptics and non-Christian deists, who read the Scriptures just as Calov did but insisted that the Scriptures were wrong. The task of these theologians, therefore, was to demonstrate that Scripture did not teach a false world picture by showing that it did not teach any world picture. Ironically, they were involved in precisely the same struggle as Calov, the struggle to uphold the Scripture principle.

An example of this conscious refusal to favor any world picture as being Scriptural is seen in Salomon Deyling's lengthy comments on Josh. 10:12-14, a passage often thought to teach a Ptolemaic world picture.[13] Deyling maintains that this passage has nothing to do with implying one world picture in favor of another.[14] The point of the story is that God miraculously intervened on behalf of His people and did so at the prayer of Joshua. With a stupendous miracle God changed the course of nature. Deyling, whose orthodoxy is unquestionable, is however most concerned to maintain that the great miracle did in fact take place, and he therefore rejects all poetic interpretations and all theories of his day which tended to explain away the true fact of God's changing the order of nature in this case (for example, the theory that after the sun had gone down, a cloud reflected it in such a way that it appeared to stand still in the sky). No, the pericope plainly intends to tell us that God entered into the affairs of men in a most dramatic way at this point in history, and we must not suppose that He would not do this through such a tremendous miracle as the one here recounted. "Nothing should be altered in the sacred history," says Deyling,[15] "nor should the ways of God and His miracles be explained away or amplified by man's ingenuity or according to man's opinions. When Scripture has spoken, then we ought to restrict ourselves to what in fact happened and not bother with what God could have done. Now the text clearly teaches that the forward movement of the sun was held up; it does not talk about the aftereffects which took place after the

---

[13] Salomon Deyling, *Observationum Sacrarum in qua Multa Scripturae Veteris ac Novi Testamenti Dubia Vexata Solvuntur* (Leipzig, 1735), I, 100 ff.

[14] Ibid., I, 103: "Res aeque erit inusitata & prorsus miraculosa quaecunque demum hypothesis, sive Ptolemaica, sive Copernicana hic admittatur."

[15] Ibid., I, 107.

sun had set, nor does it speak of a substitute sun which was produced and
then showed itself after the setting of the real and usual sun. Therefore
I would prefer to stay with the clear words of the sacred history and to
stand with André Maes,[16] a most learned man, that not only the sun and
the moon but also all the heavenly bodies were interrupted in their course
and simply rested for a while." Deyling senses that the reaction to the
pericope and his interpretation of it is that this is too great a miracle for
the purposes at hand. Was there a need for such a stupendous divine intervention? Deyling responds, "Christians should not dispute idly among
themselves whether so great a prophetic sign was needed at this particular
time or whether the whole course of nature had to be altered just to kill
a few Canaanites. The actions of God and the reasons for these actions
are impenetrable to us mortals. God does many things wisely which men
in their stupidity do not understand." These words of Deyling's indicate
that, while ingenuously refusing to become involved in the hypotheses
of astronomy as they might impinge on this Bible story, he nevertheless
insists that the story be taken seriously as a witness to a tremendous intervention of God on behalf of His people, an intervention which very definitely interrupted the course of nature.

Deyling is making no theological concession as he refuses to associate
any world picture with the Scriptures. He insists that he is understanding
the Scriptures on their own terms. And it is rather the deists (sometimes
called atheists by Deyling) who misunderstand the Scriptures.[17] Some

---

[16] André Maes, Belgian orientalist (1515/16—1631) was both a scholar and
secretary to several princes. He was one of the important figures in the edition
of the Antwerp Polyglot. See *Nouvelle Biographie Genérale,* ed. M. le Dr. Hoe-
ber (Paris: Firmin Didot Freres, 1859—63), 32, 645—46; *Allgemeine Deutsche
Biographie* (Leipzig: Verlag von Duncker & Humbolt, 1875—1902), 20, 559
to 62.

[17] At the end of his *Observationum Sacrarum Pars Prima* (I, 378 ff.) Deyling
appends a study entitled *Oratio de Israelitarum Aegyptiacorum Ingenio,* directed
against the English deists, John Marsham, John Spencer, William Nicholls, and
others who set the Newtonian world picture of the day in opposition to that of
Scripture. A more apologetic defense of Moses' knowledge of nature as reflected
in the creation account was offered by the Reformed theologian Isaac Jacquelot.
See Isaac Jacquelot, *Conformité de la foi avec la Raison, ou défence de la religion
contre les principales difficultés répondues dans le dictionnaire historique et
critique de Bayle* (1704), found in *Démonstrations evangeliques,* ed. M. l'Abée
(Paris: Petit-Montrouge, 1843), VII, 63—69. Four criticisms of Moses' account
of creation are taken up by Jacquelot. (1) That Moses had no knowledge of the
universe. For instance, he speaks of the earth and heaven as though earth were the
center of importance when the heavens are in fact infinitely larger. Therefore

of the English deists were of the opinion that Moses, who wrote the Book
of Genesis, was taught by rude men who did not amount to anything, and
his reflections on the world of nature indicate this. Deyling replies that
Moses and the patriarchs were by no means ignorant men who could not
distinguish between fact and fancy. It is rather the a priori denial, wrongly
inferred from the Newtonian physics, of any possibility of miraculous
divine intervention into space and time which prompts the deists to be
so critical of the Biblical manner of speaking when it describes God's relation to the world. Even more inexcusable to Deyling is the fact that the
deists have not read the Scriptures carefully and with sensitivity.

Deyling then offers a statement of his own position, and because of
the significance of the principle he enunciates, we quote him at some
length,[18] "We ought not be bothered by the division (in Scripture) of all
created things into heaven and earth. For Scripture sometimes conforms
to the experiences of our senses or to the ideas of sense perception as they
particularly affect us. Likewise Scripture speaks of the heavenly and earthly
bodies in no other manner than as they represent themselves to our senses,
inasmuch as whatever we know about heavenly bodies is made known to
us through our senses. Such ways of speaking are usually called 'observational' and are distinguished from the physical reality itself. Let this not
be construed as though we were saying that the divine Scripture accommodates itself to the comprehension of the masses, that is, to error, or
that it speaks erroneously, as many, especially from the school of René

Moses had no real knowledge of what he saw with his eyes. (2) The day and
night could not have been created before the light of the sun. (3) The sun and
moon are called great lights, although all the stars are much larger than the moon.
(4) the six days and the order of them make very little sense. For instance, one
day was required to create the stars, when another whole day was devoted to the
animals. In replying to these objections Jacquelot begins with the assumption that
an almighty God made the world and has revealed Himself in His Word. His
observations by way of response are quite conservative and cautious. First, he
says, we do not know it all and should admit our ignorance in the face of the
Biblical account. Second, he points out that as one speaking to men of his day
(and also ours) Moses gives a good account of creation. One can hardly expect
Moses to speak as a philosopher. It does not appear that Jacquelot takes a very
literal interpretation of the days of creation, one of the prime difficulties, and
merely takes each day as teaching us something of God's wisdom and power; and
there is nothing in all this, he thinks, which does not commend itself to the
ordinary ideas of men. The creation account, he believes, completely destroys the
doctrine of mechanism.

[18] Deyling, I, 397.

Descartes foolishly and wrongly imagine. But there is nothing wrong with our saying and admitting that the Scriptures in some places did not speak of things scientifically *(physice)* but phenomenally *(optice)*, or according to the experience of our senses and as things were apprehended by the senses. Do not all astronomical tables depend upon a place of observation? Yet these tables are not indications of error but of true observations. One errs only when one mistakes and substitutes appearance for reality. But the Spirit, who is the author of the Sacred Scriptures never does this, nor does He make any concession to commonly held error, but accommodates Himself only to our sense of sight. We might add that the sacred Scriptures were not written for the entertainment of philosophers or to develop their talents, but were addressed to the hearts of men who long for salvation and to nurture those who for the most part are simple and unlearned. I actually think that a tremendous argument for divine goodness lies in this fact that the arrangement of our universe has been described not in strict scientific terms but according to the way it is observed, lest those who are in grace and yet are weak and unskilled in philosophy be offended. Meanwhile we know that the whole Scripture has been given for them to read and understand with ease."

This statement representing the mature thoughts of orthodox Lutheranism indicates that the Scriptures were not to become a source for any world picture. For it was not the purpose of Scripture to present a world picture, but only to proclaim God as Creator and absolute Lord of all things. Therefore there should be no quarrel between the teaching of Scripture and all the various scientific hypotheses which are based on the same phenomena which Scripture describes.

There is nothing unique about Deyling's view that Scripture often speaks of the things of nature descriptively, as they appear to our senses. This was the common understanding of all the Lutheran teachers.[19] What is ironic is that Calov and his followers (Hollaz) agreed with Deyling on this principle of hermeneutics. But for some reason Calov did not follow his own principles at this point and insisted that Scripture was not

---

[19] See, for example, John Conrad Dannhauer, *Hermeneutica Sacra* (Strasbourg, 1654), p. 409; August Pfeiffer, *Thesaurus Hermeneuticus* (Leipzig and Frankfurt, 1704), p. 25; Bechmann, *Annotationes,* p. 233; Sebastian Schmidt, *Super Mosis Librum Primum, Genesis Dictum, Annotationes,* p. 12.

speaking phenomenally or poetically when it speaks of the fixity of the earth.[20]

c. The General Indifference
to the Emerging Scientific Cosmologies

Among the great majority of the Lutheran theologians of the post-Reformation era there was relative indifference and ignorance of the new scientific world pictures which were being set forth. In the case of most of them it is difficult to say just what world picture they may have held or whether they had any definite views. But it is quite clear that they did not believe that Scripture with its definite theological aim presented any unified world picture. And it is clear that they did not consider it incumbent upon them to favor or reject on theological grounds any of the cosmological hypotheses of their day.

This lack of interest in formulating any cosmology is clearly shown in Chemnitz' discussion of the hexaemeron.[21] His entire treatment of the fourth day is directed against speculation on how the heavenly bodies were created and is calculated to point out the purpose of such a creation (Ps. 136:4-9 ff.), and that God has done all in wisdom. God has placed the sun and the stars in the sky, Chemnitz says, so that, as the sun moves, seasons are brought on and man is aided in his work. And the sun rises and sets so that day and night might serve man in his work and rest (Ps. 104:23). And any other speculation on the subject he leaves to the natural sciences to explain.

The lack of interest in formulating any cosmology is shown also by the fact that, with the exception of Calov and Hollaz, none of the first-ranking Lutheran dogmaticians of the period (Heerbrand, Selnecker, Ha-

---

[20] As a basic principle of hermeneutics Calov maintains that things are often described in Scripture as they appear to the senses and not as they really are. *Systema,* I, 464: "In Scriptura nonnunquam res describitur, ut est et κατὰ δόξαν, non κατὰ τὸ εἶναι." Werner Elert (*The Structure of Lutheranism,* p. 430) makes the odd remark that "the theological intolerance of the seventeenth century vis-a-vis the astronomers runs exactly parallel to the advance of an unevangelical Biblicism." Elert offers no evidence for such a conjecture and no explanation of what he means by "unevangelical Biblicism." As a matter of fact Calov's doctrine of Scripture and his hermeneutics were the same as those Lutheran theologians' before and after him who took a more open attitude or even accepted the new world picture. See Robert Preus, *The Inspiration of Scripture* (Edinburgh, 1957), pp. 73 ff.

[21] *Loci Theologici,* I, 113. Cf. Gerhard, *Loci Theologici,* IV, 17—18.

fenreffer, Gerhard, Brochmand, Dannhauer, Kromayer, Baier, et al.) even mentions the subject in his dogmatics. We might examine the position of one representative and one of the best exegetes of the era, Sebastian Schmidt, in order to come to a clear understanding of their attitude.

Schmidt himself probably believed in the immovability of the earth, but in his comments on such verses as Heb. 1:10, which speak of the foundations of the earth, he makes no issue of this.[22] He simply makes comments like the following, which is not cosmological but theological: [23] " 'You have laid the foundations of the earth' means that You have created the earth from nothing in such a way that You have made it solid, firm, and immovable. 'For the earth abides forever.' (Eccl. 1:4)." In his comments on Is. 38:8, which Calov used to show the fixity of the earth and the movement of the sun, there is no hint of any such cosmological interest in Schmidt's commentary.[24] According to Job 38:4 Schmidt sees the earth as a firm and immovable sphere, established by God, and the mystery of how it could remain stable was unknown to man.[25] This was God's challenge hurled at Job, says Schmidt, to explain this mystery. But again it is only the theological significance of the stability of the earth, which is due to God's sustenance, that concerns Schmidt.

Schmidt's remarks introduce an important consideration at this point. They show us that it is imperative to know whether a representative theologian is speaking theologically or cosmologically as he speaks of the world and the universe. This distinction is by no means unimportant. Cosmologically the earth is not the center of the universe. Some Lutherans believed this and others denied it; most, like Schmidt, show little interest in the matter. But theologically the earth is the center of God's attention, if one is to take the Christian doctrine of creation and providence seriously. And all the Lutherans held firmly to this point. No Lutheran in the post-

[22] *In Epistolam ad Hebraeos Commentarius,* p. 105.

[23] Ibid., p. 148. Later (p. 150) he says more dogmatically, "Coeli sunt mobiles: Terra autem stat immobilis. Nitimur hic verbis, יִסַּדְתָּ, ἐθεμελίωσας, fundasti quae singula in suis linguis ejusmodi positum rei denotant, quo res immobilis persistant; nec vel per se moveantur, vel ab aliis moveri possint." But from this brief statement it is still not possible to know that Schmidt is speaking cosmologically and not theologically.

[24] Sebastian Schmidt, *Commentarius super Illustres Prophetias Iesaiae* (Hamburg and Frankfurt, 1693), p. 331.

[25] *In Librum Ijobi Commentarius,* p. 1418.

Reformation age believed in a world picture of a spacial three-story universe. No Lutheran believed that Scripture taught such a picture. Rather, all of them, including Calov, taught a doctrine of God and of Christ and of providence which transcended any observational, scientific world picture.

2. The Relationship of Lutheran Theology to the Emerging Scientific World Picture

We must now ask what is the relation, if any, between the Lutheran theological world picture and Lutheran theology as a whole to the emerging scientific world picture of the day? The answer to the question is that the classical Lutheran theology which we have been tracing is remarkably independent of any philosophical ontology and transcends completely any empirical or scientific world picture.

We have already seen this at several points in our study, for instance, in the doctrine of God's immensity and of the *unio mystica* which defied the prevailing Aristotelian doctrine of presence according to local and spatial categories. Cort Aslakssøn is most insistent that we do not confuse the various kinds of κοινωνία spoken of in Scripture with the different associations or unions which we find in the world of nature.[26] In nature we find such unions and associations as (1) physical mixtures, (2) associations by proximity (two persons working together or being together), (3) transformation (a brick being made into a fortress), (4) the union of body and soul. But God's κοινωνία is of a completely different order, for example, the essential communication of the Father's essence to the Son (Heb. 1), the mystical union by which the Spirit dwells in believers and believers have fellowship with one another (2 Cor. 13:14; 1 Cor. 1:10; 2 Peter 1:4; Phil. 1:5; 2:1), the sacramental union (1 Cor. 10:16), or the hypostatic union.[27]

[26] Cort Aslakssøn, *De Immanuele Nostro D. Jesu Christo, vero Deo et vero Homine in Una Indivisa Persona* (Frankfurt, 1620), p. 158.

[27] Jörg Baur (*Die Vernunft Zwischen Ontologie und Evangelium*, p. 106 passim) has shown with much evidence how the Lutherans, and Quenstedt in particular, are free of philosophical ontology in their theology, but attempt to stick with the Biblical position on several points in opposition to the prevailing metaphysical views of their day. In additon to the doctrine of God's presence which we have mentioned, Baur mentions the rejection of Aristotle's *prima materia,* and also the Lutheran doctrine of original sin, which made original sin a positive evil (concupiscence) and was thus opposed to the philosophical principle that every positive entity *(ens positivum)* is good. See Quenstedt, *Systema,* P.II, C.2, S.2, Q.11 (II, 135 ff.).

That the Lutheran theology transcends any world picture is seen also in the doctrine of providence, especially in the notion of God's "extraordinary providence" by which He freely helps His church by hindering, altering, and overcoming secondary causes. Such a view of providence, whereby God is engaged powerfully in the affairs of men, mitigating and even setting aside at times the laws of nature, was at complete odds with any theory of a closed universe or determinism which might have been inferred from the new physics and scientific world picture of the day (deism, Hobbes, Spinoza). As God, free and unhampered by secondary causes, works providentially among men, He is working miracles, according to the usual understanding of the term; He is performing wonderful works *(miranda opera),* which are outside the ordinary course of nature which He has established *(praeter et supra usitatum naturae ordinem a Deo institutum).*[28]

---

[28] Jacob Heerbrand, *Disputatio de Miraculis* (Tübingen, 1590), p. A2r. The Lutheran dogmaticians never offer a special discussion of miracles in their dogmatics books, probably because they saw no need of it in their day. And they say very little about miracles happening in their own day, perhaps because of their dislike of the extreme claims made throughout the Roman Catholic Church. To them a miracle was usually thought of as a *Heilswunder,* a testimony pointing to the salvation (or judgment) of man *(testimonium & confirmatio doctrinae, et ad salutem, vel perditionem hominum).* Ibid., p. Blv. And the miracles κατ᾽ ἐξοχήν, praised even in heaven (Ps. 89:5; Luke 2:13), are those things which happened on earth through Christ for our salvation: the mysteries of His incarnation and birth and passion and resurrection, the wonders of salvation. See Martini, *De Tribus Elohim,* III, 258. Viewing miracles in the light of God's economy of salvation and judgment made the Lutheran teachers very conservative, preserving an economy of miracles and suspicious of any naive claim for divine miraculous intervention in the affairs of men (Martini, ibid., II, 301). In fact they speak more of the pseudomiracles *(Miracula mendacia, miracula apparentia)* of Satan and the powers of darkness than of genuine miracles, and they warn strenuously against these deceptions and illusions *(prestigiae, illusiones, imposturae).* Heerbrand, op. cit., p. A4r. I have not found any case in their dogmatics where they allude to actual miracles of their day; their examples of miracles are always taken from the Bible. This does not imply that they were unwittingly veering toward deism. Their realistic demonology and their doctrine that diabolical miracles, although fraudulent, were indeed supernatural *(praeter ordinarium faciendi modum)* proves otherwise. It merely means that they were convinced that God in His providence and in His kingdom of grace ordinarily works through the secondary causes which He has established. And it means that God's providential activity is an article of faith, not something constantly established by miracles.

Their reason for insisting that miracles of devils were not miracles, strictly speaking, that is, not completely outside the course of nature and beyond it, was to protect God's sovereignty against any form of dualism. See Sebastian Schmidt, *Compendium Theologiae,* p. 172.

The independence of Lutheran theology from any prevailing ontology or world picture becomes particularly apparent in its Christology and its doctrine of Christ's exaltation and session at the right hand of God. That Christ is exalted to the right hand of God means that Christ rules with God in infinite power. In terms of presence this infers, according to Selnecker,[29] that "since Christ is omnipotent God, He is able to be in all places with His body or according to His human nature, all places where He wishes to be, and all this with His human nature intact, inviolate, not expanded nor diffused, and not infinitely distributed." This list of qualifications at the end of Selnecker's statement, far from making any concession to metaphysical notions of any kind, indicates that he considers his position to be incapable of any metaphysical or physical explanation and independent of any metaphysical basis, in fact, contrary to any physical or metaphysical doctrines of his day.

Christ's ascension and sitting at the right hand of God are not occurrences which can be described in terms of our three-dimensional space. True, He ascended before the eyes of His disciples, and this is a historical fact; but His being in heaven does not mean that His body is now located and circumscribed in a certain place. The right hand of God is the glorious reign of God and is everywhere. "Thus, although Christ is in heaven," Selnecker says, "He is nevertheless Lord of heaven, and heaven is not the place that encloses Him, but is enclosed by Him." [30]

Selnecker wants to make it abundantly clear that the Lutheran understanding of the Ascension into heaven and session at the right hand of God is free of the slightest metaphysical or physical connotation. He says,[31] "In this article heaven does not signify the atmosphere, the elements, the clouds, or the firmament, stars, planets, or the corporeal heavens. The ascended Christ passed through all these with His body. Neither does the term signify a physical place in some heaven or other where Christ is kept, circumscribed by His body. Rather it signifies a heavenly dwelling place and throne of God, who dwells in an inaccessible light, above all

[29] Nicolaus Selnecker, *Exegema: 1. De Unione Personali Duarum Naturarum in Christo. 2. De Idiomatum Communicatione. 3. De Coena Domini* (Wolfenbüttel, 1572), p. F5r.

[30] Ibid., p. H7r. Cf. Selnecker, *Institutiones Christianae Religionis,* II, 276; Hollaz, *Examen,* P.III, S.1, C.3, Q.151 (p. 781).

[31] Nicolaus Selnecker, *De Duobus Articulis Symboli, Ascendit ad Coelos: Sedet ad Dexteram Dei Patris, Breves Quaestiones* (Wolfenbüttel, 1572), p. F8v.

heavens, and who has entered into the glory of the Father, 'having gone into heaven . . . angels and authorities and powers being . . . subject to Him' (1 Peter 3:22)." [32]

To Selnecker there is no possibility of trying to grasp the Ascension in terms of space and time. True, he calls heaven a place, as Scripture does, but it is no *locus physicus,* no three-dimensional place which can be grasped by our present understanding. It is a place of a different order and dimension, a new exalted condition and power.

The chief objection to the Lutheran doctrine of Christ's ascension into heaven and exaltation to the right hand of power was that it violated the human nature of Christ. In reply to such an objection Selnecker makes no concession to any contemporary world picture. His theology does not violate the human nature of Christ, he contends. He grants that to have a finite and circumscribed body on earth is something quite different from being in heaven.[33] But both things must be predicated of Christ. "Christ is the Lord of heaven whom the heaven of heavens cannot hold or contain, and yet He has a true, finite, and circumscribed body which, however, in the unity of His person is of infinite and uncircumscribed power. If you ask, ποῖον σῶμα? what kind of body? I can only reply as Paul does, ἄφρον, foolish question." [34] The paradoxical nature of such a statement does not seem to bother Selnecker a bit. To him all objections to his doctrine are answered by an appeal to God's free and almighty power. "All things are possible to God, who does whatever He wishes in respect to His own body, and yet it remains His body. But since it is the body of

---

[32] Selnecker's words are representative of all the Lutheran dogmaticians on this point. See Baier-Walther, III, p. 97; Hutter, *Loci Communes Theologici,* pp. 193 ff.; Dannhauer, *Hodosophia Christiana,* p. 760.

[33] *Exegema,* p. E5r: "In coelo esse, & corpus finitum καὶ περίγραπτον habere, non significant idem. Habet Christus homo verum corpus, quia natus est homo ex Maria semper virgine. In coelo autem est, gloria & majestate & potentia divina accepta, sedens ad dexteram Patris omnipotentis."

[34] Ibid. Brenz seems almost to delight in such paradoxical language. To him the paradox is centered in the two states of Christ. In His state of exinanition Christ was subject to space and time; in His state of exaltation He was above all such limitations. Thus Christ was wrapped in swaddling clothes and lay in a manger, if you consider His humiliation. But if you consider the majesty to which He was raised, no stable could hold Him, not the whole universe. John Brenz, *De Majestate Domini Nostri Jesu Christi ad Dextram Dei Patris, et Vera Praesentia Corporis & Sanguinis ejus in Coena* (Frankfurt, 1562), p. 89.

the only-begotten God, it transcends all human and physical bodies." [35]
To the objection that because Christ was true man there could be nothing
supernatural *(hyperphysica)* about His human nature Selnecker replies
that in reference to Christ's body all sorts of things have happened which
are beyond, above, and even contrary to the usual properties of human
nature, such as His conception and birth, His transfiguration, resurrection, etc.[36]

The elements of Lutheran Christology which we have just summarized
show how the classical Lutheran theology was free from any metaphysical
orientation and not dependent upon any world picture.

Most of all, the Lutheran concepts of heaven and hell illustrate the
transcendence of Lutheran theology over all world pictures. Already at
the time of John Brenz the question was asked, may heaven be called
a place? [37] This question was, of course, closely related to Christology.
For Christ has gone to heaven with His body, which was a real body.
But He has ascended into heaven in His state of exaltation with a glorified
body which was independent and unconditioned by space and time. If
Zwingli wishes to maintain that every body occupies space, he indeed has
Aristotle on his side, says Brenz. But Brenz maintains that Christ and the
Scriptures are on his side. To be sure, heaven is God's dwelling place
and the dwelling place of His saints. But we must not, Brenz warns,

[35] *De Duobus Articulis Symboli,* p. L7r.

[36] It would be a mistake in the light of the above to conclude that there is
anything docetic about the Lutheran Christology. The human nature of Christ
was stressed most emphatically in Lutheran dogmatics, for the whole doctrine of
salvation depended upon this fact. See Hutter, *Loci Communes Theologici,* p. 123,
for an excellent discussion of this. Even more emphatic and enlightening is
Brochmand's discussion in his *Commentarius in Epistolam ad Hebraeos,* p. 176.
Here Brochmand stresses that Christ assumed not some unfallen human nature,
but human nature as it was beset by all the usual human miseries and evils and
limitations, and this that He might be a fellow sufferer *(compati posset)* in all
our misfortune and suffering (Rom. 8:3). This means that Jesus had not only
such infirmities of body and soul as hunger, thirst, the natural fear of death, etc.,
but He also lacked knowledge (Mark 11:13) and grace and He was subject to
all the usual sicknesses and diseases. If anything, Dorsch stresses all this even
more strongly. See *Synopsis Theologiae Zacharianne,* I, 208.

[37] See *De Majestate Domini Nostri Jesu Christi ad Dextram Dei Patris, et
Vera Praesentia Corporis & Sanguinis ejus in Coena,* p. 159 ff. Brenz's is perhaps
the most striking statement made on this subject, and for this reason we single
him out in our resume, even though he antedates our period of study, for the
later Lutheran dogmaticians follow his doctrine at this point very closely.

envisage saints dwelling in heaven according to physical location or movement.

God's heaven must not be understood as a place above all the heavens, a place subject to the conditions of space, where saints walk and stand and sit locally and corporally. No, it is a "heavenly kingdom which is not limited to place or intervals of places, but by God's majesty. Thus wherever God rules with His majesty, there is that heaven which is incorporeal and spiritual."

Brenz envisages hell in much the same manner. But is not such a notion a denial of much of the Biblical imagery concerning hell and a refusal to accept the literal sense of Scripture? Brenz replies, "We know on Scripture's authority that there is a hell. We know that the devils as well as wicked and impenitent men must continually be tormented there. But where does Scripture speak of this hell as a certain place? Where does it place hell locally or corporeally either inside or outside this earth?" Brenz has no metaphysical interests here as he denies that hell is subject to the conditions of space and time. He is attempting rather to transcend all physics and metaphysics by maintaining that heaven and hell cannot be comprehended under the categories of space, just as God cannot be comprehended under such conditions. Nor is Brenz veering toward Platonism or idealism at this point and implying a denial of the resurrection. It is simply his conviction that the coming of our Lord will inaugurate a complete change.

Heaven and earth as we know them will pass away and perish, and a new heaven and earth, possessing completely new conditions and dimensions, will come into being. And there we live with God in glory and in our resurrected bodies, not bodies which have been changed into spirits, but spiritual bodies which are not subject to space and time and other earthly conditions. For in heaven we require neither food nor drink nor sleep nor place nor time. What will happen there? What will it be like? We can answer better in terms of what it is not than of what it is.

But one thing is certain, says Brenz, "God will be our all in all. God will be our heaven, our earth, our place, our food, our drink, our life, our righteousness, our strength, our wisdom, our moderation, our happiness. And what more is there than this? God will be our all, and this is far more wonderful, and far more divine than anything human reason can think of or human words can express. 'For since the beginning of the world men have not heard, nor perceived by the ear, neither hath the eye seen, O God, beside Thee, what He hath prepared for him that waiteth for Him' (Is. 64:4). Therefore let Zwingli enjoy all the places in his heaven, all the sitting down and the walking around which can be seen with the eyes and heard with the ears and understood by the heart. In the obedience of faith we await those things which our blessed and only Ruler, the King of kings, and Lord of lords, will not show us in these times; for He alone has immortality and dwells in the unapproachable light, and no man has seen Him or can see Him.'"

Brenz's notions concerning heaven and hell are closely followed by all the later Lutherans. However, it was not within a Christological context that they taught a doctrine of heaven which was above space and time and all present conditions, but rather in their discussions of creation. The reason for this shift of approach was that the Socinians and Calvinists for the most part taught that God had created a *coelum empyreum* on the first day of creation. This was thought to be a created region where God dwelt together with the angels and saints.[38] In some cases this notion became rather crass and was taught along with the idea of a three-story universe which conformed to our present concept of space and time. Thus God and the angels were thought to dwell in a specific place above our earth and airy heaven.[39]

The Lutheran teachers unanimously rejected the notion of a *coelum empyreum*.[40] Heaven in which God dwells is not a place, but according to Scripture it signifies His glory and majesty (Matt. 21:25; John 6:51; Acts 3:21; 1 Cor. 15:47).[41] In Scripture heaven is often designated for the divine majesty itself or for the inexpressible glory of the deity. It is true that God is said to be in heaven and to look down from heaven (Ps. 14:2; 115:3), but "heaven" is also a word for God Himself (Matt. 21:25; Luke 20:4, 5; 15:18; Eph. 4:10; Is. 14:13).[42] Commenting on Jer. 23:24,

[38] See, for instance, John Völkel, *De Vera Religione* (Cracow, 1630), II, 5; Matthias Martini, *Quaestiones Quaedam Nobiliores, ad Explicanda Loca Difficiliora Genesis* (Bremen, 1623), p. 25.

[39] Völkel, ibid. Cf. Jacob Martini, *Synopsis Totius Religionis Photinianorum Novorum* (Wittenberg, 1633), p. 44.

[40] See Jacob Martini, ibid. Hutter, *Loci Communes Theologici,* p. 193; Selnecker, *Institutiones Christianae Religionis,* III, 274; Baier-Walther, II, 81.

[41] Jacob Martini, op. cit., p. 44.

[42] Martini, ibid., p. 45.

Jacob Martini says,[43] "It is therefore quite impossible that a created heaven should make a dwelling place for God to dwell in, as if it were a place to sit in and the earth were a footstool. For God shows here that there is no place in which He is enclosed or contained. We might note also that in another passage of Isaiah (66:1) God clearly teaches that there is no place for His rest, since all things were made by His hand and He is therefore both inside and outside of them, and since as Creator He existed prior to any creation which is placed somewhere or gives place to something else." The conclusion is that such terms as heaven, light (in which God is said to dwell), throne (on which God is said to sit), are terms for God's majesty.[44]

But if the heaven in which God dwells is His majesty, what about the heaven to which Christ, according to His human nature, ascended and in which He sits as our advocate? Is this not a created place? No, this heaven to which Christ ascended is also the majesty of God, God's direct and immediate presence (τὸ πρόσωπον τοῦ θεοῦ).[45] It is not something created or temporal and therefore subject to time or space. In his remarks on Heb. 8:1, Sebastian Schmidt says,[46] "οἱ οὐρανοί, the heavens, in which Christ sits as our high priest, are not the created heavens or a created place in the created heavens outside the earth and all things which are under the heavens, but they are the exalted majesty of God itself which at times is called the heavens in Scripture." But this heaven to which Christ ascended is more than just the direct and glorious presence of God; it is also an activity. He has appeared in the presence of God *for us.* Christ appears before God not simply to be present, but to intercede.[47] And He intercedes before God not as one who is in a state of humiliation, but as the victorious and glorified One. The session of Christ at the right hand of God in heaven was considered to be no mere inactive state, but a gracious rule.[48] Again and again in Scripture the term οἱ οὐρανοί, when not re-

[43] Ibid.

[44] Calov, *Systema,* III, 1002.

[45] Sebastian Schmidt, *In Epistolam ad Hebraeos Commentarius,* p. 975. Commenting on Heb. 9:24, Schmidt calls the heaven which Christ entered *ipsa Dei penetralis & viscera.*

[46] Ibid., p. 869.

[47] Ibid., p. 975: "Sed jam diximus, non esse apparitionem praesentiae, sed intercessionis." Cf. p. 818.

[48] Ibid., p. 154.

ferring to the universe, is taken in the sense of a relationship with God (Heb. 4:14). Commenting on Heb. 7:26, Schmidt says,[49] " 'Higher than the heavens' is nothing else than the high majesty of God. Into this it behooved our High Priest to ascend." When Christ ascended above the heavens He entered in His human nature a dimension of existence beyond space or time or any condition of our present experience.[50]

But what about the heavens in which we will dwell as God's elect? the heaven which is said to be above (Col. 3:1), the home of the Father (John 14:2), a house in the heavens not made with hands (2 Cor. 5:1), the city of the living God (Heb. 12:22), the eternal habitations (Luke 16:9), paradise (Luke 23:43; 2 Cor. 12:4), the land of the living (Ps. 116:9; 142:5)? All these phrases, Calov asserts,[51] must be understood tropically and metaphorically *(symbolice, figurate, parabolica, hieroglyphice)* for the wonderful blessings of the future life. The phrases do not refer to a created place or a created dwelling. They are figurative and parabolic expressions for eternal life. This, after all, is the only mode of speech possible for Scripture as it speaks of those things which are above our comprehension and grasp. Therefore, Calov says, when the Lutherans speak of God being *supra coelum* and of this being the future of the man in Christ they mean a "sublime state and condition." But where then are the elect who have departed this life? They are with God. "For the omnipotent God is their temple, and the Lamb is their temple (Rev. 21:22). If here in the kingdom of grace they are in Christ and Christ in them, if here they are in God and God in them, how much more will this be true there in the kingdom of glory, where God will be their all in all. And so God Himself is the heaven of the blessed." [52]

Does such a view of heaven, which removes it from the conditions of space and time and any world picture, threaten the doctrine of the resurrection? The Lutherans are convinced that it does not. Eternal life is an entirely different condition from what we experience in space and time. And our bodies will share in this new condition. They will be glorified bodies. And no further explanation can be given.[53] The heaven

---

[49] Ibid., p. 455.

[50] Selnecker, *Institutiones Christianae Religionis,* III, 274.

[51] Calov, *Systema,* III, 1005.

[52] Calov, *Systema,* III, 1006.

[53] Matthias Hafenreffer, *Loci Theologici* (Wittenberg, 1601), p. 696.

of eternal life may be called a place, a *beatorum,* in which we exist in glory with glorified bodies, but this utterly transcends the space and time of our present existence.[54]

The Lutheran idea of hell was also far removed from any physical world picture. It was not considered to be a local or corporeal place. It was not a locality in the middle of the earth, or some earthly region, or some island or lake or prison or city. Hell has its own kind of where-abouts (*suum* ποῦ), and its own kind of existence (*suum* τὸ εἶναι), without any local connotations whatever. It is rather an illocal power of the omnipotent God, a condition of being under divine wrath.[55]

The question was asked whether, according to Scripture (Matt. 25: 41), the devils do not actually suffer the sensation *(sensus)* of divine punishment and of actual fire (Is. 66:24). The answer is yes. But evil spirits have no body. And therefore it is better not to speculate, like the scholastics, about the nature of suffering, whether it is merely the apprehension of corporeal fire, or whether somehow the angels are shackled with vile bodies, or whatever the theory. It is safest to say that hellfire is used by God in a supernatural way to punish the evil angels and that we are ignorant of its nature.[56]

From the evidence just presented it should be clear that any notion of a three-story universe or any more sophisticated world picture was quite foreign to historic Lutheran theology.[57] In fact the Lutheran teachers felt that to be faithful to Scripture they should shy away from tying the

[54] Hollaz, *Examen,* P.III, S.1, C.3, Q.151 (p. 781); Quenstedt, *Systema,* P.III, C.3, Memb.3, S.1, Thesis 102 ff. (III, 380). The dogmaticians called heaven a ποῦ and hell a ποῦ not to advance any speculation about the nature of heaven or hell but to safeguard their reality. See Quenstedt, *Systema,* P.III, C.14, S.1, Theses 23,34; ibid., P.III, C.15, S.1, Thesis 20 (III, 557 ff.). The Lutherans were insistent that eternal life is enjoyed by the whole man: body and soul. But they carefully pointed out that the salvation of the body is something invisible and quite beyond our present mode of apprehension. The resurrection was also illocal, according to Quenstedt, in the sense that it was not a resurrection of bodies circumscribed according to our local physical mode of presence, but the resurrection body was present within the ποῦ of eternal life. (2 Peter 3:10 ff.)

[55] Calov, *Systema,* III, 1008.

[56] Bechmann, *Theologia Polemica,* p. 404. Quenstedt wants the question of the nature of hellfire left open. *Systema,* P.I, C.24, S.2, Q.4 (I, 570).

[57] This is also Jörg Baur's judgment, pp. 127 ff. It can be said that the theologians of the period of classical Lutheran orthodoxy are more free of the medieval notions of heaven and hell than Luther, and this is understandable inasmuch as they lived two and three generations after him.

Biblical doctrine of creation and providence, of Christ or heaven or hell, or any other article of faith, to any scientific cosmology or picture of the universe. This does not mean that they did not see certain cosmologies and world pictures as a threat to the faith. A deterministic cosmology or a world picture which absolutized time and space was indeed in conflict with revealed theology. But although God has made the world and directly sustains it at every moment, although He has made Himself known to man according to our present experience within the created order, although He became man Himself and subject to the conditions of creation, still He is transcendent, and a Christian theology will reflect this fact and not bind itself to any world picture which is constructed according to our present experience. And so Lutheran theology actually transcends all scientific world pictures.

We must ask one final question before leaving this subject. What was the posture of orthodox Lutheran theology toward the method and the advances of science? One might suppose that a theology which transcends any world picture and any empirical way of looking at things will, most likely, not feel threatened by scientific discoveries and research and opinions. This was quite true in the case of Lutheranism. But contrary to the opinion of Elert,[58] neither will such a theology *necessarily* be especially open to the breakthroughs of scientific research and development. Elert has proved his thesis that Lutherans were often interested in science and did not oppose the advances of their day, and that there is nothing in Lutheran theology to oppose such advances.[59] But neither is there anything uniquely Lutheran which would encourage special interest in science. The one aspect of creation theology which would encourage a positive attitude toward science is the doctrine of the goodness of God's creation and the divine command given to man to have dominion over the earth. But such an emphasis was not unique to Lutheranism.

But if Elert's thesis of Lutheranism's openness to science is incorrect,

[58] *The Structure of Lutheranism,* p. 425.

[59] Cf. John Warwick Montgomery, *L'astrologie et l'alchimie luthériennes a l'époque de la Réforme,* Extrait de la "Revue d'Histoire et de la Philosophie Religieuses," No. 4, 1966 (Paris: Presses Universitaires de France), pp. 324—34. John Montgomery argues against Troeltsch, who said that Lutheranism depreciated the world as a valley of tears and was therefore not open to scientific advancement. See Ernst Troeltsch, *Protestantism and Progress,* tr. W. Montgomery (Boston: Beacon Press Paperbacks, 1958), pp. 155 ff.

so is the thesis of Klaus Scholder,[60] which represents the Lutheran theologians as reactionary and incapable in principle of accepting what Kepler and Galileo were doing. He says that the radical (for its day) approach of Galileo represented a quite new approach to the gaining of knowledge, a new *Erkenntnisprinzip,* which now entered in opposition to the "Biblical Aristotelian world picture." We might respond first by saying that there was no "Biblical Aristotelian world picture" in Lutheran theology. Second, the empirical method followed so doggedly by Galileo and Kepler, a method not so different from that of Aristotle, was in principle quite acceptable to the Lutheran theologians.[61] But unfortunately the theologians, except for men like Aslakssøn who were in close contact with scientists, seldom bothered to take this recognized method of acquiring a knowledge of God's creation seriously. They possessed neither the curiosity nor the sophistication of a Galileo, and they had little appreciation of the rewards to be gained through such activity.

The point is that the so-called Copernican Revolution did not introduce anything disturbing or even new into the principles of knowledge recognized by Lutheran theologians. What was new was that the discoveries and hypotheses at times seemed at first blush to conflict with what Scripture said or implied about the world and things. But this too caused little anxiety among the Lutheran theologians, as Elert has pointed out, and for the most part little interest. For Galileo was advancing a methodology which, although not so often followed, was old and which was based in part upon the Augustinian notion that God had spoken to us in two books, the book of Scripture and the book of nature.[62] Galileo believed that the book of nature ought to be read in the language of mathematical science and empirical investigation. Scripture, on the other

---

[60] *Ursprünge und Probleme der Bibelkritik im 17. Jahrhundert,* p. 76.

[61] Melanchthon favored this position in the introduction to his *Loci Theologici Praecipui,* 1559 (CR 21, 603—4), where he contrasts the legitimate method of science, which is empirical, to the legitimate method of the church, which gains her knowledge from revelation. The general epistemological rule of Locke that all knowledge came by sensation and reflection (empiricism) was completely acceptable to the later Lutheran teachers and recognized as the basis of scientific advancement. They only warned that such a method did not provide the whole truth, for our knowledge of God came by revelation. See Valentin Loescher, *Praenotiones Theologicae contra Naturalistarum et Fanaticorum Omne Genus Atheos, Deistas, Indifferentistas, Antiscripturarios, etc.* (Wittenberg, 1708).

[62] See Crombie, *Histoire de la Science de Saint Augustin à Galilei (400 to 1650),* II, 348 passim.

hand, does not contain scientific theories, but reveals to us our eternal destiny. When speaking of natural phenomena, the Scriptures use poetic imagery or the common language of the day.[63] Like Kepler, Galileo was convinced that nothing uncovered by science would contradict Scripture but would rather confirm hundreds of passages which urge us to glorify and marvel at the supreme majesty of God. With far less enthusiasm the Lutheran theologians believed the same.

And so our conclusion is that Lutheran theology, while transcending all scientific world pictures, is not in any unique way open to the advancement of scientific knowledge or of a scientific world picture.

[63] For instance, the story of Joshua making the sun stand still is recounted as it would have appeared to the senses, according to Galileo. See Crombie, ibid., II, 408. We have already shown that this was the hermeneutical understanding of the Lutheran teachers. Kepler was probably bothered more than most of the theologians by the apparent discrepancy between scientific discoveries and hypotheses and certain statements of Scripture concerning nature. He too advocated a theory whereby Scripture accommodated itself to the popular expression of the day and to a phenomenal way of speaking when describing the things of nature. *Opera Omnia* (Frankfurt, 1858), III, 153—56.

CONCLUSION

Our practice in the preceding chapters has been to offer an objective discussion of the theology of Lutheran orthodoxy on the chief points of the articles concerning God and creation and then briefly to comment on our findings. For this reason there is no necessity for now presenting a lengthy conclusion and critique. But a few final remarks are in order.

The chief purpose of Christian dogmatics, as envisaged by the Lutheran theologians during and after the Reformation, was to summarize the Christian doctrine in an orderly way. Melanchthon's expression of such a purpose in the opening letter to his *Loci Praecipui Theologici* of 1559 actually speaks for all the following Lutheran teachers. He says,[1] "It is beneficial to set forth clear declarations as on a tablet, concerning each of the articles of Christian doctrine, and to arrange these statements in good order. We do this in order that, when we consider these things and tie them together, certain definite thoughts come to our attention, thoughts by which troubled people may be instructed, edified, strengthened, and comforted." Such a summation *(summa)* of Christian doctrine was nothing else than an orderly summation of the teachings of Scripture, according to the Lutheran dogmaticians.[2] The whole Christian doctrine was viewed

---

[1] *CR* 21, 602.

[2] This is expressed by Polycarp Leyser in his dedicatory letter to Chemnitz' *Loci Theologici* and by Chemnitz himself in his introduction to the same work. From the sheer bulk of Chemnitz' great work which sought to fulfill this aim it is quite obvious that a *summa doctrinae coelestis* was not necessarily supposed to be something brief.

as an organic body with many parts *(articuli)*. The dogmatician's objective was to present each article of faith in as complete and convincing way as possible and to relate the articles of faith to each other and to the center which was the doctrine of salvation through faith in Christ.[3]

Such a purpose, although easy to formulate, was extremely difficult to carry out; for the business of gathering the Biblical data for each article of faith and systematizing these data is of necessity selective, if not arbitrary. It becomes very difficult for a dogmatician, even in a lengthy study, to present or summarize *all* the data pertaining to an article of faith and to do so with balance.

This difficulty (and shortcoming) inherent in the dogmatic enterprise has been apparent in our present study. Although the Lutheran teachers give a very full account of the natural knowledge of God, of the name of God, and especially of the doctrine of the Trinity, there are certain aspects of the Biblical doctrine of God which are scarcely touched or only considered much later in their dogmatics, for example, the concept of God as the living God, God as a gracious God, God as the Lord of history, and the works of God.

However, simply dealing with a subject at length and gathering together masses of Biblical data pertaining to the subject does not in itself guarantee that the purpose of dogmatics will be achieved. For instance, the treatment of God's attributes, although lengthy to the point of tedium and drawing heavily from Scripture, simply does not do justice to the subject; for it is doubtful if viewing God according to a veritable proliferation of attributes helps us to see Him better and really sums up the Biblical data adequately. The fact that the dogmaticians from the time of Gerhard multiply the divine attributes and then often give only perfunctory attention to some of them would indicate that they were not unaware of the shortcomings of their approach. It might also indicate that they were rather unenthusiastic about what they were doing and were just trying to get done with a job. Certainly they realized that all theology could not be subsumed under the discussion of the divine attributes. But it never occurred to these dogmaticians to return to the simple and more

---

[3] Nicolaus Hunnius, *Diaskepsis Theologica* (Wittenberg, 1626), p. 35 passim. This position is stated by Hunnius more fully than by any of the other dogmaticians. The later Lutheran teachers all lean heavily on Hunnius at this point.

dynamic approach of Luther and Chemnitz and limit their discussion of the doctrine of God to a more thorough treatment of the Trinity.

There is no question that the earlier approach to the doctrine of God by Chemnitz, Selnecker, Heerbrand, and others, which subsumed their discussions under the doctrine of the Trinity and then made all dogmatics a sort of commentary on the creeds, is superior to that of Gerhard and the later theologians in one important respect. It gives the doctrine of the Trinity a central and formative position in the total dogmatic enterprise. The doctrine of the Trinity is not simply stated, defended, and then dropped.[4] Even the later Lutherans, commencing with Gerhard, who treat first the essence and attributes of God and only then proceed to the Trinity, do not by any means minimize the importance of the Trinitarian doctrine in itself or as it affects all theology. We notice how even these later theologians in their scholastic manner ascribe, not willy-nilly but deliberately and with care, all the *opera ad extra* of God (for example, the inspiration of Scripture, conversion, justification, etc.) to the Trinity and to each person of the Trinity.[5] And they too make all of dogmatics a tracing of the working of the economic Trinity. This is done much more consciously than in modern Lutheran dogmatics. The strong insistence upon the fact that the doctrine of the Trinity was adumbrated in the Old Testament and the fact that the Old Testament Scriptures are in theological agreement with the New Testament serves also to underline the central place of the doctrine of the Trinity in Christian theology. Without any doubt we can assert that the Post-Reformation era, more than any other, emphasized and demonstrated with solid Biblical support the fundamental importance of the doctrine of the Trinity not only for Christian worship and piety, but also for carrying out the work of Christian dogmatics. In this respect the contribution of classical Lutheran theology is significant indeed. But this superior feature of the old Lutheran dogmatics cannot hide the failure to discover and pursue the many Biblical motifs which could have enhanced and completed the treatment of the doctrine of God.

[4] This is a criticism leveled by Karl Rahner against much of Roman Catholic dogmatics in his *The Trinity* (London: Burns & Oates, Ltd., 1970), pp. 14 ff.

[5] For example, Hollaz, *Examen*, P.III, S.1, C.6, q.8, p.857. Here, as in innumerable cases, Hollaz, like Baier and the other later dogmaticians, offers and interprets Scripture passages which ascribe conversion to each of the Three Persons in the Trinity.

The triune God is the God of both Testaments and of all history. The Logos is the one revealer of God in both Testaments and of all history. All this was most important to historic Lutheran theology, as we have seen, and shows the importance of all theology being carried out from a Trinitarian perspective. Thus we see post-Reformation Lutheranism rehabilitating the doctrine of the Trinity not only by offering a firm Biblical basis for it, but by making all theology Trinitarian.

As the Lutheran teachers proceed to the doctrine of creation they do better. Their treatment is not nearly so scholastic and it is more directly Biblical. And furthermore, their discussions are much more practical. One of the important principles enunciated in the prolegomena of Lutheran dogmatics was that theology was a *habitus practicus* θεόσδοτος. A classic statement of this was expressed by Chemnitz:[6] "We must at all times bear in mind that the Son of God did not proceed from the hidden seat of the eternal Father and reveal the heavenly doctrine in order to sow hotbeds for all sorts of disputations which a person plays at to show off his talents, but in order that men might be taught about the true knowledge of God and about all those things which it is necessary to follow for eternal life. Therefore we must pay special care to each *locus* of doctrine; we must pay special attention to how and in what manner the doctrine which has been handed down to us may be put to use in the serious exercise of repentance, faith, and obedience and prayer. In this way our minds make progress in both doctrine and piety." This principle, if it means anything, should have made itself felt in every *locus* in Christian doctrine. But we do not see much in the old Lutheran treatment of the doctrine of God which is practical in the sense of Chemnitz's statement — not even in the earlier treatment of Heerbrand, Selnecker, and Chemnitz himself.

The attempt to make theology practical is much more apparent in the Lutheran doctrine of creation. The lack of speculation on the precise cosmological implications of the days of creation, the lack of interest in wedding the Biblical doctrine of creation to any world picture, the homiletical and doxological tone of the discussions on the hexaemeron and of the entire doctrine join to make the doctrine of creation something which can be used by the Christian — used to show him God's wonderful good-

---

[6] *Loci Theologici,* I, 17. Cf. Calov, *Systema,* I, 26 ff.; Quenstedt, *Systema,* P.I, C.1, S.1, Thesis 30 (I, 11).

ness and power and wisdom, used to show him his unique importance in God's eyes and his unique purpose in the universe, and used to show him why his life should be lived in love and praise of God.

The practical nature of theology is brought out even more distinctly in the doctrine of providence as it seeks to show God's immanent and loving care for all creation and especially for those who trust Him. If this use of the doctrine is disturbed somewhat by the dogmaticians' attempt to answer the many problems connected with the doctrine, it is only because the old Lutherans felt that such problems must be faced in order to make the doctrine of providence truly meaningful and practical.

This brings us to one of the more commendable aspects of the Lutheran doctrine of creation, namely, its setting in a soteriological and eschatological context. The synthetic *(loci theologici)* method of the earlier representatives of our period (Selnecker, Gerhard, Chemnitz) was calculated to bring all theology and the articles of faith under the light of the Gospel.[7] The later analytical method of Calov, Quenstedt, Dannhauer, and others was an attempt to bring all Christian doctrine under the light of final causes, namely salvation. This is why most of them discussed eternal life immediately after the article of creation and providence.[8] All creation and God's *creatio continua* were seen in God's economy as serving man in this life and especially in his pursuit of eternal life. Such a soteriological and eschatological perspective should pervade all theology, according to historic Lutheranism. The effort to carry out this aim is seen in the fact that the *causa finalis* of almost every article treated by the Lutheran teachers is man's salvation, eternal life, communion with God. True, this *causa finalis* is often stated in a perfunctory manner as the dogmaticians fill out the scheme of causal factors which they

---

[7] Balthasar Meisner, *Anthropologia Sacra* (Wittenberg, 1663), Decas. III, Disp. 24, p. 139: "This article (justification through faith) is the central point of theology according to which all other articles of faith are adjusted; it is the sacred ocean into which all other doctrines flow; it is the treasure chest of our faith which keeps safe and unharmed all the other doctrines." Cf. Chemnitz, *Loci Theologici,* II, 200; Quenstedt, *Systema,* P.III, C.8, S.1, Thesis 1. Other similar statements are listed in Baier-Walther, III, 240—99.

[8] Quenstedt considers eternal life immediately after the *locus* on creation but takes up the other eschatological themes such as Antichrist, resurrection, final judgment, etc., at the end of his dogmatics after the *locus* on the church. Cf. also John Deutschmann, *Theologia Positiva Primi Theologi Adami Protoplasti* (Wittenberg, 1694); Kromayer, *Theologia Positivo-Polemica.* Baier and Dannhauer take all of eschatology up at this early point in dogmatics.

had adopted. But the constant pointing to the end of the road, to the goal of the believer's pilgrimage, and the reiteration at every point in Christian theology of man's eschatological purpose is always clearly discernible. This emphasis is no doubt even more apparent in the hymns and sermons and devotional literature of the day, but one cannot miss the same pre-occupation with this theme as one reads almost anywhere in the post-Reformation Lutheran dogmatics. Soteriology and eschatology or, one might say, creation viewed soteriologically and eschatologically sets the stage for all the discussion of all theology — of all the articles of faith.

All this does not mean that Lutheran theology after the Reformation had become so "spiritual" as to be disinterested in the Christian's life in the world here and now. The preoccupation with salvation and the life to come did not imply an escape from the obligations of life here and now. The Lutheran creation theology taught that man is to enjoy life and creation as God's gift now. This doctrine was fortified by the strong emphasis (often in response to Roman Catholic polemics) on the doctrine of good works done willingly and joyfully in this life,[9] and by lengthy discussions on the many aspects of the Christian life, on the home *(de statu domestico)*, and on the state *(de magistratu politico)*. The fact that an unrealistic quietism sometimes manifested itself in Lutheran circles (for example, in the court of Elector John George of Saxony during the Thirty Years' War) was not due to an overemphasis on the "other world" in Lutheran theology but was the result of putting into practice some of the Lutheran reformers' strong statements on the distinction between ecclesiastical and civil power (Augsburg Confession, XXVIII, 11-17 passim). No, it was the definite aim of the Lutheran dogmaticians to have the soteriological and eschatological perspective of theology activate and motivate the man of God in this life on earth.[10]

---

[9] One of the most eloquent dissertations on good works and the Christian life is expressed by Jasper Brochmand in his *In Canonicam et Catholicam Jacobi Epistolam Commentarius* (Copenhagen, 1640), p. 153 passim. To Brochmand the Christian's joy in life is his joy in good works. Brochmand's purpose in writing this commentary is, among other things, to show that Lutheranism takes James very seriously at this point.

[10] But lacking is an emphasis upon the social aspects of the Christian life. For instance, the goal of the Christian life is said to be an inner change in man (Baier-Walther, III, 303, 312). But no mention is made of any social goal for good works. However, when providence is discussed, the question is asked why God prolongs the life of believers, and the reply is given, "God prolongs life for believers either to reward their obedience or for the public good" (ibid., II,

One significant discovery in our studies is worthy of mention in conclusion because of its obvious significance for theology today. The reader will have noticed throughout our survey a good bit of emphasis upon controversies carried on between the Lutherans and the Socinians. It is interesting that these controversies in every case were very definitely tied to hermeneutics. This fact ought not be dismissed as irrelevant to our day. The history of Socinian-Lutheran polemics offers a clear example of two opposing approaches to Scripture and theology, approaches which came to deeply divergent dogmatic conclusions.

Today it can hardly be denied that Protestant and of late also Catholic exegesis follows at least as closely in the train of Socinian hermeneutics as in the tradition of the classical Lutheran or Protestant hermeneutics which we have observed in operation in our present study. How many Protestant or Roman Catholic exegetes today, for instance, would follow the old Lutherans as they found their doctrine of the Trinity, the deity of Christ, and the personality of the Holy Spirit in the Old Testament? Even the 17th-century Lutheran George Calixt could not accept such an approach.

But the hermeneutical approach to Scripture which we have observed among the post-Reformation Lutherans was not something which could just be discarded or even modified, for it was a part of the heritage of the Reformation and of the Lutheran Confessions.[11] There is no question but that the dogmaticians whom we have studied considered themselves and genuine Lutheranism bound not only to a doctrine but to a hermeneutic. To abandon the hermeneutics which they believed was Christ's hermeneutics and that of the New Testament would result in abandoning the Christian doctrine as well. To see that Christian theology is bound to definite hermeneutics one need merely witness, the Lutherans argued, that as the Socinians departed from the traditional hermeneutics of the

---

178). But this is about as far as the dogmaticians ever go in speaking of the social aspects of the Christian life. The social implications of the Gospel were usually discussed under the *locus* on civil government.

[11] For an excellent survey of the hermeneutics of the Lutheran Confessions see Ralph Bohlmann, *Principles of Biblical Interpretation in the Lutheran Confessions* (St. Louis: Concordia Publishing House, 1968). Bohlmann shows that according to the Lutheran Confessions the Reformation theology was dependent upon certain definite hermeneutical principles, such as the clarity of Scripture, the Christocentricity of all Scripture, the analogy of Scripture, the unity of Scripture, and the principle of deriving all theology from the *sensus literalis*. There is no doubt that the later Lutheran dogmaticians share these convictions. See Robert Preus, *The Theology of Post-Reformation Lutheranism,* I, pp. 315—39.

Reformation and the church catholic they rejected the Trinity and the deity of Christ.

That the old Lutherans saw such a close relationship between Biblical hermeneutics and doctrine is the only explanation for them taking the Socinian theology so seriously. The Socinians, living as they did in a virtual ghetto existence, were at that time no real threat to evangelical Lutheranism. They had little direct contact with most of the Lutherans. And they had a lot of trouble even getting their books published. The strenuous and lengthy Lutheran attack against Socinianism was due to the clear perception of the Lutheran teachers that the Socinian hermeneutics could only lead to the kind of doctrine the Socinians were advancing; and the Lutherans never tired of pointing this out.

Today we see the Socinian hermeneutics with its rejection of the hallowed interpretations of the past, its virtual refusal to read the Old Testament in the light of the New, its playing down of the *analogia Scripturae,* its failure to find the doctrine of the Trinity in the Old Testament (or even in the New), and its critical approach to the synoptic problem as remarkably modern for its day. The Lutherans of the 16th and 17th centuries saw this approach to Scripture as leading only to a denial of the Christian doctrine of God as well as other articles of faith. Today we who commit ourselves to the doctrine of the Trinity must ask ourselves seriously just how much of the old Protestant hermeneutics can be discarded without losing also the Biblical basis for the Christian doctrine of God.

BIBLIOGRAPHY

PRIMARY SOURCES

Aslakssøn, Cort. *De Creatione Disputatio Prima.* Copenhagen, 1609.

―――. *De Immanuele Nostro D. Jesu Christo, vero Deo et vero Homino in Una Indivisa Persona.* Frankfurt, 1620.

―――. *De Mundo.* Copenhagen, 1605—7.

―――. *De Natura Coeli Triplicis.* Sigena of Nassau, 1597.

―――. *De Statu Christi* θεάνθρωπον. Copenhagen, 1622.

―――. *Physica et Ethica Mosaica.* Copenhagen, 1613.

Joh. Guieliemi Baieri (Baier, John William). *Compendium Theologiae Positivae,* denuo edendum curavit C. F. G. [sic] Walther. St. Louis, 1879.

Balduin, Friedrich. *Commentarius in Omnes Epistolas Pauli.* Frankfurt, 1664.

Barclay, Robert. *An Apology for the True Christian Divinity.* London, 1825.

Bechmann, Friedemann. *Annotationes Uberiores in Compendium Theologicum Leonhardi Hutteri.* Frankfurt and Leipzig, 1690.

―――. *Theologia Polemica.* Jena, 1719.

Beza, Theodore. *Ad Acta Coloquii Montischelgardensis Tubingae Edita Theodori Bezae Responsionis Altera.* Geneva, 1588.

Brenz, John. *De Majestate Domini Nostri Jesu Christi ad Dextram Dei Patris et Vera Praesentia Corporis & Sanguinis ejus in Coena.* Frankfurt, 1562.

Brochmand, Jesper E. (Casparus Erasmus). *Universae Theologiae Systema.* Ulm, 1658.

―――. *Commentarius in Epistolam ad Hebraeos.* Copenhagen, 1706.

―――. *Definitiones Articulorum Fidei.* Copenhagen, 1628.

————. *In Canonicam et Catholicam Jacobi Epistolam Commentarius.* Copenhagen, 1640.

Bucan, William. *Institutiones Theologiae.* Geneva, 1609.

Calov, Abraham. *Apodixis Articulorum Fidei.* Lüneberg, 1684.

————. *Biblia Testamenti Veteris Illustrata.* Dresden and Leipzig, 1719.

————. *Commentarius in Genesin.* Wittenberg, 1671.

————. *Consensus Repetitus Fidei Vere Lutheranae.* Wittenberg, 1666.

————. *Consideratio Arminianismi.* Wittenberg, 1655.

————. *Socinismus Profligatus, hoc est, Errorum Socinianorum Luculenta Confutatio.* Wittenberg, 1668.

————. *Systema Locorum Theologicorum.* Wittenberg, 1655—77.

————. *Theologia Naturalis et Revelata.* Leipzig, 1646.

————. *Veritas Religionis Christianae per Praecipua Capita, adversus Judaeos ex Sacro Ebraeo Codica.* Wittenberg, 1679.

Catechesis Racoviensis, seu Liber Socinianorum Primarius. Frankfurt and Leipzig, 1739.

Chemnitz, Martin. *Loci Theologici.* Wittenberg, 1653.

————. *Examen Concilii Tridentini.* Berlin, 1861.

Chytraeus, David. *Opera.* Leipzig, 1594.

Cundisius, Gottfried. *Notae et Observationes quibus Compendium Theologicum Dn. D. Leonhardi Hutteri Illustratur.* Leipzig, 1705.

Dannhauer, John Conrad. *Hodosophia Christiana, seu Theologia Positiva.* Strasbourg, 1649.

————. *Christosophia seu Sapientiarum Sapientia, de Salvatore Christo, ejus Persona, Officio, Beneficiis, Explicita atque Variis Corruptelis Purgata.* Strasbourg, 1638.

————. *Hermeneutica Sacra.* Strasbourg, 1654.

Dedekenn, George. *Thesauri Conciliorum et Decisionum.* Jena, 1671.

Deutschmann, John. *Antiquissima Theologia Positiva.* Wittenberg, 1694.

————. *Disputatio Theologiae Biblicae de Providentia Divina ex Rom. xi. 36.* Wittenberg, 1688.

————. *Theologia Positiva Primi Theologi Adami Protoplasti.* Wittenberg, 1694.

Deyling, Salomon. *Observationum Sacrarum in qua Multa Scripturae Veteris ac Novi Testamenti Dubia Vexata Solvuntur.* Leipzig, 1735.

Dorsch, John George. *Synopsis Theologiae Zacharianae.* Frankfurt, 1683.

Enyedim, George. *Explicationes Locorum Scripturae, Veteris et Novi Testamenti, in quibus Dogma Trinitatis Stabiliri Solet.* Groningen, 1670.

Episcopius, Simon. *Opera Theologica.* Amsterdam, 1650.

Geier, Martin. *Opuscula Philologica.* Amsterdam, 1695.

Gerhard, John. *Annotationes Posthumae in Epistolam ad Colossenses.* Jena, 1660.

———. *Commentarius super Epistolam ad Ebraeos.* Jena, 1666.

———. *Confessio Catholica.* Erfurt, 1679.

———. *Loci Theologici,* denuo ed. . . . J. F. Cotta. Tübingen, 1762.

Gerlach, Stephan. *Theses de Providentia Dei.* Tübingen, 1591.

Hafenreffer, Matthias. *Loci Theologici.* Wittenberg, 1601.

Heerbrand, Jacob. *Compendium Theologiae.* Tübingen, 1573.

———. *Disputatio de Miraculis.* Tübingen, 1590.

Hollaz, David. *Examen Theologicum Acroamaticum.* Rostock and Leipzig, 1741.

Hunnius, Giles. *Articulus de Providentia Dei et Aeterna Praedestinatione Filiorum Dei ad Salutem.* Frankfurt, 1596.

———. *Opera Latina.* Wittenberg, 1607.

Hunnius, Nicholas. *Diaskepsis Theologica de Fundamentali Dissensu Doctrinae, Evangelicae Lutheranae, et Calvinianae, seu Reformatae.* Wittenberg, 1628.

Hutter, Leonard. *Loci Communes Theologici.* Wittenberg, 1619.

Jacquelot, Isaac. *Conformité de la foi avec la Raison, ou défence de la réligion contre les principales difficultés répendues dans le dictionaire historique et critique de Bayle (1704),* in *Démonstrations evangelique.* Ed. M. d'Abee. Paris: Petit-Montrouge, 1843.

Keckermann, Bartholomew. *Systema Sacrae Theologiae.* Hanover, 1602.

———. *Systema Theologicum.* Geneva, 1602.

Kepler, John. *Opera Omnia.* Frankfurt, 1858.

Kromayer, Jerome. *Theologia Positivo-Polemica.* Frankfurt and Leipzig, 1687.

Loescher, Valentin. *Praenotiones Theologicae contra Naturalistarum et Fanaticorum Omne Genus, Atheos, Deistas, Indifferentistas, Antiscripturarios, etc.* 5th ed. Wittenberg, 1752.

Martini, Cornelius. *Compendium Theologiae et Epitome Theologiae Naturalis.* Wolfenbüttel, 1650.

Martini, Jacob. *De Tribus Elohim.* Wittenberg, 1619.

———. *Partitiones & Quaestiones Metaphysicae.* Wittenberg, 1615.

———. *Synopsis Totius Religionis Photinianorum Novorum.* Wittenberg, 1633.

Martini, Matthew. *De Deo, Summo Illo Bono et Causa Omnis Boni, Libelli Duo.* Bremen, 1616.

————. *Quaestiones Quaedam Nobiliores, ad Explicanda Loca Difficiliora Genesis.* Bremen, 1623.

————. *Quaestiones Theologicae & Philologicae in Librum Josuae.* Bremen, 1624.

Martyr, Peter. *Loci Communes.* Zürich, 1580.

Meisner, Balthasar. *Anthropologia Sacra.* Wittenberg, 1663.

————. *Philosophia Sobria.* Rinteln, 1626.

Mentzer, Balthasar. *Opera Latina.* Frankfurt, 1669.

Osiander, John Adam. *Collegium Theologicum Systematicum.* Stuttgart and Frankfurt, 1684.

————. *Theologicum Systema seu Theologia Positiva Acroamatica.* Tübingen, 1679.

Pfeiffer, August. *Thesaurus Hermeneuticus.* Leipzig and Frankfurt, 1704.

Polanus, Amandus. *Institutiones Theologicae.* Geneva, 1609.

Quenstedt, John Andr. *Theologia Didactico-Polemica sive Systema Theologicum.* Wittenberg, 1685.

Schaafman, Andrew. *Libri II Controversiarum de Peccatorum Causis.* Frankfurt, 1597.

Scherzer, John Adam. *Systema Theologiae.* Leipzig and Frankfurt, 1698.

Schmidt, Sebastian. *Commentarius Super Illustres Prophetias Iesaiae.* Hamburg and Frankfurt, 1693.

————. *Compendium Theologiae.* Strasbourg, 1697.

————. *Disputatio de Christo ex Matth. XVI. 16.* Strasbourg, 1690.

————. *In Epistolam D. Pauli ad Hebraeos Commentarius.* Strasbourg, 1680.

————. *In Librum Ijobi Commentarius.* Strasbourg, 1705.

————. *Super Mosis Librum Primum, Genesis Dictum, Annotationes.* Strasbourg, 1697.

Selnecker, Nicolaus. *De Duobus Articulis Symboli, Ascendit ad Coelos: Sedet ad Dexteram Dei Patris, Breves Quaestiones.* Wolfenbüttel, 1572.

————. *Exegema: 1. De Unione Personali Duarum Naturarum in Christo. 2. De Idiomatum Communicatione. 3. De Coena Domini.* Wolfenbüttel, 1572.

————. *Institutiones Christianae Religionis.* Frankfurt, 1573.

————. *Recitationes Aliquot.* Leipzig, 1581.

Smaltz, Valentin. *Refutatio Disputationis de Spiritu Sancto.* Cracow, 1613.

————. *Refutatio Thesium de Sacrosancta Imitata Divinae Essentiae et in eadem Sacrosancta Personarum Trinitate a Jacobo Schappero Propositarum.* Cracow, 1614.

————. *Responsio ad Scriptum Hermani Ravenspergeri.* Cracow, 1613.

Socinus, Faustus. *Opera Omnia.* Amsterdam, 1656.

Solida, *Verboque Dei & Libro Concordiae Christianae Congrua Decisio Quatuor Illorum inter Aliquos Theologos Augustanae Confessionis Nuperrime Controversorum Capitum Principaliorum, de Vera Descriptione & Fundamento Praesentiae Dei, Ejusque Filii Jesu Christi apud Creaturas.* Leipzig, 1624.

Thumm, Theodore, *Impietas Weigliana.* Tübingen, 1622.

Vasquez, Gabriel. *Commentariorum ac Disputationum in Primam Partem S. Thomae Liber I.* Alcolá, 1597.

Voet, Gisbert (Voetius). *Selectarum Disputationum Theologicarum Pars Prima.* Utrecht, 1648.

Völkel, John. *De Vera Religione.* Cracow, 1630.

Vorst, Conrad. *Epitome Exegeseos Apologeticae.* Steinfurt, 1611.

————. *Tractatus Theologicus de Deo.* Steinfurt, 1606.

Walther, Michael. *Officina Biblica.* Wittenberg, 1703.

SECONDARY SOURCES

Anselm of Canterbury. *Pourquoi Dieu s'est Fait Homme.* Trad. de René Roques. Paris: Les Editions du Cerf, 1963.

Barth, Karl. *Church Dogmatics.* Trans. G. T. Thomson, G. W. Bromily, et al. Edinburgh: T. & T. Clark, 1936—69.

Baur, Jörg. *Die Vernunft Zwischen Ontologie und Evangelium: Eine Untersuchung zur Theologie Johann Andreas Quenstedts.* Gütersloh: Verlagshaus Gerd Mohn, 1962.

Bohlmann, Ralph. *Principles of Biblical Hermeneutics in the Lutheran Confessions.* St. Louis: Concordia Publishing House, 1968.

Brunner, Emil. *Revelation and Reason.* Trans. Olive Wyon. Philadelphia: The Westminster Press, 1946.

Crombie, A. C. *Histoire de Science de Saint Augustin à Galiléi (400—1650).* Paris: Presses Universitaires de France, 1959.

Elert, Werner. *Der Christliche Glaube.* Berlin: Furche Verlag, 1941.

————. *The Structure of Lutheranism.* Trans. Walter A. Hansen. St. Louis: Concordia Publishing House, 1962.

Flew, Anthony, and Alesdaire MacIntyre. *New Essays in Philosophical Theology.* London: SCM Press, 1955.

Fraenkel, Peter. *Testimonia Patrum, the Function of the Patristic Argument in the Theology of Philip Melanchthon.* Geneva: Librairie E. Droz, 1961.

Garstein, Oskar. *Cort Aslakssøn.* Oslo: Lutherstiftelsen, 1953.

Hägglund, Bengt. *Die Heilige Schrift und ihre Deutung in der Theologie Johann Gerhards.* Lund: CWK Gleerups Förlag, 1951.

Hooykaas, R. *Natural Law and Divine Miracle.* Leiden: H. J. Brill, 1959.

Koester, Arthur. *The Sleepwalkers.* New York: Macmillan, 1959.

————. *The Watershed: a Biography of Johannes Kepler.* New York: Doubleday & Co., 1960.

Moldaenke, Günter. *Schriftverständnis und Schriftdeutung im Zeitalter der Reformation. I. Matthias Flacius Illyricus.* Stuttgart, 1936.

Montgomery, John Warwick, ed. *Crisis in Lutheran Theology.* Vol. 2. Grand Rapids: Baker Book Company, 1967.

————. *The 'Is God Dead?' Controversy.* Grand Rapids: Zondervan, 1966.

Pelikan, Jaroslav. *From Luther to Kierkegaard.* St. Louis: Concordia Publishing House, 1963.

Pieper, Francis. *Christian Dogmatics.* Trans. Theodore Engelder et al. St. Louis: Concordia Publishing House, 1950—53.

Prestige, G. L. *God in Patristic Thought.* London: S.P.C.K. Press, 1950.

Preus, Robert. *The Inspiration of Scripture.* Edinburgh: Oliver & Boyd, 1957.

————. *The Theology of Post-Reformation Lutheranism: A Study of Theological Prolegomena.* St. Louis: Concordia Publishing House, 1970.

Ritschl, Otto. *Dogmengeschichte des Protestantismus.* Leipzig: J. C. Hinrichs'sche Buchhandlung, and Göttingen: Vandenhoeck & Ruprecht, 1908—27.

Rogness, Michael. *Melanchthon, Reformer Without Honor.* Minneapolis: Augsburg Publishing House, 1969.

Schlink, Edmund. *Theology of the Lutheran Confessions.* Trans. Paul F. Koehneke and Herbert J. A. Bouman. Philadelphia: Muhlenberg Press, 1961.

Scholder, Klaus. *Ursprünge und Problem der Bibelkritik im 17. Jahrhundert.* Munich: Chris. Kaiser Verlag, 1966.

Troeltsch, Ernst. *Protestantism and Progress.* Trans. W. Montgomery. Boston: Beacon Press Paperbacks, 1958.

Van Buren, Paul M. *The Secular Meaning of the Gospel.* New York: The Macmillan Company, 1963.

Wilber, E. M. *A History of Unitarianism.* Cambridge: Harvard University Press, 1946.

INDEX

Names and Subjects

SCRIPTURE PASSAGES